MORE THAN A MENU

2

MORE THAN A MENU

Food and its Meaning in Asian Cultures across the U.S.

First edition, Spring 2021
By: Media Narrative Project

Introduction by: Michael A. Longinow, Ph.D
Foreword by: Bryan Moe
Dedication by: Angela Hom

Publisher: Ingram Books, LightningSource,
LaVergne, Tennessee , USA

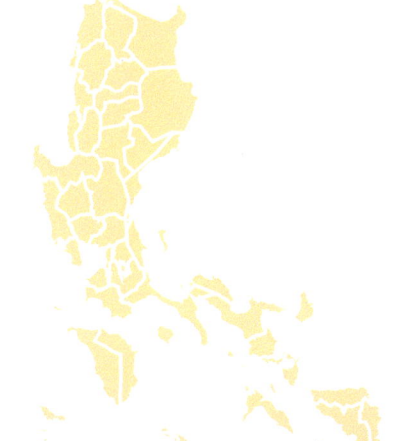

Department of Digital Journalism and Media - Biola University

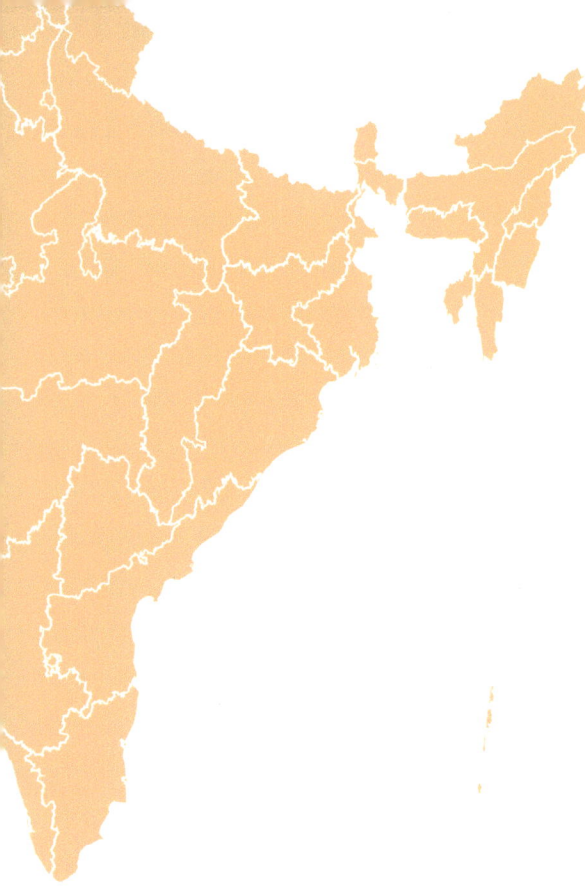

advisors
Michael Longinow
Tamara Welter (Design)

cover photo
Corrie Myhr

© 2021 Biola Avenue Press
Department of Digital Journalism & Media

Published by Biola Avenue Press
Imprint of the Department
of Digital Journalism & Media
Biola University

13800 Biola University Drive,
La Mirada, CA 90639

Printed in the United States of America

ISBN 978-0-9839572-6-3
Requests for information should be addressed
to: Dr. Michael Longinow, Chair
Department of Digital Journalism & Media
Biola University
13800 Biola University Drive,
La Mirada, CA 90639

Dedication

This book is dedicated to those who have been affected by anti-Asian attacks because of COVID-19. Those who lost their lives due to hate, those who have been attacked out of fear, those who have been silenced, and those who are fighting for justice.

-Angela Hom

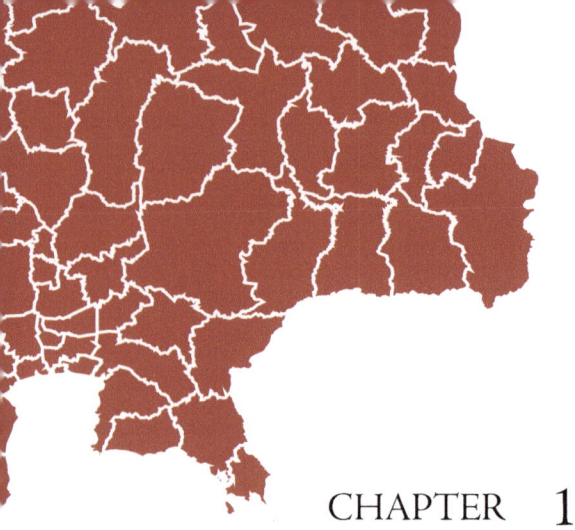

TABLE OF

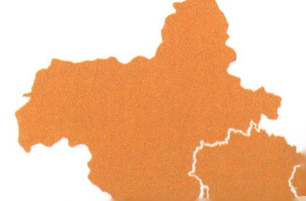

CONTENTS

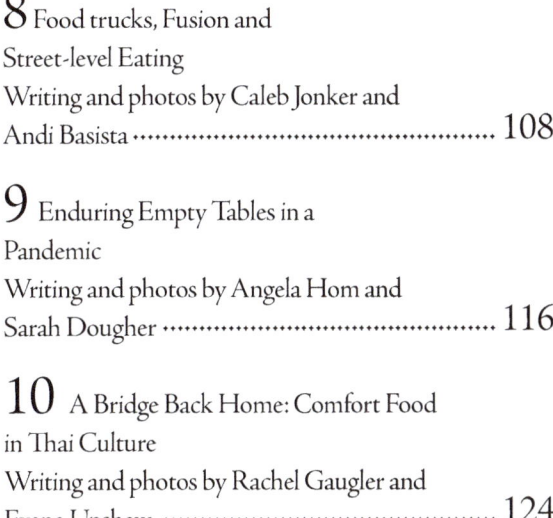

MULTIMEDIA

Introduction to the team of students
who produced the narrative book project

Chapter summaries

Audio podcast by Sarah Dougher,
interviewing student team members

Team Journey Blog

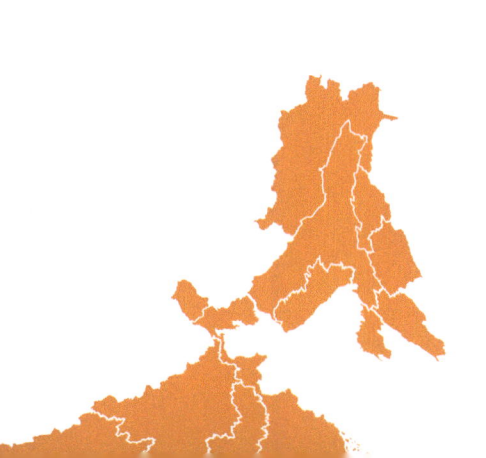

MORE THAN A MENU:
Food and its Meaning in Asian Cultures across the U.S.

Foreword

by Bryan Moe

All food has meaning. And we need, from time to time, to pull back a little bit to see we are swimming in a sea of that meaning. The meanings may change with the tide, but the waves are relentless, always there, waiting for us to decode and engage. Lucky for us, food is an invitation to discovery — of self, of others, and more importantly of how we all fit together.

Food is one of the reasons we get up and go to work every day — to make sure it is available for ourselves and loved ones. Too often a lack of it is a reason to cause harm to others and even fight wars.

In this book, a collection of student writers, photojournalists and multimedia storytellers have found windows of meaning in the food and the people who prepare and serve that food in culturally diverse Asian communities across the U.S. and in Southern California. By using all of their senses these students have asked deep questions about how food plays into identity, security, authenticity, and faith. Now more than ever their insights are needed to give us another glimpse into lived stories in and around food. The stories they found reveal struggle, pain, love, and the overcoming of obstacles, of barriers.
 Right now, during a pandemic, when it feels like the heat has been turned to high on social discord, perhaps food is a way to bring the temperature back down, or at least repurpose it into flames that grill up some seasonal veggies.

Even if we don't break physical bread with our neighbors every day, these stories serve as a kind of shared communion. With this communion we can lift up the voices that don't get heard enough; maybe the glimpse in these pages will create enough attention to our problems of alienation to push forward some solutions for greater unity. Even if it is one Spring Roll or meat filled bun at a time.

Bryan W. Moe is an Assistant Professor in Communication Studies. His research finds itself at the intersection of rhetoric, social movements, and food. Recent publications include chapters in and Handbook for Food and Popular Culture (2018) and Global Brooklyn: Designing Food Experiences in World Cities (2021).

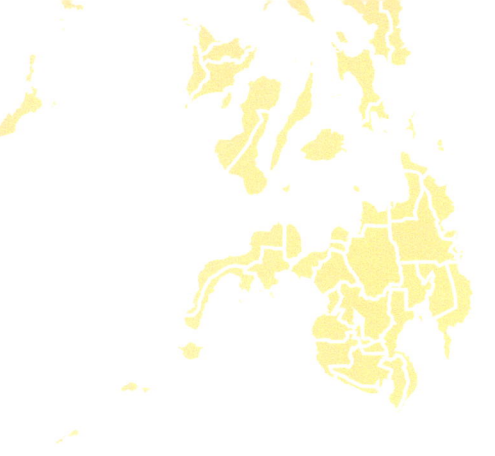

Acknowledgements

This book would not have been possible without the collaborative guidance of Dr. Tamara Welter and her patient nudging of design students in the hard work, under tight deadlines, of crafting pages that combine photo storytelling with the power of color, typography, line and form. Dr. Welter and her students have collaborated in the work of Biola Avenue Press since its inception.

This year, the work of her students complements that of student writers and photojournalists in the 2021 Media Narrative Project class. Those storytellers, over a period of less than three months, read widely, chased down elusive interviewees, and did on-the-street journalistic reporting — under constraints of a global pandemic — with remarkable perseverance and courage. They worked as a team, learning from each other. But they learned most of all from people whose cultures and ways of understanding food traditions and faith experiences differ from their own. By means of computer technology, they worked from points as far distant as Richmond, California, New York City and Seoul, South Korea.

The combined work of all these students adds to an ongoing literature of Asian cultural understanding in the United States. Viewed through the lens of food, it bears new exploration, for it goes to press in a dark moment of our nation's history, a time of unspeakable violence and public hatred of people from Asian backgrounds (including restaurant owners) in many parts of the U.S.

The project was enriched by the cooperation of Dr. Christina Lee Kim and Dr. Stan Ng, faculty members at Biola University whose guest appearances in the Media Narrative Project class helped students grasp the psychology of Asian hospitality culture and Asian restaurants as businesses. Their insights into how to approach sources for interviews was invaluable. Suggestions by Dr. Nancy Wang Yuen, Biola faculty member and renowned expert on Asian cultures, helped refine the scope of this project.

The project was also made possible by the support of the Division of Communication within the School of Fine Arts and Communication at Biola University, an institution whose mission, in brief, is to think biblically about everything, embracing the diversity of all humankind in an invitation to know God, through Jesus Christ, in our individual cultures and journeys.

Introduction

By Michael A. Longinow, Ph.D

Journalists must care. And that's hard. (Not all journalism does.) But for those of us who pursue journalism from a stance of abandonment to Christ and His call to love, we can do no other.

The Jewish philosopher and theologian Elie Wiesel was fond of telling interviewers that the opposite of love is not hate. It is indifference. And we live in a time when indifference is easy because we're tired. The numbers, the data, the charts showing deaths, infections, tracing of disease spread — it wears us out. The global pandemic shut us away in our rooms, put us behind masks, isolated us. At the printing of this book, it will have been more than a year since the dispersion began. Only now are we emerging into open spaces, and indoor spaces. And yet fear remains. In the middle of all that, perhaps because of the weariness and isolation, anger has erupted over injustices we have been silent about too long. In the summer of 2020, streets in downtown centers across the U.S. (and in cities across the world) filled with protesters chanting the names of Black women and men who had been killed by police. Less prominently, but no less tragically, there have been protests in the weeks before this book went to press about violence against people of Asian background. Some of those attacks, verbal and otherwise, have been against people who run restaurants serving Asian food.

This book is not about anger. Rather, it is about pursuit of understanding, of caring to know and explain. Most of the students who did this book's reporting do not have Asian family heritage. And it is from that lack of personal expertise that they brought honest questions, curiosity, a willingness to learn, to set aside cultural expectation.

This book's in-depth reporting and visual storytelling come at a moment of significance for our nation and world. It is a time of renewed attention to conscience. Bill Kovach and Tom Rosenstiel, in The Elements of Journalism, tell us that journalists must be allowed to "exercise their personal conscience." And we have done so. May the ideas in these pages begin, and continue, important conversations about cultural meaning, about hospitality across barriers, and about daring to love in ways that are delicious and meaningful.

Michael Longinow, born in Chicago, grew up in a mixed ethnicity home where Ukrainian varenkes and Russian borscht alternated with the skirt steak and cilantro of Mexican tacos at family gatherings. To eat together was to truly be family.

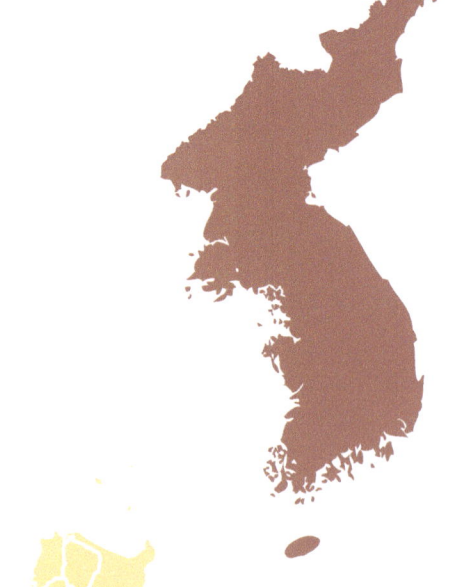

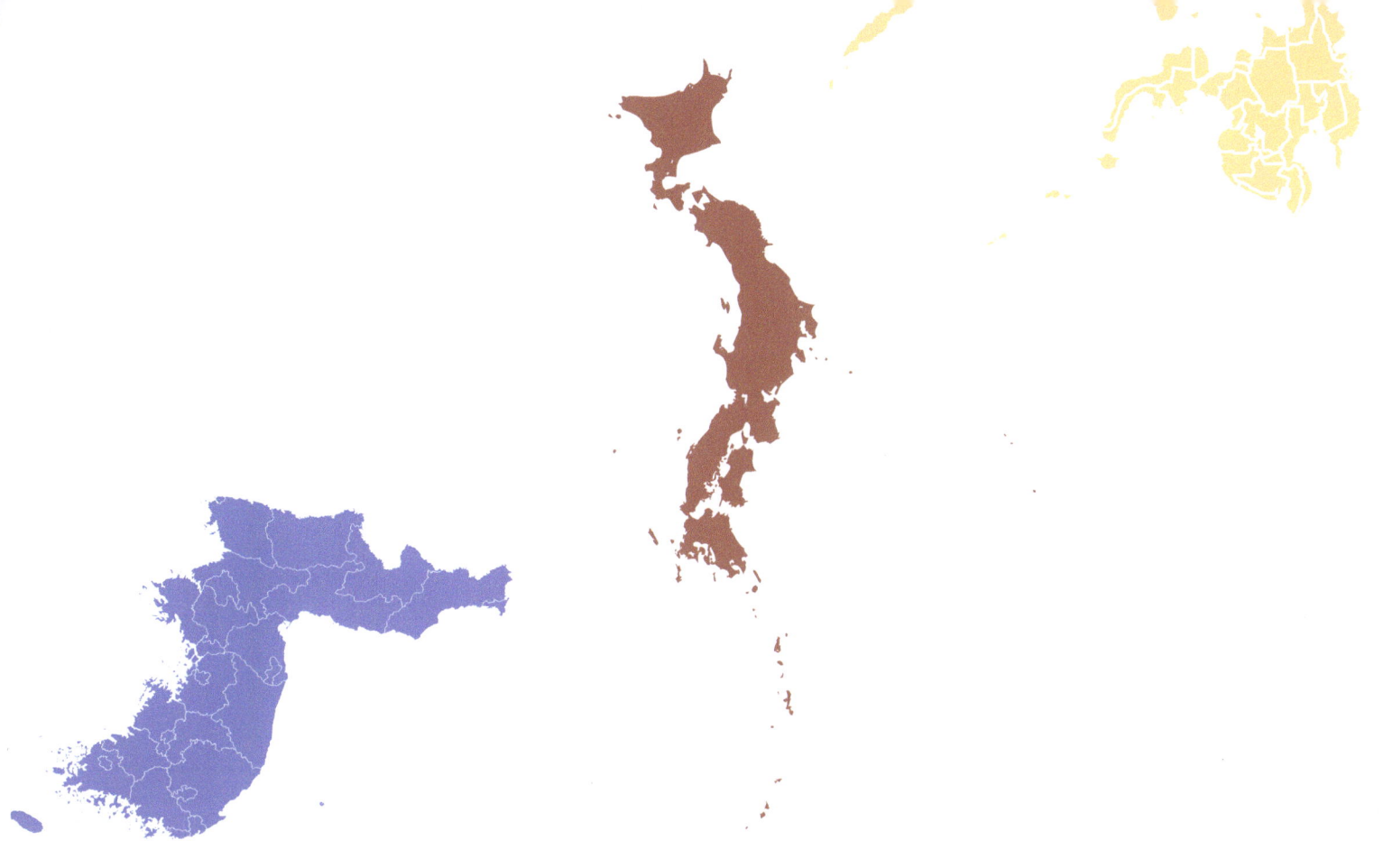

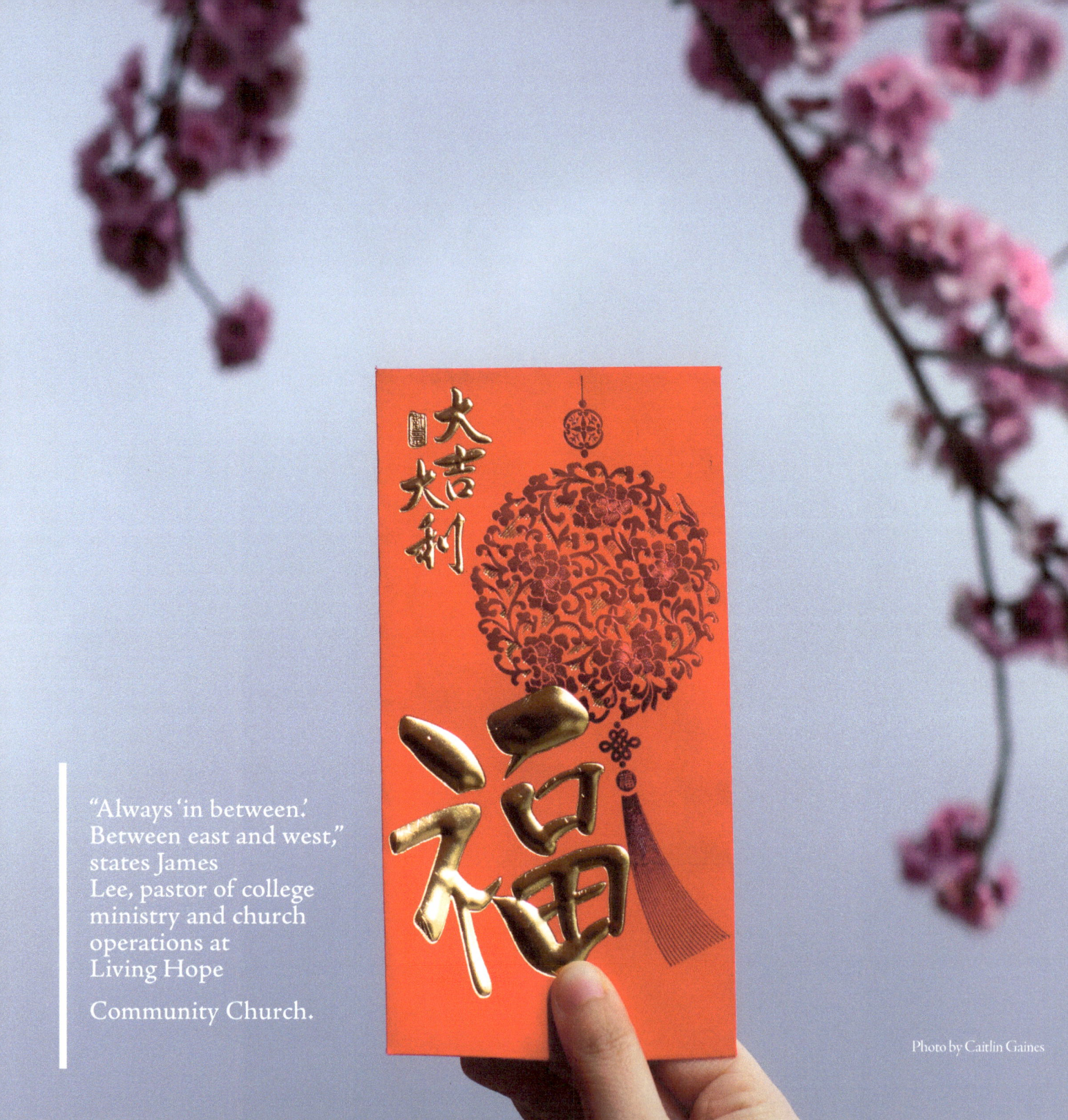

"Always 'in between.'
Between east and west,"
states James
Lee, pastor of college
ministry and church
operations at
Living Hope

Community Church.

1. Between East and West

By: Angela Hom

The struggle many Asian Americans experience is feeling like an imposter. The idea of not fully feeling that they are Asian, nor American enough. The world tells them that they should blend in, but it also screams that they do not belong here. The struggle to find this new identity and claim it as their own is something that Ian Lam, a junior elementary education major at Biola University, knows very well.

"Being an American born Chinese makes me feel that I don't really fit in either culture entirely because there's a part of me that will always feel foreign when I'm in the U.S. or in Hong Kong," explains Lam.

Lam was born in Thousand Oaks, CA in 1999. His parents decided to take him out of his environment and travel across the world more than 7,000 miles away to a land of a new language, new surroundings and little time to claim his bearings. Hong Kong was a place foreign to Lam, yet he called it home for seven years.

"In my first couple years in Hong Kong, I often couldn't understand or relate to a lot of the things my peers talked about during recess or hangout times because I only understood English," says Lam. "After I moved to the states seven to eight years later, my community felt pretty foreign as well because a lot of people here don't speak Cantonese or understand Chinese."

Lam had just adjusted to the previously foreign Hong Kong when his parents decided to move back to the United States in 2014. Just when Lam thought he had found a community to identify with, it was pulled from him yet again. He explained it is a "reverse culture shock".

"I just always felt American during my time in Hong Kong. I never really identified as a Hong Konger, at least for the first couple years. As time went by and I spent more time with my friends over there, I slowly started to view Hong Kong as my home as I got more fluent with the language over there," explains Lam. "Back then my English was not really good; I had a thick accent. I didn't know anybody at all, everybody spoke English."

Lam emphasized that language was the biggest driving factor of belonging. For both of Lam's worlds, this was a crucial factor to feeling like he belonged in the countries he was in.

Feeling like they belong is something many Asian Americans do not get the privilege of knowing. No matter where they are, there is always a disconnect between their own upbringing and their lives in the United States. The phrase many Asian Americans have come to know too well is "Go back to where you came from." But for many, the United States is their home and the only thing they know. This develops what is known as perpetual foreigner syndrome.

According to Thierry Devos and Mahzarin Banaji, perpetual foreigner syndrome means, "members of ethnic minorities will always be seen as the 'other' in the White Anglo-Saxon dominant society of the United States, which may have negative implications for them."

"When people say, 'China is our home and [they] tell us to go back to China,' that is definitely not true. China has a different culture to even Asian Americans too," says Lam. "We grew up with a mix of both cultures. If we go to a totally different country that speaks a totally different language, we'll just be foreigners as well. I think it's important for a lot of people to understand that. Asian Americans don't particularly fit in one culture."[1]

HISTORY

Historically Asian Americans have been discriminated against for many reasons: fear of communism, xenophobia, economic and employment reasons, and many more. Yet, this is not just an occurrence of the past. George Santayana, a Spanish philosopher, claimed history is doomed to repeat itself. Just because Asian discrimination and anti-Asian racism is not prominent in our everyday, does not mean it is not happening today.

The term Asian American highlights two cultures combining into something beautiful. But where does this term originate? The origins of the term can be traced back to 1968 when activist Yuji Ichioka rallied his fellow Asian Americans for justice.[2] Inspired by the Black Power movement, Ichioka wanted to reclaim Asian identity within the United States. He coined the term Asian American as an act of rebellion against the term oriental.[3] The term oriental was used to attack and discriminate against Asians at the time, implying that Asians were not from the United States, that they were the other. The overall movement was an act to end injustice for all Asian Americans, newly immigrated or American born.[4]

But how did Asian Americans get to where they are today? It all began in the 19th century.[5] This was when the first wave of Chinese immigrants came to the United States seeking a better life and the promise of fortune from the Gold Rush. These rumors were completely blown out of proportion, so White settlers implemented laws to prevent Chinese immigrants from becoming American citizens (Naturalization Act of 1790). Throughout the decades following 1790, Asians were discriminated against and seen as the other in the country they were seeking a new future in. Leading the community to now, where there is still a sense of isolation towards those who do not fit into the mold of America.

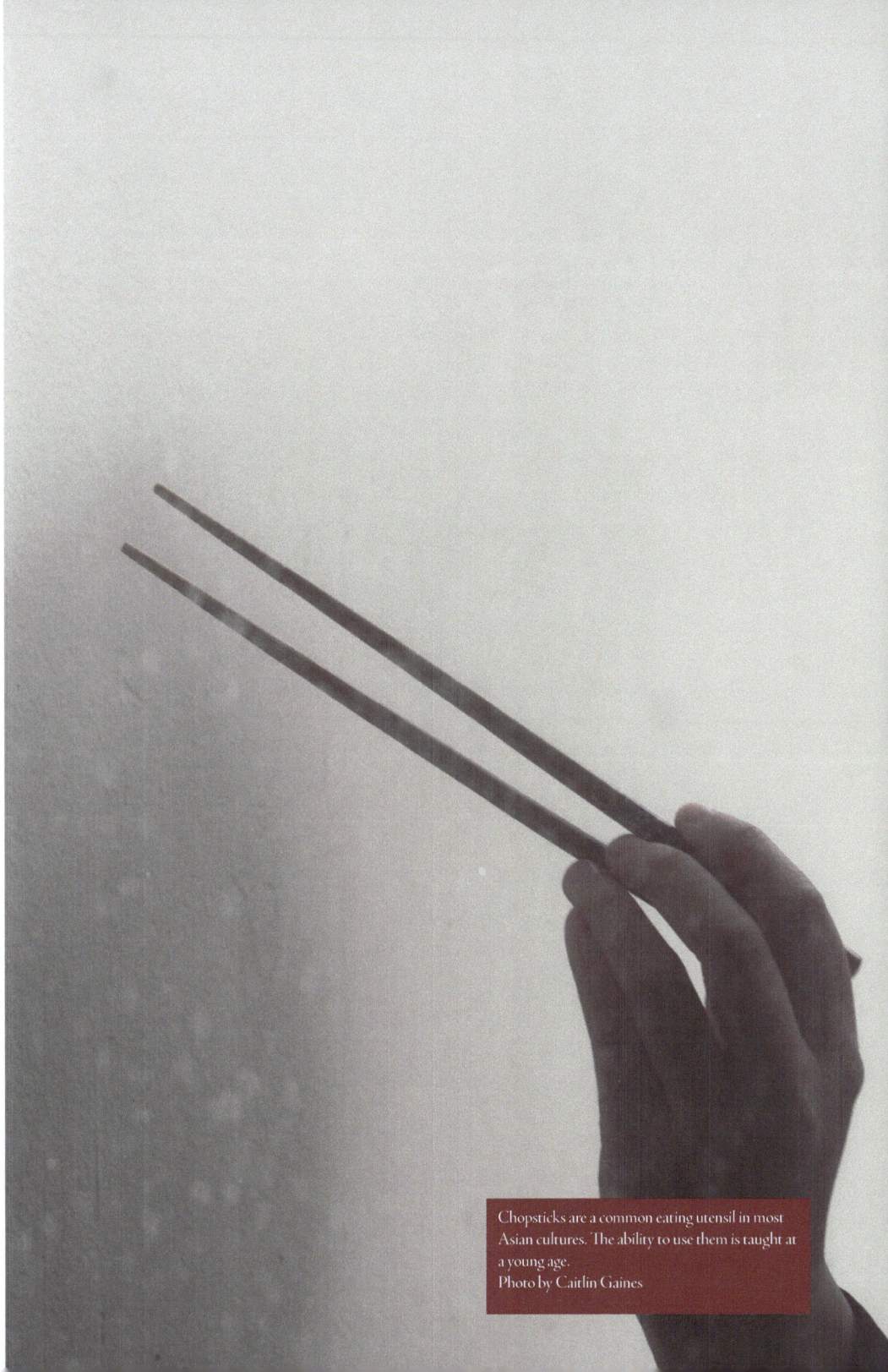

Chopsticks are a common eating utensil in most Asian cultures. The ability to use them is taught at a young age.
Photo by Caitlin Gaines

HIGH EXPECTATIONS

Many Asian immigrants are thriving in the United States today, instilling in their children the same work ethic that carried them through the gold rush. Though not every Asian household is thriving, statistically Asians in the U.S. are more well off than any other racial group. According to Statista.com in 2019, Asian American households' annual median income was $98,174.[6] Yet this is only the median. The number does not reflect the many different Asian groups within America as well as those households who are above and, especially, below the median.

"It's interesting because the wealth gap in Asians is crazy," explains Kim Huynh, a recent graduate from University of San Diego. "On one hand, my experience is privileged, but my cousin's family goes through a lot because they don't speak English and are less well off."

According to Pew Research, "Only four Asian origin groups had household incomes that exceeded the national median for Asian Americans overall: Indians ($100,000), Filipinos ($80,000) and Sri Lankans and Japanese (both $74,000). By contrast, most of the other 15 [Asian] origin groups were well below the national median for Asian Americans, including the two with the lowest median household incomes – Nepalese ($43,500) and Burmese ($36,000)."

Despite Asians only making up 5.9% of the American population according to the U.S. Census Bureau,[7] Asian household incomes on average exceed all other race groups in the nation.[8] This statistic forces many Asian American children to strive for high expectations placed on them by their parents.

Many Asian immigrants fought for their place in the United States, seeking a better life for themselves and their families. What Huynh described is what many immigrant children experience every day. There is this high expectation placed on them in order to achieve and excel in society to provide for their families in the future. These expectations apply pressure on many children making them feel as if they can never be enough.

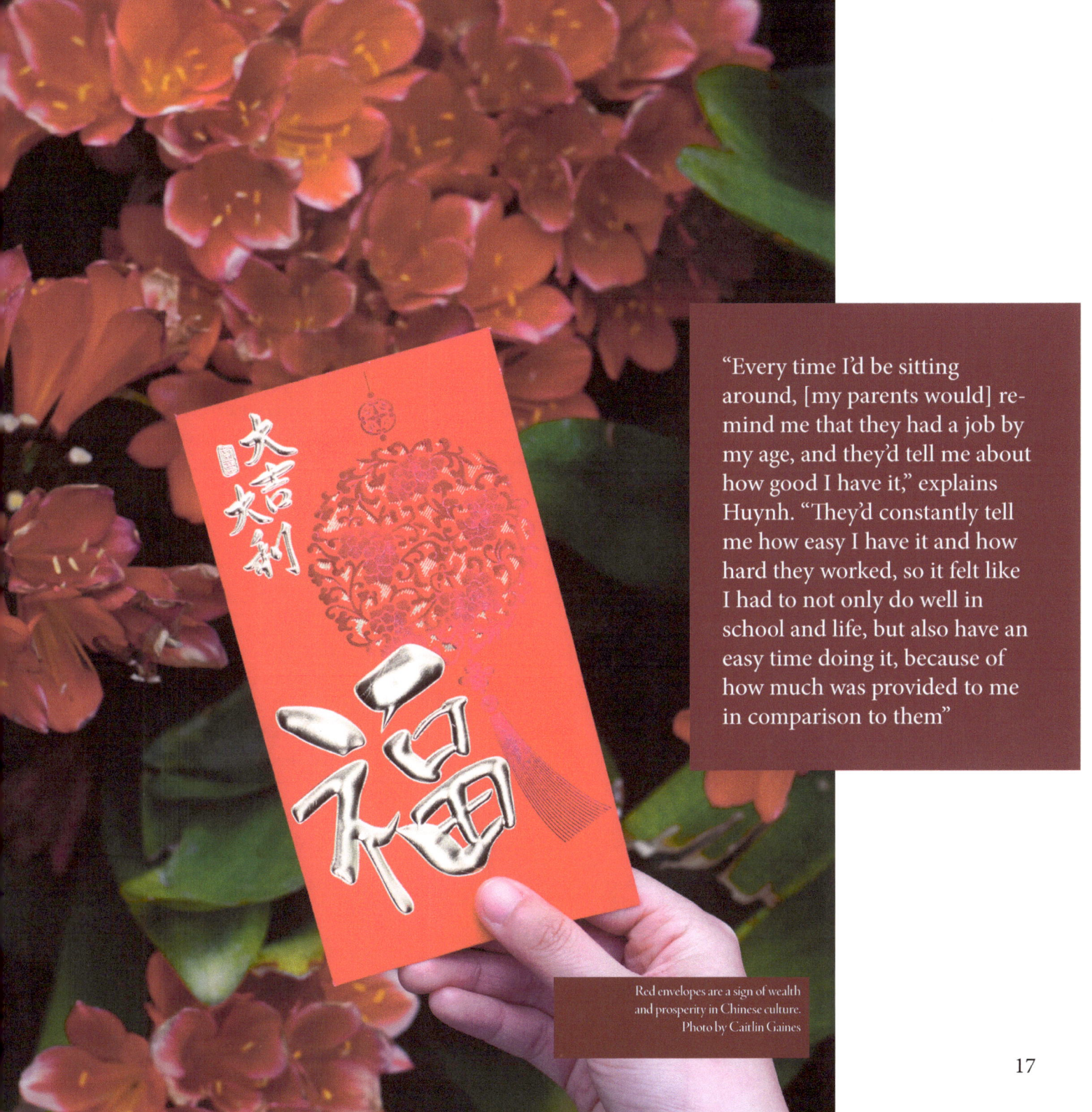

大吉大利

福

"Every time I'd be sitting around, [my parents would] remind me that they had a job by my age, and they'd tell me about how good I have it," explains Huynh. "They'd constantly tell me how easy I have it and how hard they worked, so it felt like I had to not only do well in school and life, but also have an easy time doing it, because of how much was provided to me in comparison to them"

Red envelopes are a sign of wealth and prosperity in Chinese culture.
Photo by Caitlin Gaines

CAUGHT BETWEEN

Being Chinese American myself encompasses the feeling of being in-between claimed by many minorities in America. Growing up in a predominantly Asian community provided me with the opportunity to surround myself with people who look and act like me but stepping into the real world was an entirely different monster. I am seen as the other by those outside my little bubble; not fitting in anywhere I turn. Even though I had rarely received any anti-Asian hate in my life, I had to come to terms with my own identity of being both Asian and American. Knowing that I will never fit in completely in America or China but acknowledging that I am a beautiful combination of both cultures. Caught between two distinct cultures. The world telling you that you need to blend in while your conscience telling you to be yourself. This is what it is like to be Asian American.

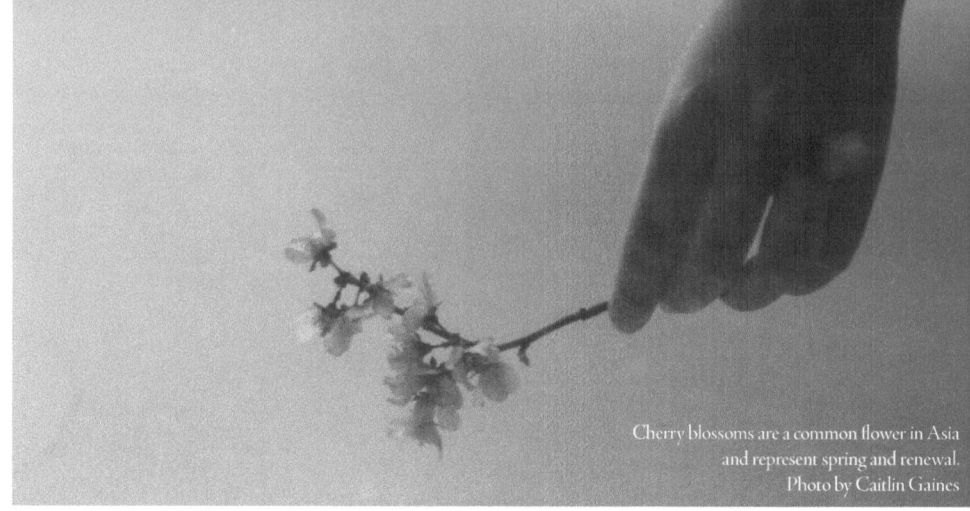

Cherry blossoms are a common flower in Asia and represent spring and renewal.
Photo by Caitlin Gaines

Diving into a table full of dim sum on Lunar New Year but also celebrating Thanksgiving for Chinese Americans. Playing yutnori for New Years and also laughing with friends between rounds of Mario Kart. Going to learn Vietnamese at Vietnamese school right after coming back from a six-hour day of American school. These are just a couple of experiences many Asian Americans have come to accept as their normal.

Food and pastimes are a window into someone's culture and the combination of both American and Asian culture is what many Asian Americans know well.

There are so many aspects that make up the Asian American identity. The pressures of familial and societal norms weigh on the generations to come. There will always be a disconnect of culture, but the Asian American community has come to accept their displacement and embrace what makes them unique. Being of both Asian and American cultures and using their experiences to form a new identity.

REFERENCES

1. Devos, T., & Banaji, M. R. (2005). American = white? Journal of Personality and Social Psychology, 88(3), 447-466. doi:10.1037/0022-3514.88.3.447
2. Rao, S. (2018, August 1). The term 'Asian American' was meant to create a collective identity. What does that mean in 2018? The Washington Post. https://www.washingtonpost.com/lifestyle/style/the-term-asian-american-was-meant-to-create-a-collective-identity-is-it-necessary-in-2018/2018/07/27/c30e7eb0-8e90-11e8-b769-e3fff17f0689_story.html.
3. Wang, Y. (2019, March 30). The long history and slow death of a word once used to describe everyone and everything from Egypt to China as well as rugs. The Washington Post. https://www.washingtonpost.com/news/morning-mix/wp/2016/05/13/the-long-history-and-slow-death-of-a-word-used-to-describe-everyone-from-turks-to-the-chinese/.
4. Rao, S. (2018, August 1). The term 'Asian American' was meant to create a collective identity. What does that mean in 2018? The Washington Post. https://www.washingtonpost.com/lifestyle/style/the-term-asian-american-was-meant-to-create-a-collective-identity-is-it-necessary-in-2018/2018/07/27/c30e7eb0-8e90-11e8-b769-e3fff17f0689_story.html.
5. The Journey from Gold Mountain: The Asian American Experience. (2006). Japanese American Citizens League.
6. Department, P., & 20, J. (2021, January 20). Median household income by race or ethnic GROUP 2019. Retrieved February 24, 2021, from https://www.statista.com/statistics/233324/median-household-income-in-the-united-states-by-race-or-ethnic-group/
7. U.S. census bureau QUICKFACTS: United States. (n.d.). Retrieved February 23, 2021, from https://www.census.gov/quickfacts/fact/table/US/RHI225219
8. Budiman, A., Cilluffo, A., & Ruiz, N. G. (2020, May 30). Key facts about Asian origin groups in the U.S. Pew Research Center. https://www.pewresearch.org/fact-tank/2019/05/22/key-facts-about-asian-origin-groups-in-the-u-s/.

This is the Asian American experience.

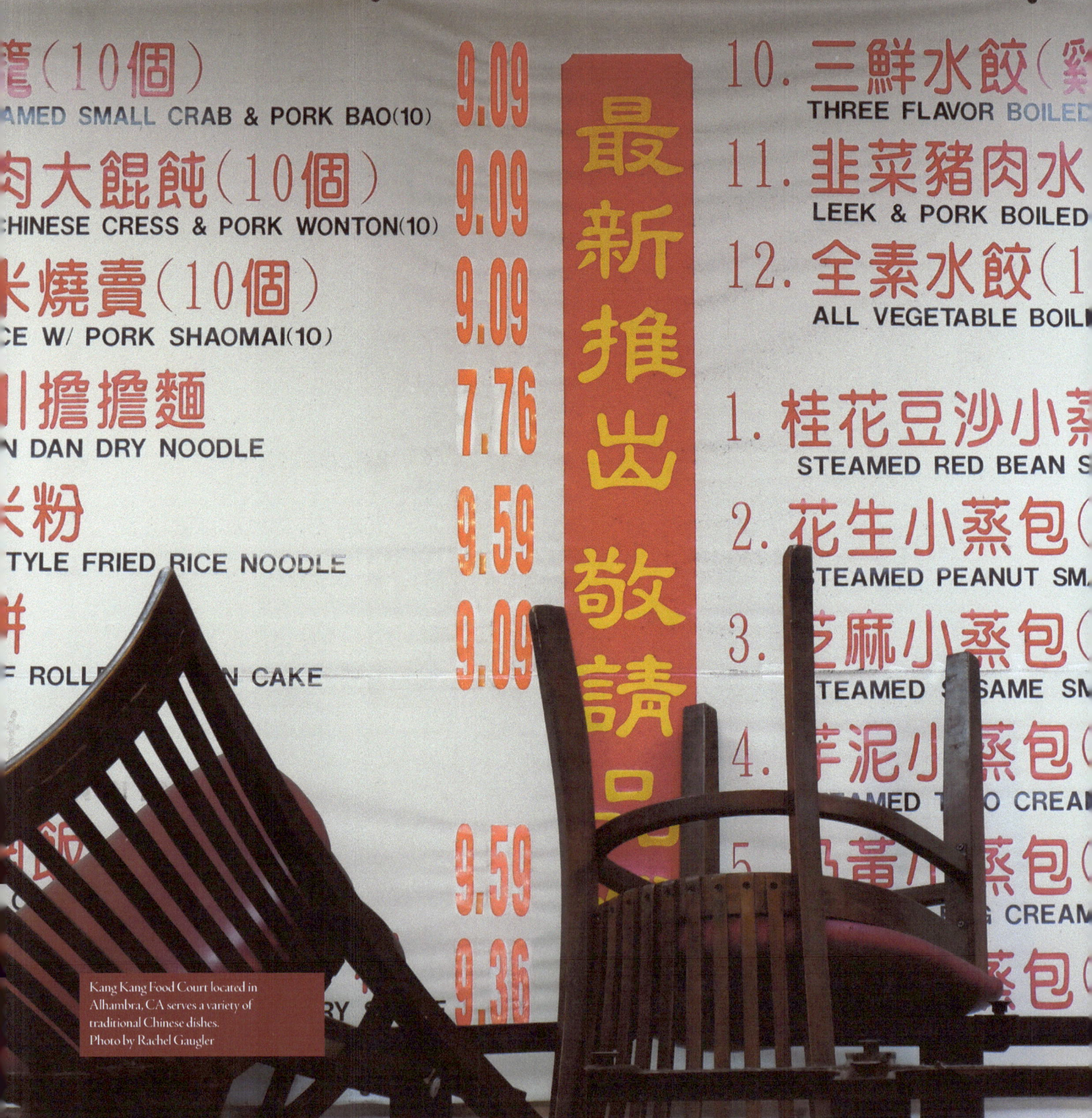

（10個）　9.09
...AMED SMALL CRAB & PORK BAO(10)

肉大餛飩（10個）　9.09
...HINESE CRESS & PORK WONTON(10)

米燒賣（10個）　9.09
...CE W/ PORK SHAOMAI(10)

川擔擔麵　7.76
...N DAN DRY NOODLE

...粉　9.59
...TYLE FRIED RICE NOODLE

...　9.09
...F ROLLE... ...N CAKE

9.59

9.36

最新推出敬請品...

10. 三鮮水餃（...
THREE FLAVOR BOILED...

11. 韭菜豬肉水...
LEEK & PORK BOILED...

12. 全素水餃（1...
ALL VEGETABLE BOIL...

1. 桂花豆沙小蒸...
STEAMED RED BEAN S...

2. 花生小蒸包（...
...STEAMED PEANUT SMA...

3. 芝麻小蒸包（...
...TEAMED S...SAME SM...

4. 芋泥小蒸包（...
...AMED T...O CREAM...

5. ...黃小蒸包（...
...CREAM...

...包（...

Kang Kang Food Court located in Alhambra, CA serves a variety of traditional Chinese dishes.
Photo by Rachel Gaugler

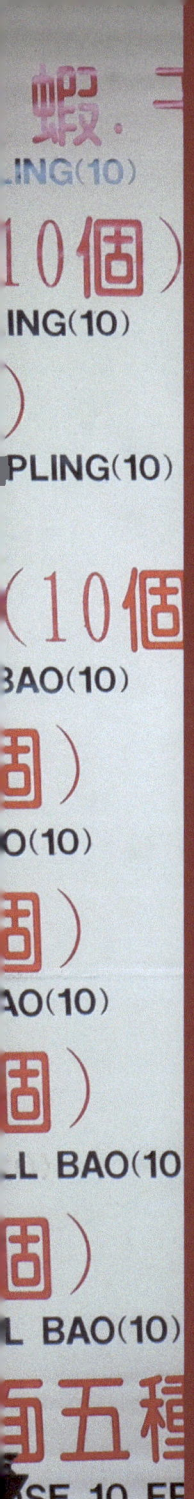

2. The landscape of Flavors: the Asian Foodscape in the U.S.

By: Rachel Gaugler

As one person rolls up their sleeves to wash the cabbage, another hunches over the kitchen counter to prepare the paste of red pepper, garlic, ginger, sugar and fish sauce. Just a few feet away, another person packages the sour, funky fermented mix of vegetables into containers for their neighbors to bring home, all the while sharing stories and singing songs. This is the picture of gimjang, a kimchi making party and an event that Jennifer Kim, a second-generation Korean-American, recalls fondly. This is jeong.

Jeong is a term that describes intimate feelings arising from one's relationship with another person, and the desire to do something for them, such as making extra kimchi and sharing it with family and friends. Kim described jeong as the feeling associated with being part of a family or community.

> "It is the community and local history that determine whether a neighborhood becomes a food oasis or a food desert."
> - Simon Vonthron

早點 BREAKFAST

Breakfast Choose 3 Items
Served with Porridge

0. 菜飯糰	Fried Rice Cake	1.83
1. 油條	Twisted Cruller	1.83
2. 燒餅	Baked Pancake	1.83
3. 飯糰（鹹、甜、素）	Rice Roll	3.20
4. 熱豆漿	Sweet Soybean Milk	2.28
5. 鹹豆漿	Salted Soybean Milk	3.20
6. 冰豆漿	Cold Soybean Milk	2.28
7. 稀飯（白、綠豆、小米、鹹）	Porridge	1.83 2.28
8. 蛋餅	Pan Fried Egg Cake	4.57
9. 薄餅煎蛋	Pan Cake with Egg	4.57
10. 荷包蛋	Pan Fried Egg	2.28

快餐或早點：$5.28
三菜或兩菜一點心，附送稀飯

早、晚快餐 FAST FOOD FOR LUNCH & DINNER

花式眾多，精心烹製，大眾品味，經濟實惠，每日進貨，新鮮健康。

任選四菜附送白飯	$7.08 Choice of 4 Items with Steamed Rice
任選三菜附送白飯	$6.35 Choice of 3 Items with Steamed Rice
任選二菜附送白飯	$5.71 Choice of 2 Items with Steamed Rice
任選一菜附送白飯	$5.02 Choice of 1 Item with Steamed Rice
大碗單菜	$4.52 Family Size 1 Item
白飯	$1.60 Steamed Rice

台灣小吃 TAIWANESE FOOD

21. 蚵仔煎	SPan Fried Oyster Cake with Egg	8.17
26. 魚丸湯	Taiwan Style Fish Ball Soup	8.17
27. 糯米大腸	Sweet Rice with Chitterlings	8.17
28. 台灣肉粽(1)	Taiwan Meat with Glutinous Rice(1)	3.43
29. 控肉飯、麵、米粉	Stewed Pork Rice/Noodle/Rice Noodle	9.09
30. 豬腳飯、麵、米粉	Pork Feet Rice/Noodle/Rice Noodle	9.09
31. 冬菇肉燥飯、麵、米粉	Minced Meat & Mushroon Rice/Noodle/Rice Noodle	9.09
32. 魷魚羹飯、麵、米粉	Squid Stew Soup Rice/Noodle/Rice Noodle	9.36
33. 台南擔仔麵、米粉	Taiwan Style Meat w/Noodle/Rice Noodle	7.53
34. 大腸麵、麵線、米粉	Chitterlings Noodle/Thin Noodle/Rice Noodle	9.36
35. 台式雲吞湯、麵、米粉	Taiwan Style Wonton Soup/Noodle/Rice Noodle	7.76 9.36
36. 乾麵、乾米粉	Dry Noodle or Rice Noodle	7.99
37. 海鮮湯烏冬	Seafood Udon Soup	10.05
38. 海鮮炒烏冬	Stirred Fried Udon with Seafood	10.05
39. 蚵仔麵線	Oyster Thin Noodle	9.36
40. 當歸鴨麵線	Danguei Duck Thin Noodle Soup	10.05
41. 酸菜肚片湯	Preserved Vegetable Pig Stomach Soup	8.68
42. 魷魚羹湯	Squid Stew Soup	8.68
43. 肉羹飯、麵、米粉	Pork Stew Soup Rice, Noodle or Rice Noodle	9.36
44. 台式排骨乾麵	Taiwan Style Pork Chop with Dry Noodle	9.36

北方小吃 FOOD IN NO...

51. 牛肉捲餅(2)	Simmered Beef	
53. 京都肉餅	Jing Dong Meat	
54. 家常餅（一張或半張）	Chinese Pie (Wh...	
55. 家常餅套餐（附醬豬肉、醬、蔥段）	Chinese Pie w/Sim...	
56. 蔥油餅	Green Onion Pan...	
57. 鮮肉白菜水餃(10)	Pork & Napa Boi...	
53. 鍋貼(8)	Pan Fried Dumpl...	
59. 三鮮水餃(10)	Thrcr Flavor Boil...	
（蝦、豬肉、雞蛋）	(Shrimp, Scallops...	
60. 全青水餃(10)	All Vegetable Boi...	
61. 韭菜豬肉水餃(10)	Leek & P... Boil...	
62. 韭菜盒子(4)	Leek Cake (4)	
63. 酸菜羊肉砂鍋	Sour Vegetable w/La...	
64. 酸菜白肉砂鍋	Sour Vegetable w/P...	
65. 酸采豆腐砂鍋	Sour Vegetable w/T...	
66. 紅燒牛肉刀削麵	Dow Xiao Noodle ...	
67. 酸菜羊肉刀削麵	Dow Xiao Noodle S...	
68. 打鹵刀削麵	Dow Xiao Noodle ...	
69. 炸醬刀削麵	Dow Xiao Noodle ...	
70. 酸辣湯	Hot & Sour Soup	

江南小吃 FOOD IN EAS...

76. 薺菜大餛飩(10)	Shanghai Style Chinese...	
77. 豬肉糯米燒賣(10)	Glutinous Rice w/...	
78. 上海蟹粉小籠湯包(10)	Shanghai Steamed S...	
79. 上海生煎包(8)	Shanghai Pan Frie...	
80. 上海小籠湯包(10)	Shanghai Steame...	
81. 三鮮小餛飩(12)	Three Flavor Mini...	
82. 菜肉大餛飩(10)	Vegetable & Pork...	
83. 上海炒年糕	Shanghai Fried Ri...	
84. 上海湯年糕	Shanghai Rice Ca...	
85. 鹹豬肉、雞肉、排骨菜飯	Salted Pork/Chicken/...	
86. 上海粗炒麵	Shanghai ried N...	
87. 蔥油拌麵	Scallion & Vegetab...	
88. 蘇州燜肉湯麵	Suzhou Steamed ...	
89. 現炒雪菜肉絲湯麵、米粉	Preserved Veg. & Shredde...	
90. 現炒鱔糊湯麵、米粉	Shredded Eel Nood...	
91. 燻魚麵、米粉	Smoked Fish Noo...	
92. 辣醬麵	Noodle in Special ...	
93. 咖哩牛肉麵、米粉	Curry Beef Noodle...	
94. 榨菜肉絲麵、米粉	Preserved Veg. & Shred...	
95. 榨菜肉絲湯	Preserved Veg. & ...	
96. 青菜豆腐湯	Chinese Green & T...	
97. 油豆腐細粉湯	Fried Bean Curd & ...	
98. 咖哩牛肉細粉湯	Curry Beef & Verm...	
99. 上海鮮肉包、素菜中包(1)	Shanghai Medium ...	
100. 蘿蔔絲、紅豆沙酥餅(1)	Backed Turnip/ Re...	
101. 紅豆湯圓(4)	Red Bean Rice Ba...	
102. 鮮肉湯圓(4)	Pork Rice Ball Sou...	
103. 上海鮮肉粽(1)	Shanghai Pork Glu...	
104. 桂花紅豆沙小蒸包(10)	Steamed Red Bea...	
105. 花生、...	

...N CHINA

...n Cake (2) ..	9.09
...	8.17
...	6.40 5.25
...Green Onion.	9.36
...	5.94
...g (10)	7.53
...	8.45
...(10)	8.22
...g (10)	7.53
...(10)	7.99
...	8.22
...ole..19.18	16.44
...role.16.44	14.61
...ole 14.61	12.79
...	10.05
...e and Lamb	10.96
...l Soup	9.59
...Sauc..	9.59
...	8.17

...CHINA

...Wonton (10) ..	9.09
...ai (10)	9.09
...ork Bao (10) ..	9.09
...o (8)	9.09
...o (10)	8.17
...)	5.48
...)	8.17
...	9.36
...	9.36
...egetable Rice..	9.36
...	9.36
...Noodle	8.22
...e Soup ..	9.36
...ice Noodle Soup	9.36
...odle Soup..	15.53
...oodle Soup.	9.59
...e	9.36
...odle	9.09
...dle/Rice Noodle	9.09
...Pork Soup ...	8.17
...	7.31
...Soup 5.48	8.45
...5.93	9.09
...le Bao (1) ...	1.37
...ke (1)	1.37
...	6.85
...	6.85
...(1) ...	3.43
...(10) ...	8.68

廣式香港 東南亞小吃
FOOD IN SOUTHERN CHINA HONG KONG & ASIA

108.	干炒牛河	Beef Chow Fun Dry Style 9.59
109.	海鮮炒河粉	Seafood Chow Fun 10.50
110.	什錦炒河粉	Assorted Meat Chow Fun 10.50
111.	黑椒牛腩飯	Beef Rice in Black Pepper Sauce 9.59
112.	牛肉燴飯	Beef Rice in Brown Sauce 9.59
113.	沙茶牛肉飯、麵	Satay Beef Rice/Noodle 9.59
114.	海鮮燴飯	Rice Covered by Seafood in Wine Sauce .. 10.50
115.	蘿蔔糕 (4)	Turnip Cake (4) 5.94
116.	星洲炒米粉	Singapore Style Fried Rice Noodle 9.59
117.	黑椒豬排飯、湯麵、湯米粉	Pork Chop Rice/Noodle/Rice Noodle in Black Pepper Sauce .. 9.59
118.	黑椒雞腿飯、湯麵、米粉	Chicken Thigh Rice/Noodle/Rice Noodle in Black Pepper Sauce .. 9.59
122.	康康雲吞 (10)	Kang Kang Wonton (10) 9.13
123.	康康雲吞、米粉、河粉	Kang Kang Wonton Noodle/Rice Noodle/Fun 9.13
124.	康康雞肉半麵	Kang Kang Chicken Noodle 9.13
125.	康康豬手、米粉、河粉	Kang Kang Pig Feet Noodle/Rice Noodle/Fun 9.36
126.	康康牛腩麵、米粉、河粉	Kang Kang Beef Noodle/Rice Noodle/Fun .. 9.36
127.	濕炒豆豉牛河	Beef Chow Fun in Black Bean Sauce Wet Style .. 9.59
128.	紅燒羊腩湯麵、米粉、河粉	Lamb Noodle/Rice Noodle/Fun in Brown Sauce 10.27
129.	咖哩雞腿飯	Chicken Thigh & Rice in Curry Sauce 9.36
130.	咖哩豬排飯	Pork Chop & Rice in Curry Sauce 9.36
131.	咖哩牛腩飯	Beef & Rice in Curry Sauce 9.59
132.	雞絲涼麵	Chicken Cold Noodle 9.36

本店傳統小吃
HOUSE SPECIALTIES

133.	四川擔擔麵 (花生)	Szechwan Dan Dan Dry Noodle (Peanuts) ... 7.76
134.	牛肉麵	Beef Stew Noodle 9.59
135.	排骨飯、麵、米粉	Pork Chop Rice/ Noodle/ Rice Noodle 9.09
136.	雞腿飯、麵、米粉	Chicken Thigh Rice/ Noodle/ Rice Noodle ... 9.09
137.	什錦湯麵、米粉	Assorted Meat Noodle/ Rice Noodle 10.00
138.	海鮮湯麵、米粉	Seafood Noodle/ Rice Noodle 10.00
139.	火腿蛋炒飯	Ham & Egg Fried Rice 9.09
140.	楊州炒飯	Yang Zhou Fried Rice 9.09
141.	雞肉炒飯、麵、米粉	Chicken Fried Rice/ Noodle/ Rice Noodle .. 9.09
142.	牛肉炒飯、麵、米粉	Beef Fried Rice/ Noodle/ Rice Noodle 9.59
143.	肉絲炒飯、麵、米粉	Pork fried Rice/ Noodle/ Rice Noodle 9.09
144.	蝦仁炒飯、麵、米粉	Shrimp Fried Rice/ Noodle/ Rice Noodle ... 10.00
145.	什錦炒飯、麵、米粉	Assorted Meat Fried Rice/ Noodle/ Rice Noodle 10.00
146.	海鮮炒飯、麵、米粉	Seafood Fried Rice/ Noodle/ Rice Noodle 10.00

Kang Kang Food Court located in Alhambra, CA serves a variety of traditional Chinese dishes.

For collectivist cultures that emphasize relationships and interconnectedness, one way jeong is expressed is through the sharing of recipes from one generation to the next. Another way is through the sharing of meals between restaurant owners and their customers. As they open the doors and invite people into their family-owned businesses, they demonstrate jeong. This is a picture common to many restaurants found especially within ethnic enclaves across the U.S., shaping the culture of the Asian "foodscape."

Food studies scholar Simon Vonthron defines the term "foodscape" as emphasizing the connection between people, food and places.[1] The Asian foodscape, in particular, focuses on the relationships between Asian-American communities and traditional food of their culture. Vonthron explains that ethnic foodscapes help to shape the social identities of communities living within these neighborhoods. Increasingly, food has become the main connection between first, second and even third generation Asian-Americans with their homeland.

TRADITIONAL OR TRENDY?

Since the 19th century, when the first Chinatown was established in San Francisco, the Asian "foodscape" across the U.S. has evolved dramatically. In the past several decades, we have seen a rise in Asian-American populations in metropolitan areas like New York City and Los Angeles, but also in unexpected places like St. Paul, Minnesota and Houston, Texas. As the Asian-American population grows, so does the cuisine, leaving room for both a celebration of diverse palates and the downward spiral of food tokenization.

As we dive into the food scene of Asian enclaves in the U.S., how do we navigate the dichotomy of traditional and trendy?

We can start by defining food tokenism. In a blog post[2] about ethnic food "trends," food journalist Pelin Keskin describes tokenism as when "someone from another race who doesn't understand the cultural nuances...speaks for you or cooks the food that's so personal."

Food tokenism is the unfortunate, but common side effect of the rising food media scene. It is a form of discrimination as it often celebrates the dish but not the culture, and perpetuates a different, "trendifying" culture of traditional dishes. With little focus on the people who created those cuisines, ethnic food "trends" tend to cater to the privileged consumer. As ethnic food becomes "trendy," more faces grace the streets of ethnic enclaves, and the celebration of community ethnic identity is replaced by a new, hipster one.

When considering the changing landscape of Koreatown, for example, Kim wonders how individuals who grew up in Korea would feel about their cultural hub expanding to foreigners.

"Everywhere they go, they may feel like they are surrounded by non-Koreans and are losing touch with their homeland," said Kim.

Further, as the food that was once too smelly or spicy for the mainstream white folk becomes the new food trend—such as kimchi as a probiotic—there's a hypocritical undertone.

Now, the kimchi that brought such shame in the school cafeteria can be found in the shape of a burger in an upscale neighborhood in Washington, explains Ruth Tam. In an article[3] for Chicago Tribune, Tam describes her hesitation at seeing some of the foods that she grew up with in an immigrant home become the next trend in food media.

"This cultural appropriation stings because the same dishes hyped as 'authentic' on trendy menus were scorned when cooked in the homes of the immigrants who brought them here," explained Tam. "Fashionable food from foreign cultures may satisfy a temporary hunger, but if you're trying it for shallow reasons, you'll be culturally unfulfilled in the long run."

Although the "trendifying" of Asian foods may be argued as an economic advantage as it brings in business, food blogger Ann-Derrick Gaillot explains that it can monetize food in ways that don't benefit the communities which created them. For example, when an ethnic dish becomes trendy, people from outside of the immigrant community tend to hop on the new fad and profit off of monetizing that community's culture. Essentially, it's a "colonization attitude that is still present in the food world," explains Gaillot.

"I'm hoping that we get to the stage where we respect authentic food financially as much as we do socially," said Keskin.

Even as we continue to explore Asian culture through the lens of Asian cuisine, our goal is not to speak for the people we interview but rather bring attention to their stories, restaurants, and most importantly, foods. We want to celebrate the people behind the cutting board. By the end of this book, our hope is that readers will not only have greater knowledge of the restaurants they so often order from, but an appreciation for the history and story behind them and a desire to learn more. So, in this quest for more knowledge, let's begin by taking a brief look at the current Asian demographic in the U.S.

CHANGING NEIGHBOR-HOODS: A CLOSER LOOK AT THE ASIAN-AMERICAN DEMOGRAPHIC

According to the 2010 census, there are 17.3 million Americans of Asian ancestry. California has the largest Asian population with nearly 5.6 million people, roughly 14.9% of the state's population. Out of these 5.6 million, the largest groups are Filipino (26%), Chinese (23%) and Indian (10%). The second largest Asian population is in New York, another cultural hub. With close to 1.6 million people, New York's Asian population is largely made up of individuals from Korea (10%), China (37%) and India (23%). In New York City alone, there are 1.2 million Asians concentrated in neighborhoods like Jackson Heights and Flushing. The third largest Asian population is in Texas. According to the South China Morning Post[4], Texas' Asian population increased 72% from 2000 to 2010 with nearly 1.2 million Asians of largely Chinese, Vietnamese and Indian descent.

With more than thirty ethnically Asian groups represented in the U.S.—many of these craving cultural hubs of their own—the number of ethnic enclaves is on the rise. But, what exactly is an ethnic enclave? An ethnic enclave is a re-creation[5] of the remembered homeland by incoming immigrants and a pathway[6] back into one's home country.

In an article[7] about Asian enclaves throughout the U.S., David Johnson explains that enclaves were formed as a result of immigrants from Asia or the Pacific Islands desiring to be a part of already established ethnic communities, where common language and culture "made them feel at home."

For many immigrants, ethnic enclaves are primarily a place of refuge. For others, they're a place of prosperity. In a book[8] about social justice, Michael Liu and Kim Geron describe three different types of ethnic enclaves—traditional enclaves, economic enclaves and ethnoburbs.

In the next few sections, we'll explore these three types of ethnic enclaves and the Asian communities that primarily fall within them.

ENCLAVES AS REFUGE

The traditional enclave refers to the neighborhood communities forged before World War II by Chinese, Japanese and Filipino immigrants. Whether it was Little Manila formed in the bayou of New Orleans in the 1750s or the first Chinatown established in San Francisco in 1849, these traditional enclaves were formed as refuges from racism and increasing anti-Asian sentiment in the U.S. These neighborhoods were a means for protection and through both a shared community and food, immigrants grew to be resilient.

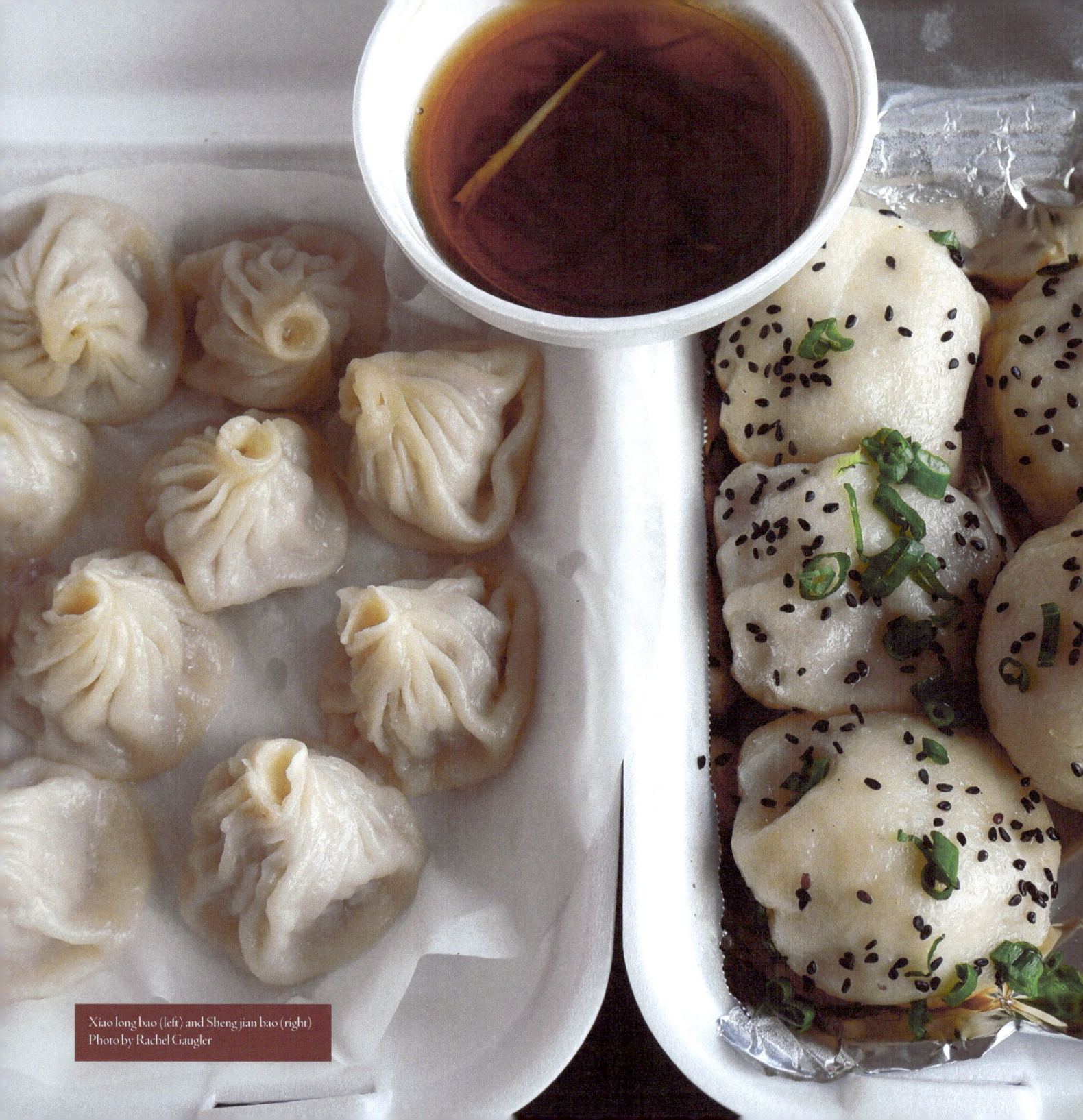

Xiao long bao (left) and Sheng jian bao (right)
Photo by Rachel Gaugler

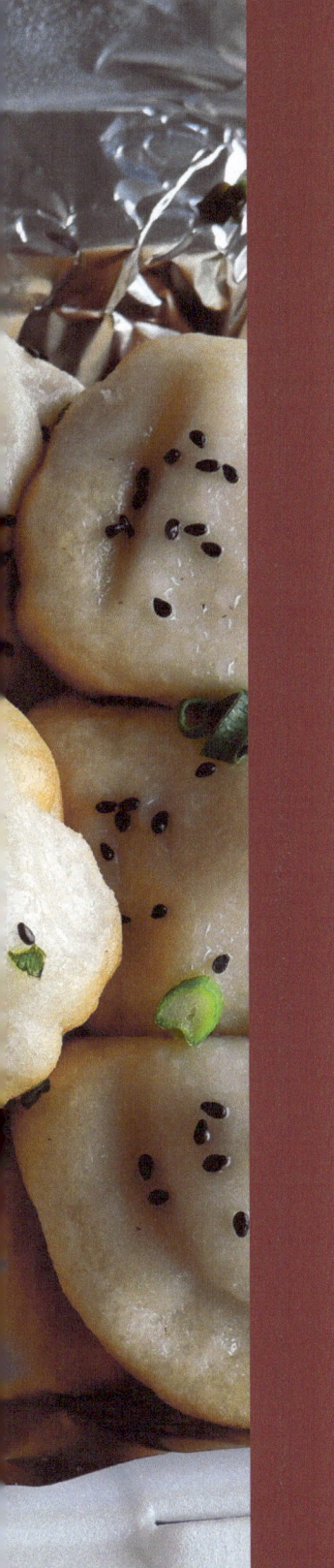

CHINATOWN

Chinatowns have been in the U.S. for more than 170 years. The first one was established in 1849 in San Francisco (SF) when, according to the Time magazine, the first Chinese immigrants to the U.S. went into the business of providing services for the miners as traders, grocers, merchants and restaurant owners. In 1882, the Chinese Exclusion Act was passed and anti-Chinese sentiment grew, despite the hordes of miners at so-called "chow chow houses."[9] In the 20th century, Chinese chop suey joints were received with greater favor by young urbanites who found these places to be hip and affordable. Although Chinese food has been westernized over the years to cater to the tastes of consumers, in recent decades, the U.S. is seeing a rise in authentic Chinese cuisine.

For example, you can now find traditional Cantonese at one of Chinatown's oldest restaurants, R&G Lounge, on Kearny Street in San Francisco and mooncakes at the Eastern Bakery on Grant Avenue. So, although rooted in racism and established as a refuge from discrimination of a dominant culture, Chinatown is the origin for many of the well-known flavors and recipes of Chinese-American food today with dishes such as chop suey, egg foo yung and moo goo gai pan. As immigrants fanned out around the country, Chinatowns mushroomed all over the United States, including in Manhattan, NY, which contains the largest Chinese population outside of Asia.

FILIPINOTOWNS / LITTLE MANILAS

Another example of a traditional enclave is Filipinotown or Little Manila. Ethnographer David Johnson[10] explains that in the 1700s, Filipino sailors arrived in New Orleans, Louisiana, forming the first Little Manila and Bayou Cholas, the oldest Asian communities in the U.S. After the U.S. won control over the Philippines after the Spanish-American war, Filipino immigration to the U.S. increased and laborers came to work in agriculture in Hawaii and California. Although Filipino grocery stores, office complexes, schools and restaurants emerged in a concentrated area east of downtown Los Angeles in the 1900s, Frank Shyong of the Los Angeles Times explains that it wasn't until 2002 that it was officially recognized as Historic Filipinotown, or HiFi[11], giving the neighborhood a name and identity. At the same time, another Filipino enclave was forming 3,000 miles away in Woodside, Queens. New York based journalist Marjorie Cohen describes in an article[12] for Brick Underground that Woodside's Little Manila dates back to the 1970s, right after passage of the 1965 Immigration and Nationality Act. As Filipino doctors and nurses began to arrive in NYC, they settled near Elmhurst Hospital and formed a community on the strip of Roosevelt Avenue from 61st Street to 70th Street. Little Manila is home to many restaurants and mini marts.

"Having a place that the community can be reminded of home while sharing our culture with the various nationalities that visit us daily is our motivation and brings us joy," said Dizon.

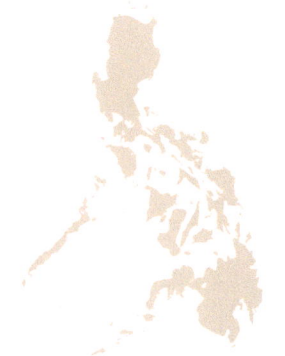

JAPANTOWNS / LITTLE TOKYO

Like Chinatown and Little Manila, Japantowns have a long history, embedded with forces of racism and exclusion. San Francisco's Japantown (JTown) or Nihonmachi, was created in 1906 when the number of Japanese on the U.S. mainland outnumbered Chinese. Urban Japanese businesses boomed in San Francisco and Los Angeles. However, when California passed the Alien Land Law in 1913, which prohibited "aliens ineligible for citizenship" from owning or holding long-term leases on land, Nihonmachis in New York, San Francisco, Los Angeles, Portland and Seattle provided space for Japanese-Americans to find housing and jobs. They became social hubs for Japanese immigrants.[13]

What do Japantowns look like today? JTowns can be found throughout the U.S., most notably in San Francisco, Los Angeles and San Jose. The Japanese community in Los Angeles is centered near downtown and is known as Little Tokyo. This town emerged in 1886 when a former sailor, Hamanosuke "Charles Hama" Shigeta, opened Kame Restaurant on East First Street. Today, it is a neighborhood lined with old-school ramen joints and new craft breweries. Visitors can try out Daikokuya, if looking for a ramen spot, or Sushi Gen in the Arts District. Like many of the other enclaves, JTown is not only a cultural hub, but a culinary corner of the Asian-American experience.

ENCLAVES AS OPPORTUNITY

The economic enclave is made up of ethnic entrepreneurs from newly arriving immigrant and refugee populations, such as South Asians, Koreans and refugees from Southeast Asia. Examples of these enclaves include Little Saigon in Westminster, California and Little India in Artesia, California. As these communities grow in size and attract individuals from other cities, the restaurant business flourishes.

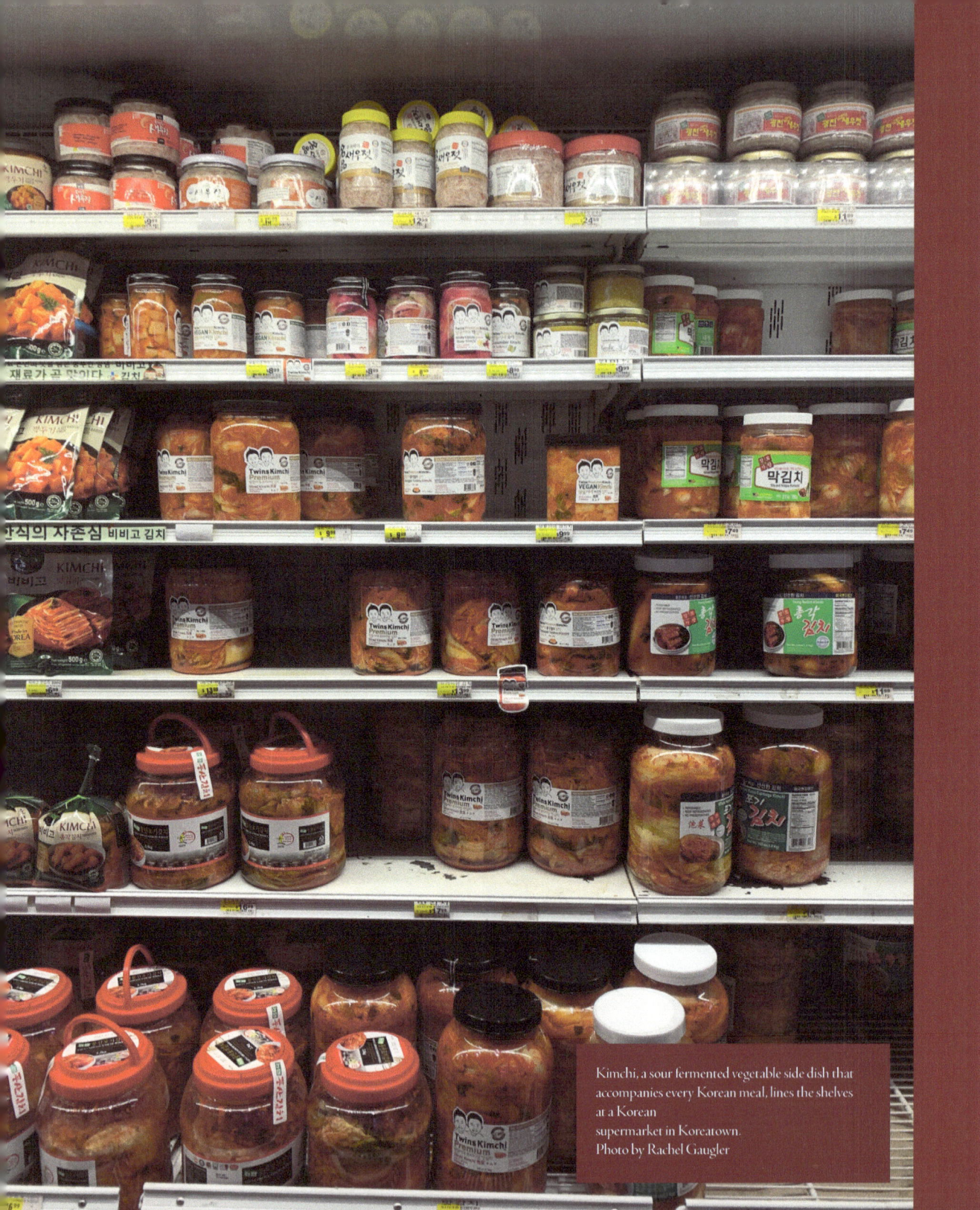

Kimchi, a sour fermented vegetable side dish that accompanies every Korean meal, lines the shelves at a Korean supermarket in Koreatown.
Photo by Rachel Gaugler

KOREATOWNS

Although the first Korean settlement in the U.S. was established in Riverside, California, in the early 1900s, it wasn't until the early 1970s that Koreatown officially emerged in Los Angeles with various restaurants and supermarkets spanning over three square miles. Sandra Chen, writer for Neighborhoods, discusses Koreatown's History[14] as Told Through Its Restaurants. She explains that the LA K-Town is made up of "hundreds of local eateries offering anything from traditional Korean food such as bibimbap, oxtail soup, and Korean barbecue to diverse options like tacos, steak, fried chicken, and even vegan burgers." Some restaurants that trace the town's history include The Prince Restaurant, a famous bar and lounge that marks a time in Koreatown's history when the neighborhood was transitioning from upscale American suburb to a more diverse destination and Dong Il Jong, one of the oldest restaurants in K-Town. In addition to Los Angeles, Koreatowns also developed in areas such as San Francisco, Orange County, New York City, Houston and Philadelphia. Sophie-Claire Hoeller, in an article about ethnic neighborhoods in New York City, pinpoints New York as the home to over 140,000 Korean residents—the second largest Korean population in the US—who frequent K-Town on West 32nd Street often, giving the area a "super local and authentic vibe."

LITTLE INDIA

"The first time I went there, I thought I was in Delhi," said Sanjoy Chakravorty, professor of geography and urban studies at Temple University, of Little India in Edison, New Jersey, in an interview with NBC news.

The economic enclave of India is born from the earliest Indian immigrants who came to the U.S. in the late 1800s and early 1900s and worked as farm laborers in California. After 1965, more Indian professionals, such as doctors, engineers and scientists started arriving in larger numbers, forming South Asian clusters in three major areas: Jackson Heights in Queens, New York, Devon Avenue in Chicago, Illinois and in Edison, New Jersey. Like the rich culture of India, Little India in Jackson Heights is bright with colors and enriched with the smell of curries and spices. Sweet shops, curry houses and eateries selling chutney, a family of Indian condiments, such as a ground peanut garnish or mint dipping sauce that you may accompany a samosa with, line the streets of this bustling neighborhood. Artesia, California is also home to a Little India of its own. Spanning across five streets on Pioneer Boulevard, Little India is full of stores filled with a rainbow of hand-crafted fabrics and all the spices necessary to cook an Indian meal, as well as restaurants filled with the sweet aroma of Indian curries.

LITTLE SRI LANKA

Little Sri Lanka is another Asian-American enclave that has become the ""emotional heart of a growing community," according to The New York Times' Rachel Khona.[15] Whether you're looking for pineapple curry, kottu—a dish made from godhamba roti and stir fried with vegetables, eggs, meat and spices—or rice flour bowls, Little Sri Lanka in Staten Island, New York has it all. Though only spanning across a few neighborhoods in this NYC borough, Little Sri Lanka's restaurants allow for authentic Sri Lankan dining experiences, complete with elongated triangular-shaped metal chairs, menus of home-cooked meals and chefs that grew up cooking with relatives in the motherland.

LITTLE SAIGONS

Little Saigons are home to Vietnamese residents. The Vietnamese population of Little Saigon is largely made up of refugees who emigrated to the U.S. after the end of the Vietnam War in 1975. In 1987, Little Saigon was established as an official Vietnamese enclave and quickly grew into a commercial and residential hub, and is now home to the largest Vietnamese population outside of Vietnam. Cathay Chaplin, in a blog post[16] about the tradition behind this corner of the world, visits Little Saigon through the lens of her grandfather.

"The area is a kind of sacred ground, evidence that South Vietnam still exists, not only in the mind of its people, but as a place in the world," said Chaplin of Little Saigon. "After my grandparents and their eight children settled in San Diego following the end of the Vietnam War, visits to Little Saigon were the closest they ever got to going to home again — seeing not only distant friends and relatives, but the cultural markers of a country that no longer existed."

Although Little Saigon in Orange County is the most established Vietnamese town, other pockets of largely Vietnamese communities can be found in San Jose, Atlanta, Sacramento, Denver, Oklahoma City and New Orleans.

LITTLE CAMBODIA

Similar to Little Saigons, Cambodian enclaves were formed when Cambodians came to Long Beach as refugees 40 years ago after the Khmer Rouge regime took both lives and cultural vibrancy in Cambodia. Today, Long Beach is home to the largest population of Cambodians anywhere in the US. Eater's Sarah Bennett explains[17] that those who fled Cambodia did their best to rebuild the only way they knew how—through food. Through neighborhood markets selling tropical fruits and spices and restaurants serving Cambodian specialities, such as a spice-rubbed whitefish steamed in coconut milk curry, Cambodia Town brings locals and visitors alike through the tangy, fishy, spicy, herbal flavors of Southeast Asian cuisine.

"Today, Long Beach as a whole has become a destination for homesick Cambodians seeking flavors of home, and for Westerners eager to dine on Khmer food for the first (or millionth) time," said Sarah Bennett of Eater Los Angeles.

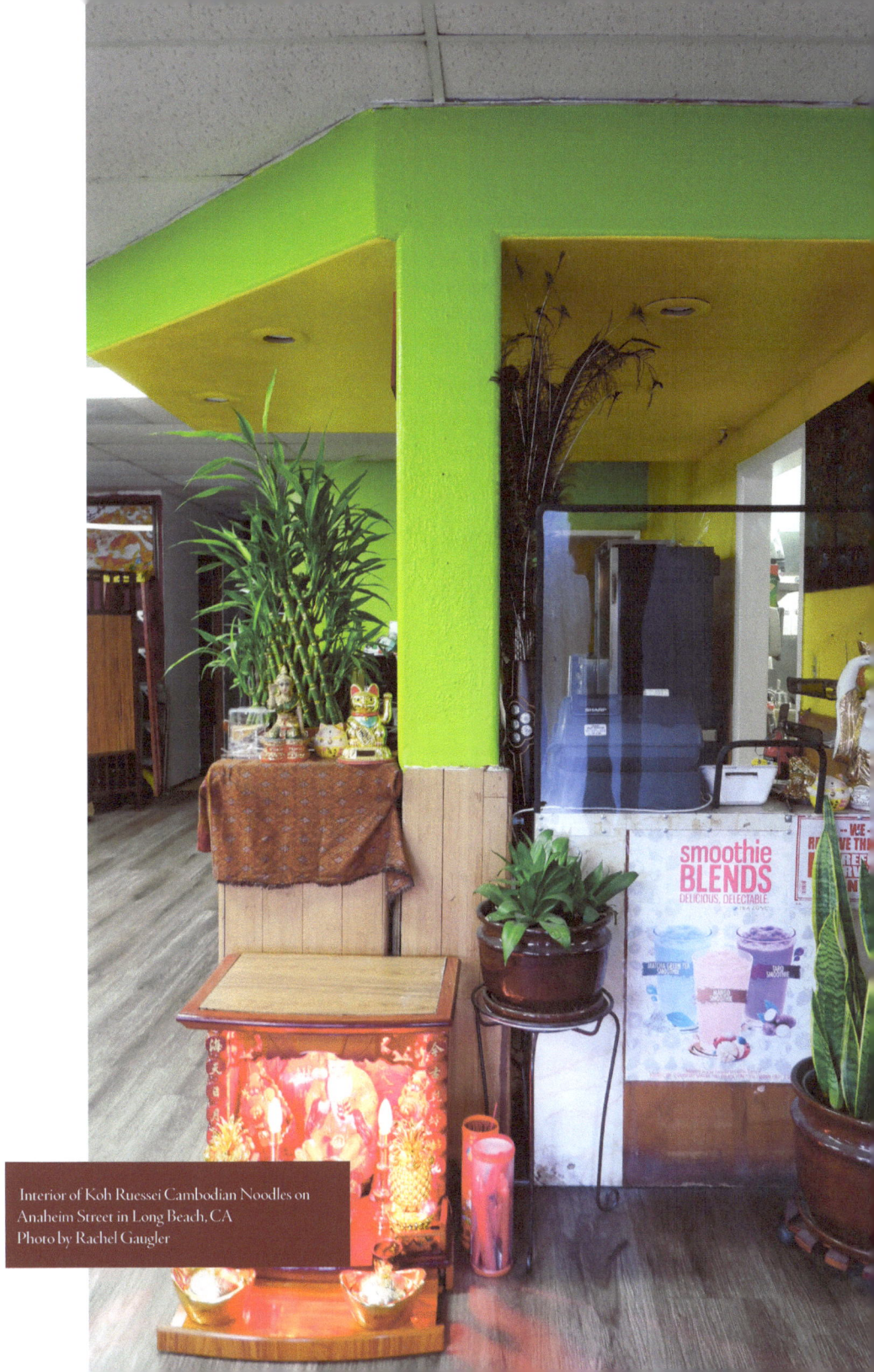

Interior of Koh Ruessei Cambodian Noodles on Anaheim Street in Long Beach, CA
Photo by Rachel Gaugler

THAI TOWN

While LA's Thai Town only stretches across half a mile in East Hollywood, its existence has been symbolic and influential in Thai culture on a much grander scale, locally and transnationally.[18] LA's Thai Town became the first officially recognized Thai Town in the world in 1999. With restaurants like Hollywood Thai, Night+Market and Siam Sunset, all regions of Thailand are highlighted in the Thai foodscape in East Hollywood. Visitors and locals can get sticky rice dishes of northeast Thailand and thick rich curries of southern Thai cuisine. As younger chefs emerge, the food scene is shifting to an authentic take on childhood and household dishes through the lens of being second-generation Thai-Americans.

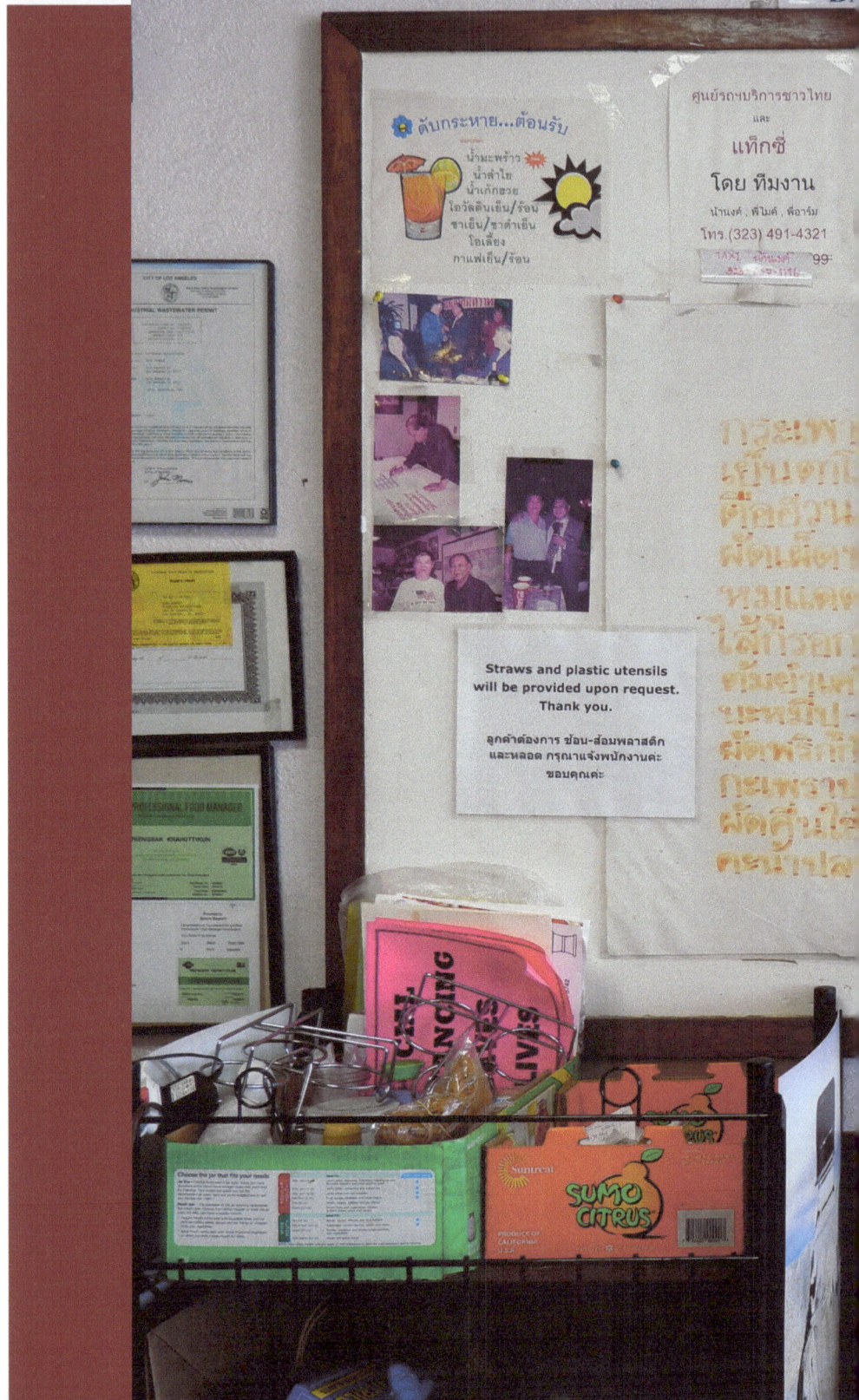

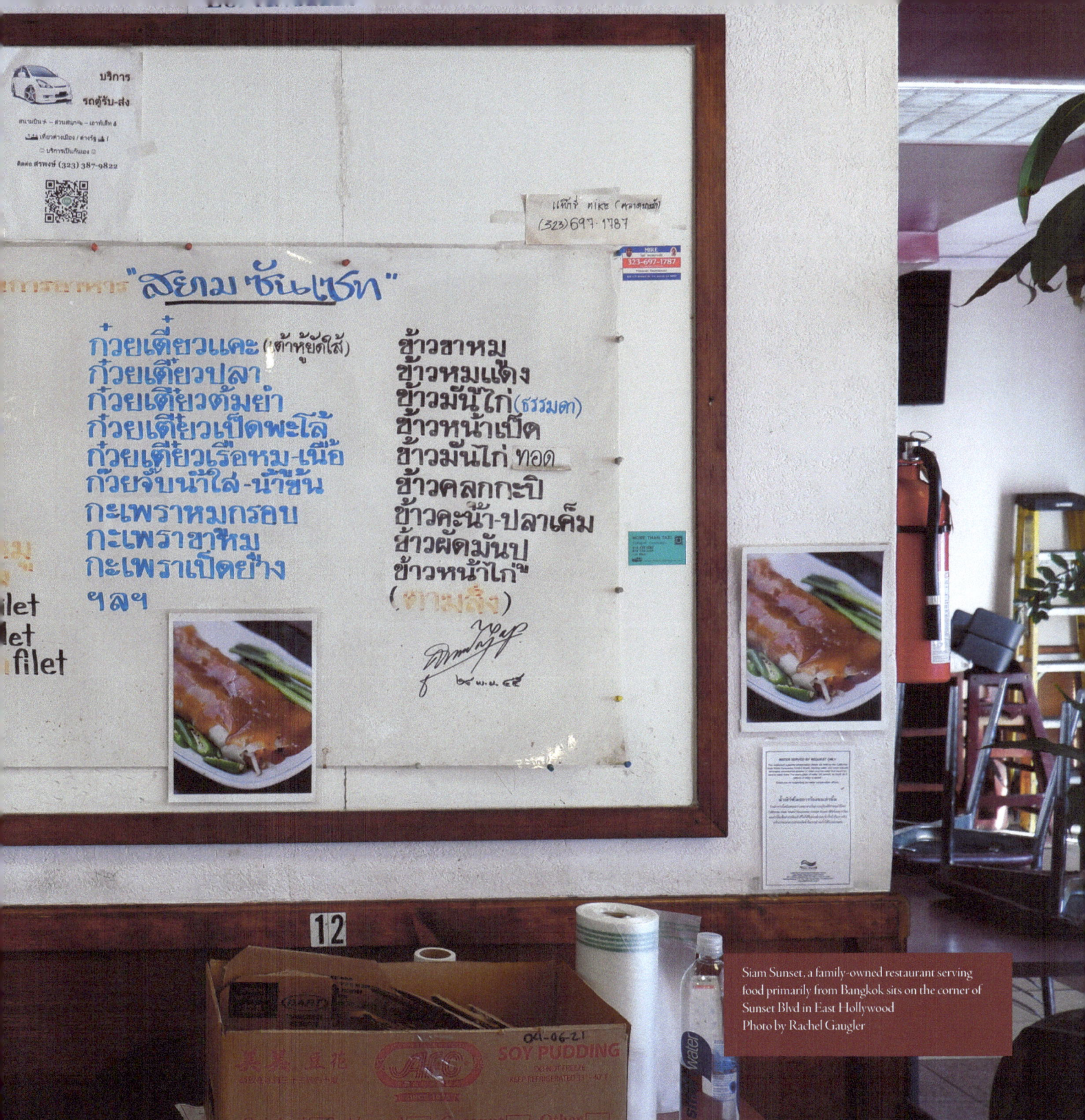

บริการ
รถตู้รับ-ส่ง

ติดต่อ สุรพงษ์ (323) 387-9822

แท็กซี่ mike (ตลาดหมอช้ำ)
(323) 697-1787

รายการอาหาร "สยาม ซันเซ็ท"

ก๋วยเตี๋ยวแคะ (เต้าหู้ยัดไส้)
ก๋วยเตี๋ยวปลา
ก๋วยเตี๋ยวต้มยำ
ก๋วยเตี๋ยวเป็ดพะโล้
ก๋วยเตี๋ยวเรือหมู-เนื้อ
ก๋วยจับน้ำใส-น้ำข้น
กะเพราหมูกรอบ
กะเพราขาหมู
กะเพราเป็ดย่าง
ฯลฯ

ข้าวขาหมู
ข้าวหมูแดง
ข้าวมันไก่ (ธรรมดา)
ข้าวหน้าเป็ด
ข้าวมันไก่ ทอด
ข้าวคลุกกะปิ
ข้าวคะน้า-ปลาเค็ม
ข้าวผัดมันปู
ข้าวหน้าไก่ ฯ
(ตามสั่ง)

filet
filet
filet

12

SOY PUDDING

Siam Sunset, a family-owned restaurant serving food primarily from Bangkok sits on the corner of Sunset Blvd in East Hollywood
Photo by Rachel Gaugler

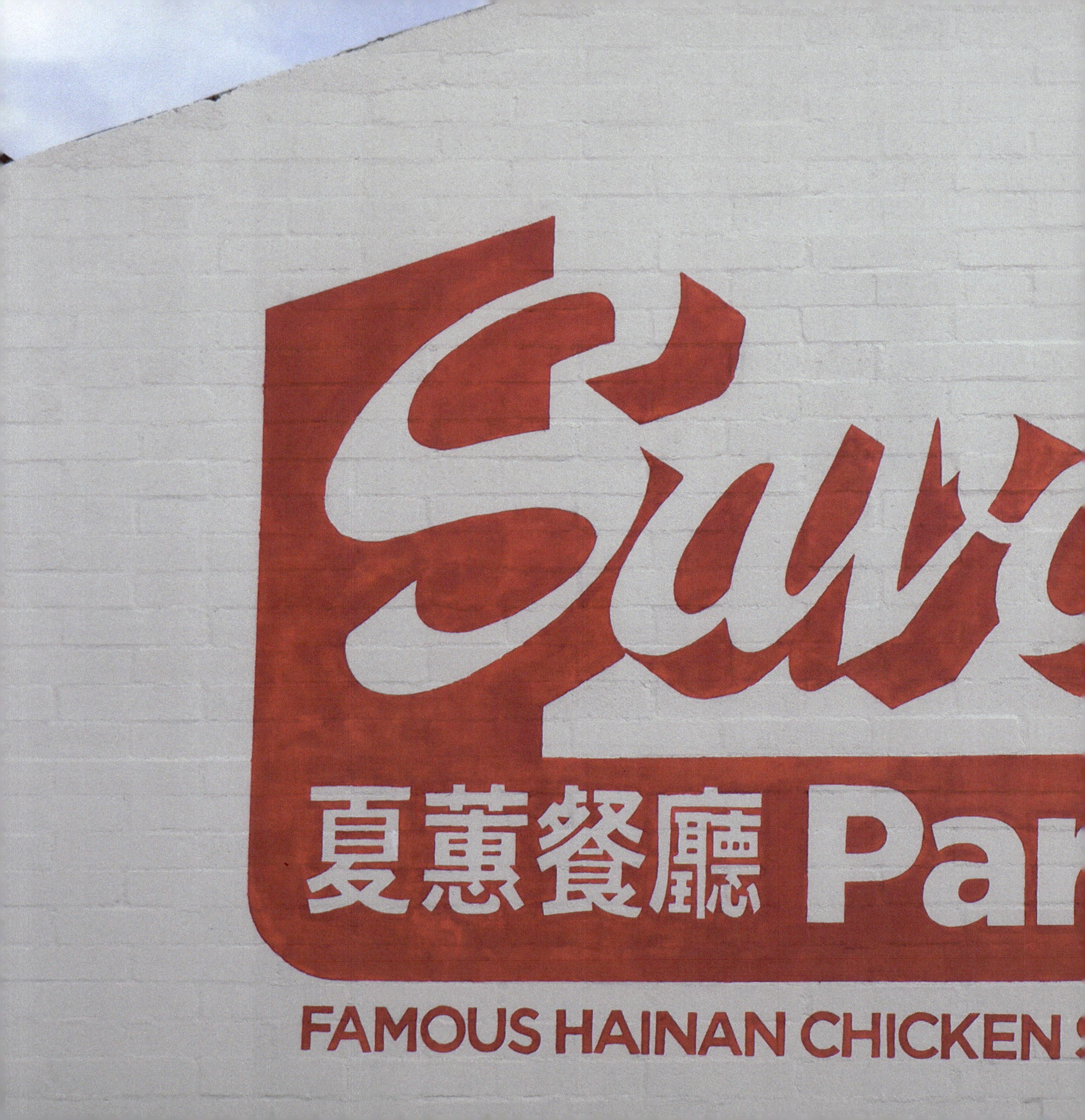

Suga

夏蕙餐廳 Par

FAMOUS HAINAN CHICKEN

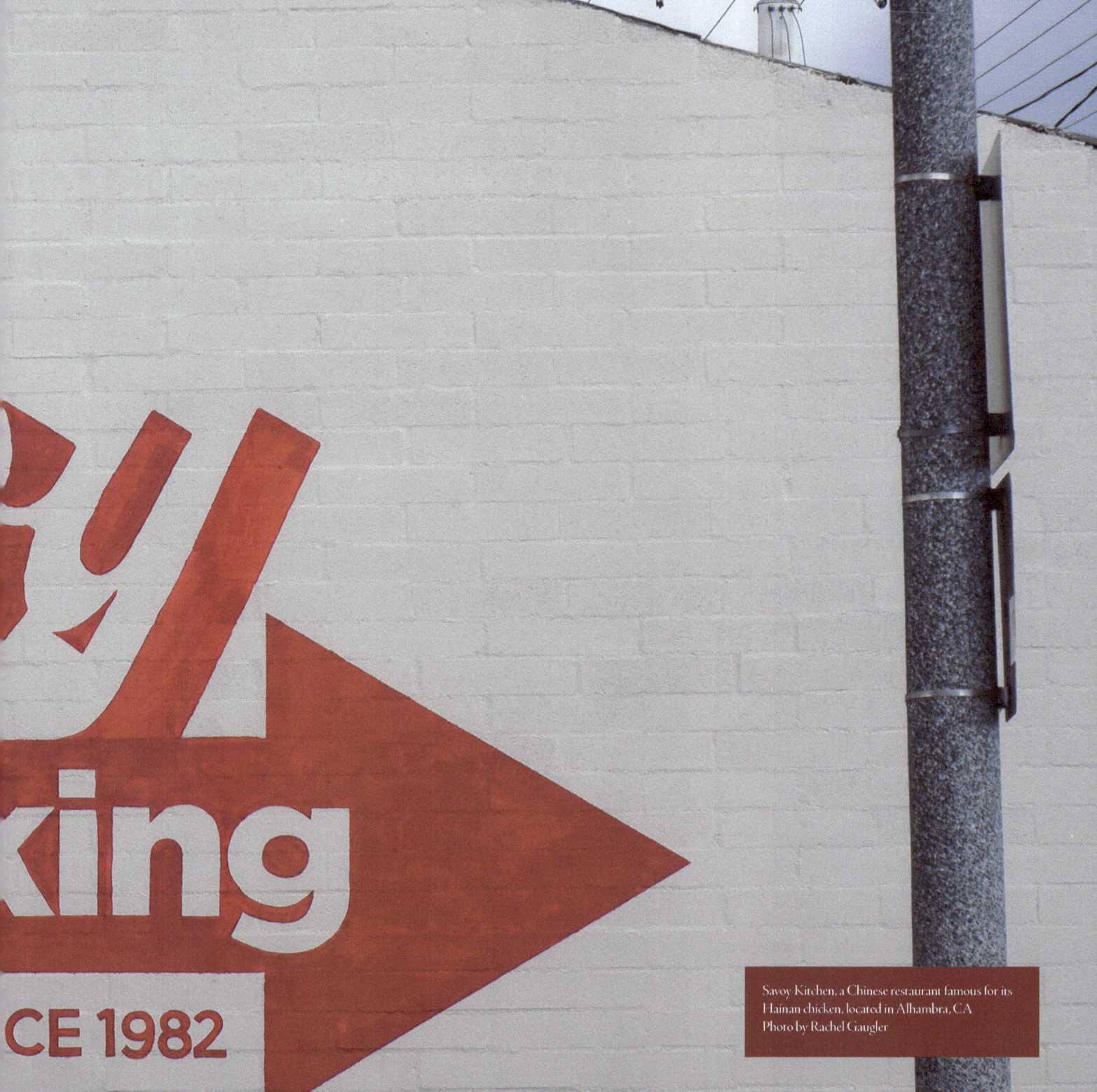

Savoy Kitchen, a Chinese restaurant famous for its
Hainan chicken, located in Alhambra, CA
Photo by Rachel Gaugler

ENCLAVES AS COMMUNITY

The last kind of enclave is an ethnoburb, which is a suburban ethnic cluster of residential areas and business districts in large metropolitan areas. Ethnoburbs are typically made up of multiethnic communities, in which one ethnic minority group has a significant concentration, but not necessarily a majority.

SAN GABRIEL VALLEY

San Gabriel Valley (SGV), also known as the 626, is an example of a Chinese ethnoburb. With Vietnamese boba stands, delicious dim sum eateries and coconut jelly and red bean dessert spots, SGV is a cultural hub of Asian flavors. Yiran Wang, writer for AHBE LAB, describes SGV as "a unique combination of immigrant tastes and Los Angeles infrastructure, a neighborhood that looks like a 1950s suburb, yet smells like an enticing Sichuan hotpot." To Wang, the foodscape of SGV is an "ever evolving landscape of flavors." Wang's description of "immigrant tastes" highlights the crux of the Asian-American enclave—the satisfaction of the craving for familiar tastes, language and company. When faced with a different dominant language and unfamiliar foodscape, ethnic enclaves maintain a continued connection to the homeland, provide a sense of familiarity, recreate the look and feel of cities abroad and provide[19] the social connections necessary to overcome linguistic, cultural and legal barriers.

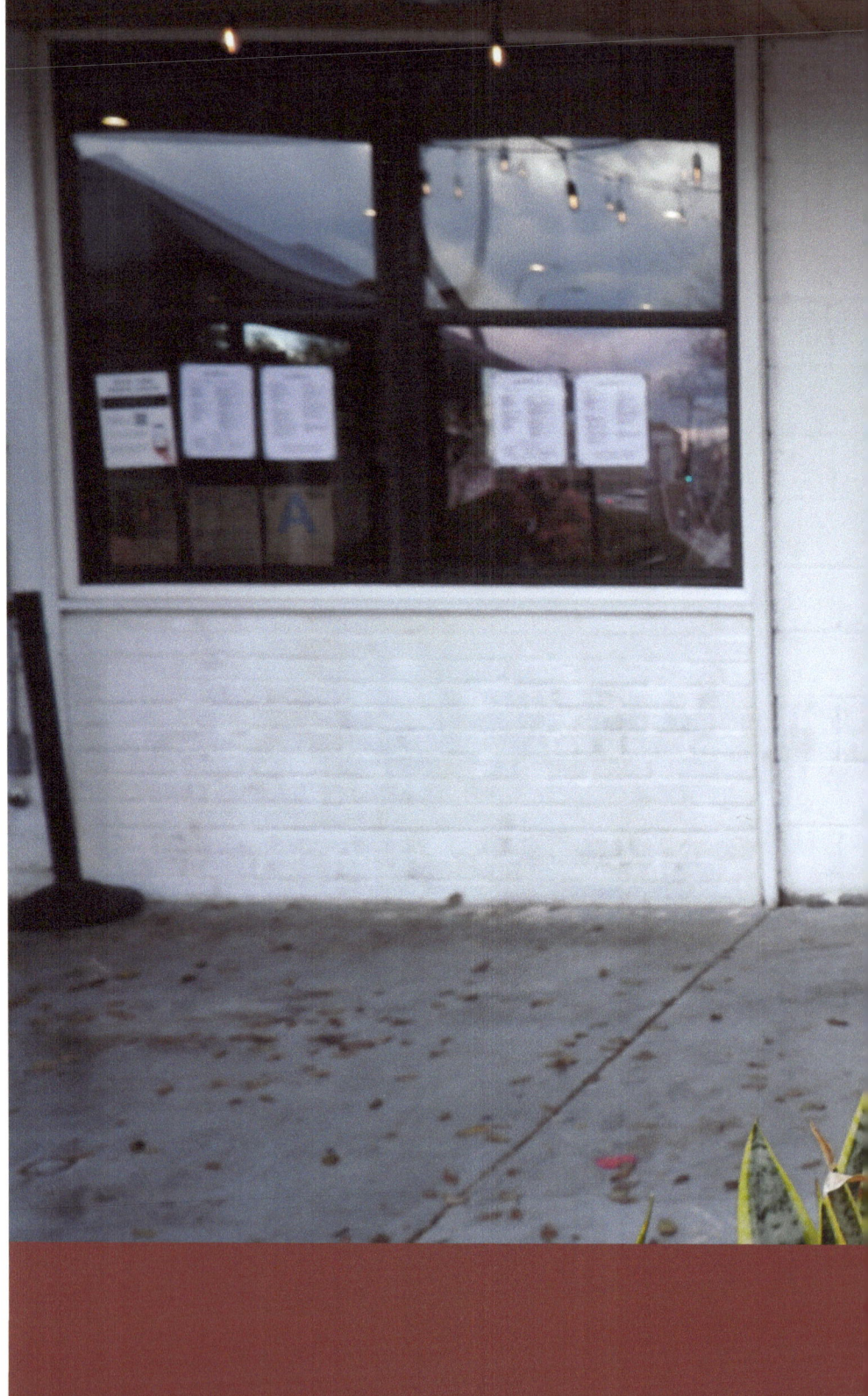

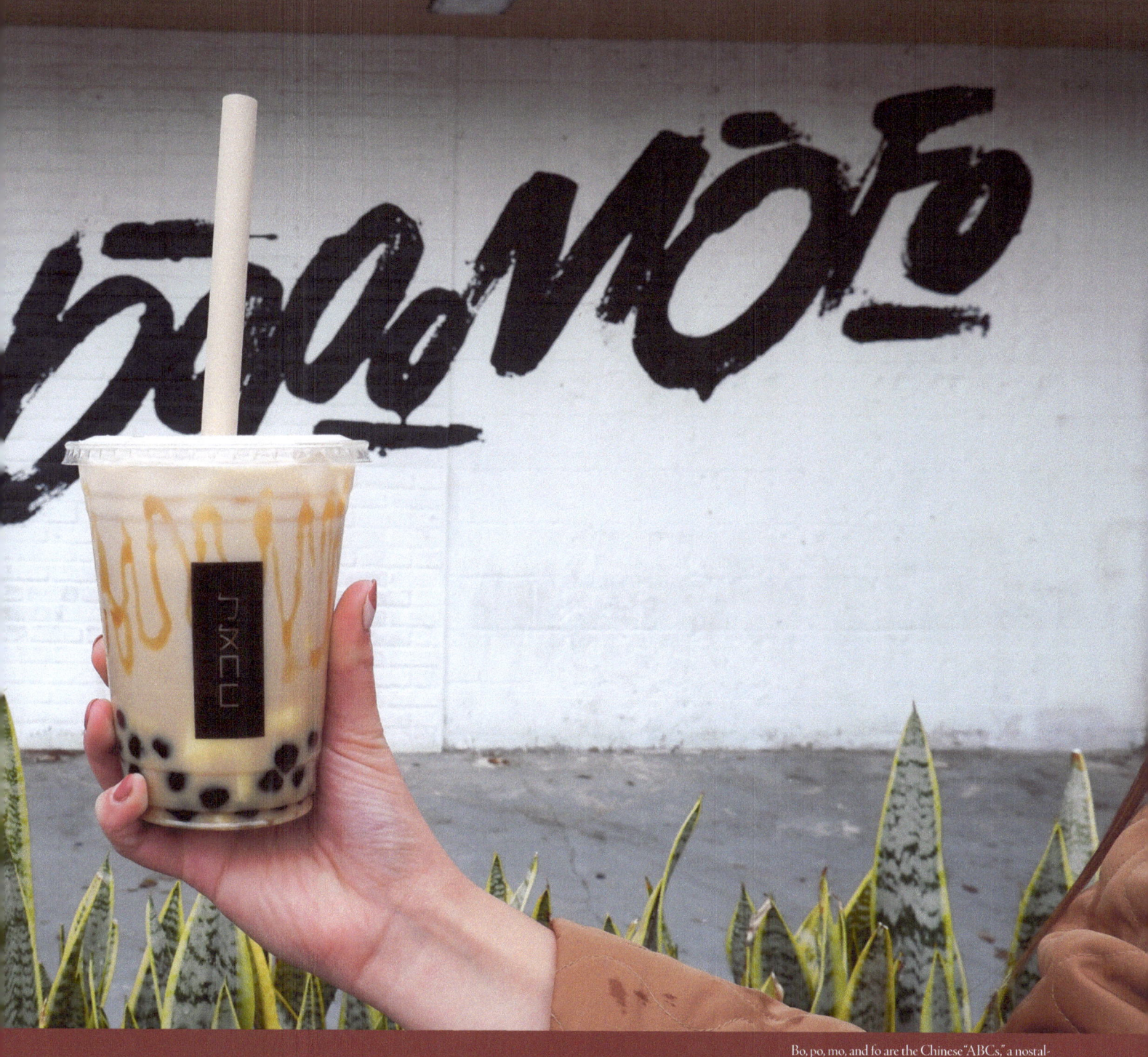

Bo, po, mo, and fo are the Chinese "ABCs," a nostalgic and basic foundation for Asian-Americans
Photo by Eleazar Lee

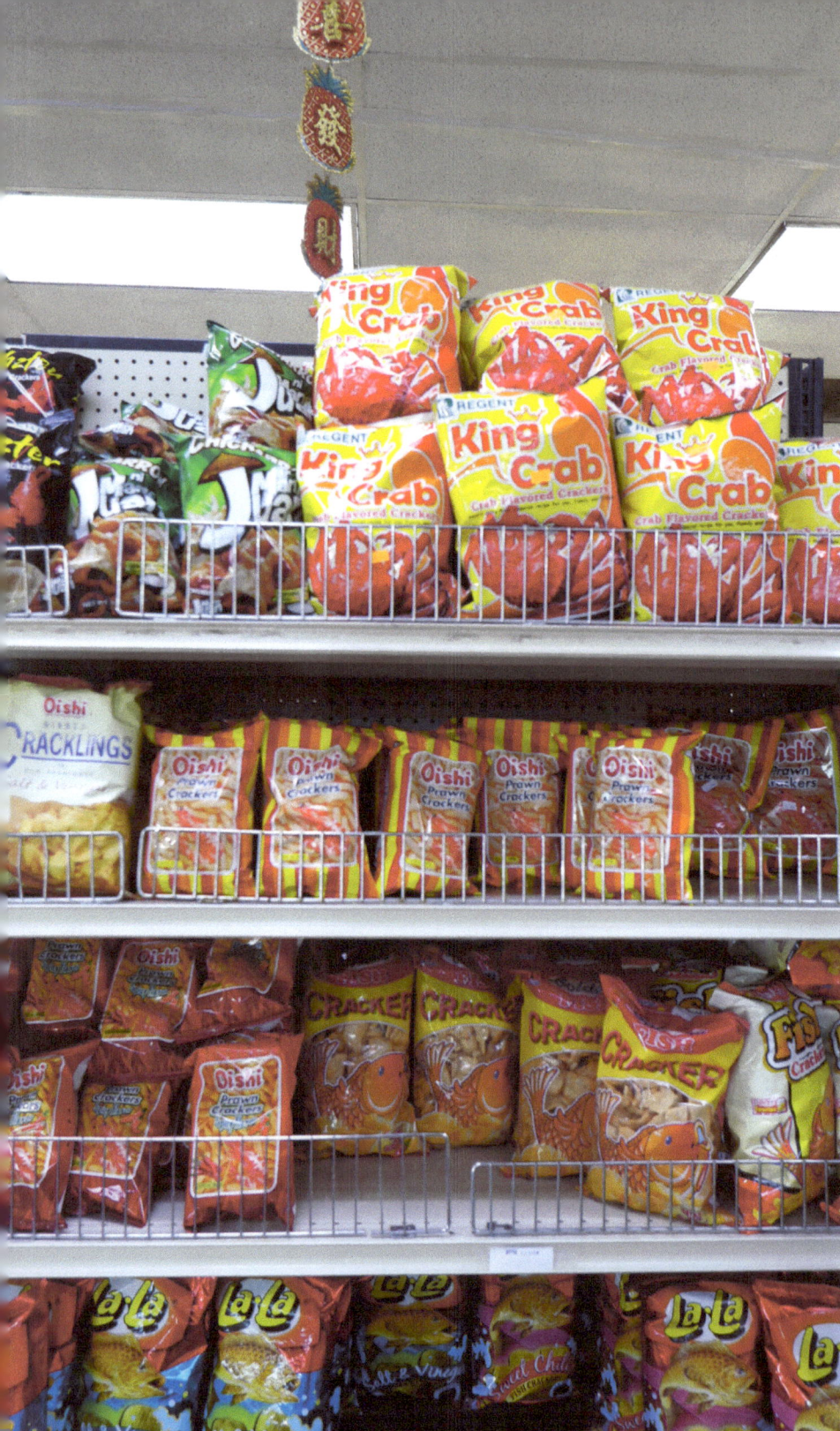

Oishi Prawn Crackers, based in the Philippines, is a flavorful seafood snack enjoyed across Asia
Photo by Rachel Gaugler

REMEMBERED HOMELAND

Whether it's a ramen joint in Monterey Park, a supermarket in Long Beach or a boba spot in Alhambra, ethnic enclaves are pictures of a remembered homeland. They are places of refuge, opportunity and community. For an immigrant or a second, even third, generation Asian-American, ethnic enclaves provide familiarity, comfort and a gateway to a home across the oceans. For those outside of these Asian-American communities, enclaves provide a window into a different corner of the world, a corner where jeong is alive and well.

Whether one is visiting a home away from home or is simply looking to explore a new culture and food, these enclaves are to be treated with respect. After all, restaurant owners are extending an invitation and it is the customer's responsibility to know how to respond.

"If you go into some Asian restaurants, it feels like they just opened their home up to you," explains Kim. "You see one of the kids at a table doing homework and a relative in the back cooking. One of their kids is serving you. You feel like you're an extension of that family."

REFERENCES

1. Vonthron, Simon, et al. "Foodscape: A Scoping Review and a Research Agenda for Food Security-Related Studies." PLOS ONE, vol. 15, no. 5, 2020, doi:10.1371/journal. pone.0233218.
2. Gaillot, Ann-Derrick. "Understanding 'Ethnic' Food Trends." The Outline, The Outline, 25 May 2017, theoutline.com/post/1584/ethnic-food-trends-jamaican-patties.
3. Tam, Ruth. "You Shame My Culture's Food - Then Make It Trendy." Chicagotribune.com, 1 Sept. 2015, www.chicagotribune.com/opinion/commentary/ct-food-gentrification-asian-cuisine-20150901-story.html.
4. Hernández, Marco. "Asian-American." South China Morning Post, multimedia.scmp.com/news/world/AsianAmerican/.
5. "Ethnic Enclaves." Immigration to the United States, immigrationtounitedstates.org/484-ethnic-enclaves.html#:~:text=Significance%3A%20Ethnic%20enclaves%20have%20long,assimilation%20into%20United%20States%20society.
6. Published by Keelan Cook Keelan Cook leads the Peoples Next Door project and is an Associate Director with the Union Baptist Association in Houston, et al. "What Is an 'Ethnic Enclave,' and Why Should I Care?" The Peoples Next Door, 22 Feb. 2017, keelancook.com/2017/02/22/what-is-an-ethnic-enclave-and-why-should-i-care/.
7. "Chinatowns and Other Asian-American Enclaves." Infoplease, Infoplease, www.infoplease.com/history/apa-heritage/chinatowns-and-other-asian-american-enclaves.
8. Changing Neighborhood: Ethnic Enclaves and the ... - JSTOR. www.jstor.org/stable/29768486.
9. Rude, Emelyn. "Chinese Food in America: A Very Brief History." Time, Time, 8 Feb. 2016, time.com/4211871/chinese-food-history/.
10. "Chinatowns and Other Asian-American Enclaves." Infoplease, Infoplease, www.infoplease.com/history/apa-heritage/chinatowns-and-other-asian-american-enclaves-0.
11. "Shyong: Here's How HiFi, or Historic Filipinotown, Got Its Name." Los Angeles Times, Los Angeles Times, 6 Jan. 2020, www.latimes.com/california/story/2020-01-06/filipinotown-cool-enclaves.
12. "Woodside's Little Manila Offers a Piece of the Philippines in Queens." Brick Underground, 18 Dec. 2017, www.brickunderground.com/live/little-manila-in-Queens.
13. Kandil, Caitlin Yoshiko. "How 1800s Racism Birthed Chinatown, Japantown and Other Ethnic Enclaves." NBCNews.com, NBCUniversal News Group, 13 May 2019, www.nbcnews.com/news/asian-america/how-1800s-racism-birthed-chinatown-japantown-other-ethnic-enclaves-n997296.
14. Chen, Sandra ChenSandra. "Koreatown's History as Told Through Its Restaurants." Neighborhoods.com, Https://Static.neighborhoods.com/Neighborhoods-Default-Logo.pngNeighborhoods.com, 1 May 2020, www.neighborhoods.com/blog/koreatowns-history-as-told-through-its-restaurants.
15. Khona, Rachel. "On Staten Island, Savoring Flavors of Sri Lanka." The New York Times, The New York Times, 15 July 2015, www.nytimes.com/2015/07/19/travel/on-staten-island-savoring-flavors-of-sri-lanka.html.
16. Chaplin, Cathy. "There's No Place Like Little Saigon." Eater, Eater, 11 July 2018, www.eater.com/2018/7/11/17555520/california-vietnamese-food-little-saigon-orange-county.
17. Bennett, Sarah. "The Heart of Cambodian Culture in America Beats Through Long Beach." Eater LA, Eater LA, 17 May 2017, la.eater.com/2017/5/17/15645728/cambodian-cuisine-long-beach-los-angeles-feature.
18. Trinh, Jean. "The Decades-Long Evolution of Thai Cuisine in Los Angeles." KCET, 19 Jan. 2021, www.kcet.org/shows/the-migrant-kitchen/the-decades-long-evolution-of-thai-cuisine-in-los-angeles.
19. Published by Keelan Cook Keelan Cook leads the Peoples Next Door project and is an Associate Director with the Union Baptist Association in Houston, et al. "What Is an 'Ethnic Enclave,' and Why Should I Care?" The Peoples Next Door, 22 Feb. 2017, keelancook.com/2017/02/22/what-is-an-ethnic-enclave-and-why-should-i-care/.

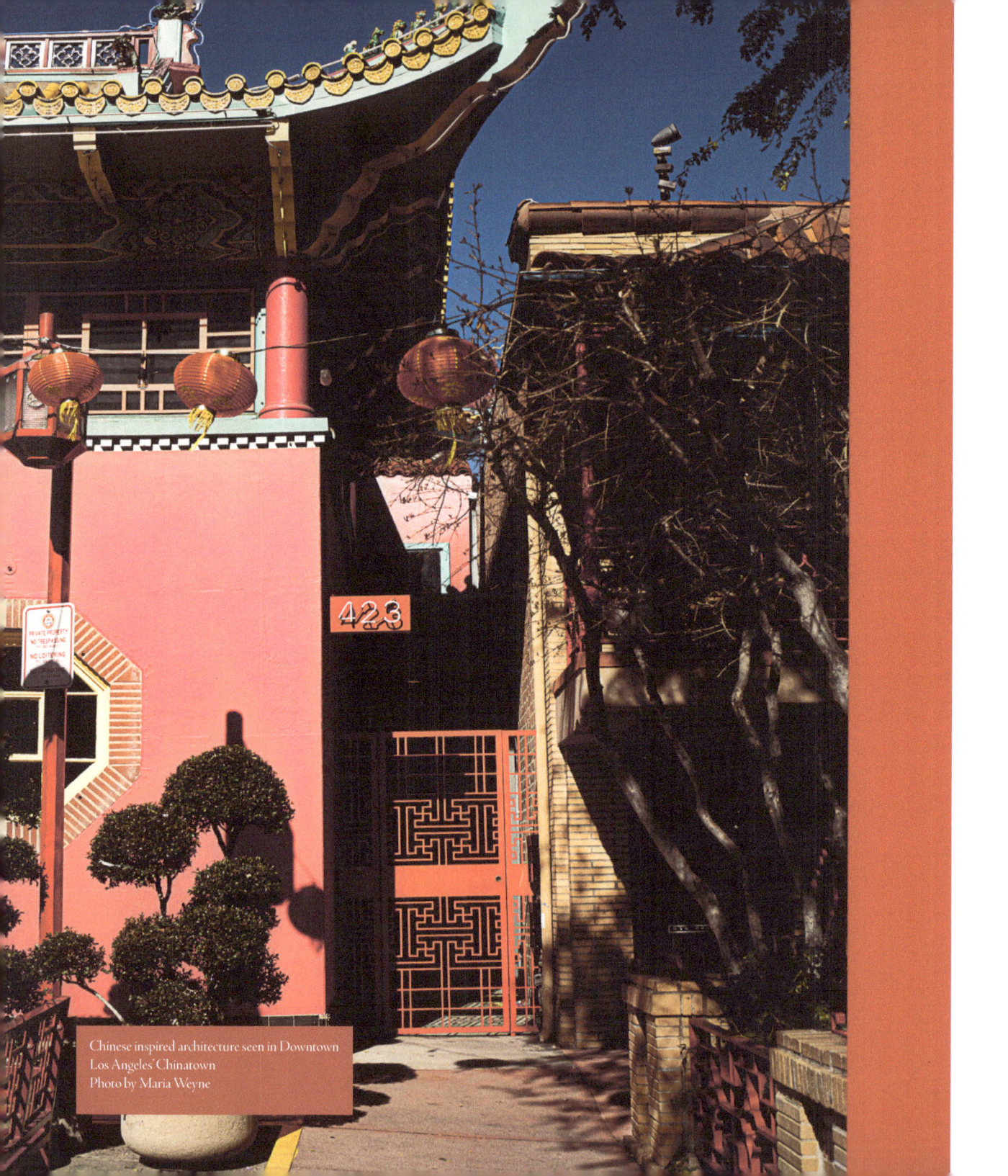

Chinese inspired architecture seen in Downtown
Los Angeles' Chinatown
Photo by Maria Weyne

3. Chinese Food —But Not Really

By: Bethsabe Camacho and Evana Upshaw

The heavy door swings open, and the smell of fried food smacks you in the face. You stand at the very back of the line, debating if you will get a bowl or a plate. Finally, you are next in line to order and the server asks you if you would like a sample. You choose to get the plate with chow mein instead of the fried rice, and a double entree of orange chicken. This is the story of a well-known American phenomenon—dining at Panda Express.

Virtually none of these dishes would be available to you in China. They are a product of a fusion of tastes created to satisfy the American palate.

How was America able to transition from intense and explicit anti-Chinese sentiment, to filling their cities with Chinese restaurants that outnumber the number of Burger Kings, Kentucky Fried Chickens, McDonald's and Wendy's, combined? Producer and author Jennifer 8. Lee says that there are about 50,000 Chinese restaurants in the United States—the Chinese restaurant scene is an American cultural staple.

Stan Ng's family immigrated from China in the 1970s when communist rule began to take over. Though his family was considered wealthy, they lost everything and an opportunity to go to America knocked on their door. They arrived in Los Angeles' Chinatown and worked several service jobs that allowed them to pay the bills while keeping their head down. Before Ng's birth, his grandfather bought the Chinese restaurant called Golden Chicken Inn in the predominantly Latino city of Oxnard.

Ng, now the director of engineering programs at Biola University, grew up spending the majority of his extra time at the Golden Chicken Inn. Being raised in the Chinese restaurant

"Soy sauce on rice is like ranch on toast." - Jason Wu

43

industry, he is intimately familiar with the joys and hardships of the immigrant working-experience in the United States.

THE CHINESE EXPERIENCE IN THE UNITED STATES

To tell the story of Chinese food in America, one has to know the story of Chinese-American immigrants.

The California Gold Rush in the 1840s came with an influx of people from across the world yearning to strike it rich. Thousands of Chinese men immigrated to the United States and settled along the West Coast, but like many others, they found the gold business unprofitable. They then found work in the construction of the railroad lines, laundry and other low-wage jobs. But anti-Chinese prejudice quickly took hold, and immigrants faced incredible amounts of violence. According to the Library of Congress, those who committed crimes against Chinese people were not held accountable for their actions. In fact, "a case can be made that Chinese immigrants suffered worse treatment than any other group that came voluntarily to the U.S." A series of state and federal laws were enacted that explicitly targeted Chinese immigrants, culminating in the 1882 Chinese Exclusion Act. The legislation made it impossible for Chinese immigrants to obtain U.S. citizenship and for Chinese laborers to enter America.

This hatred and violence drew the Chinese community together, and immigrants built societies for themselves that were made by and for their own communities. According to Time magazine, it was a mix of yearning for tastes of home and the traditional virtues of hospitality and cultural traditions that brought the explosion of Chinese food in the U.S. Today, we see evidence of these ethnic enclaves in Chinatowns across America. They are safe spaces for newly arrived Chinese immigrants to get connected, find work and live in a familiar community.

THE BIRTH OF A NEW CUISINE

Chinese-Americans quickly realized that in order for their restaurants to make it in the U.S., they had to appeal to American tastes, explains the documentary The Search for General Tso (2014). According to Chinese family bloggers The Woks of Life, Chinese cuisine typically involves large leafy greens (like bok choy, Chinese broccoli and Chinese water spinach), dry spices (like red Sichuan peppercorn, star anise, curry powder and Chinese cinnamon), oils (like sesame oil and hoisin sauce), aromatics (like garlic, ginger root, green onions and shallots) and meats like pork, chicken, sea cucumbers, scallops, Jinhua ham and a range of other proteins.

By contrast, the American palate leans heavily on dairy (like milk, cheese and cream), sugar, salt, potatoes and meats like beef, chicken, shrimp and pork. Easily recognizable vegetables include carrots, peppers, onions and broccoli. Chinese-Americans, understanding this, got innovative and created a middle ground that ultimately made Americans more comfortable with their foods.

"Americanized Chinese food" is a term commonly used among Chinese Americans to describe this middle ground. Chi Kao, who was born in Taiwan and moved to the United States after attending college there, said she once went to a Chinese restaurant in a rural town and wanted sweet and sour pork. The waiter abruptly told her, "Don't order that! That's for Americans." Kao insisted that she wanted the sweet and sour pork. He then proceeded to speak to her in Mandarin Chinese, saying adamantly, "No! That's for Americans!" Situations like this have happened to her more than once.

PANDA EXPRESS

Chinese-born American Andrew Cherng, alongside his father, Master Chef Ming-Tsai, founded the Panda Restaurant Group in 1973. According to the DigiLab exhibit at the University of Georgia, the first restaurant opened was the Panda Inn, in Pasadena, California. The idea was a more formal, sit-down dining approach to Chinese food. In 1983, Cherng and his wife Penny were invited by the manager of the Glendale Galleria mall to create a fast-food version of the Panda Inn, thus, the invention of Panda Express.

When Asians crave Chinese food, the last place to satisfy their cravings would be Panda Express. Jason Wu, a California native of Tawainese background describes how he would never classify Panda Express as Chinese food. In fact, he says that "Taco Bell or Chipotle is to Mexican food, as Panda Express is to Chinese food."

The idea behind Cherng's restaurant ventures was to use Chinese flavor and ingredients to suit American tastes. If people hesitated to try Chinese food because of their unfamiliarity with the ingredients, the idea was to function as a first introduction to Chinese cuisine, according to the food site Mashed.

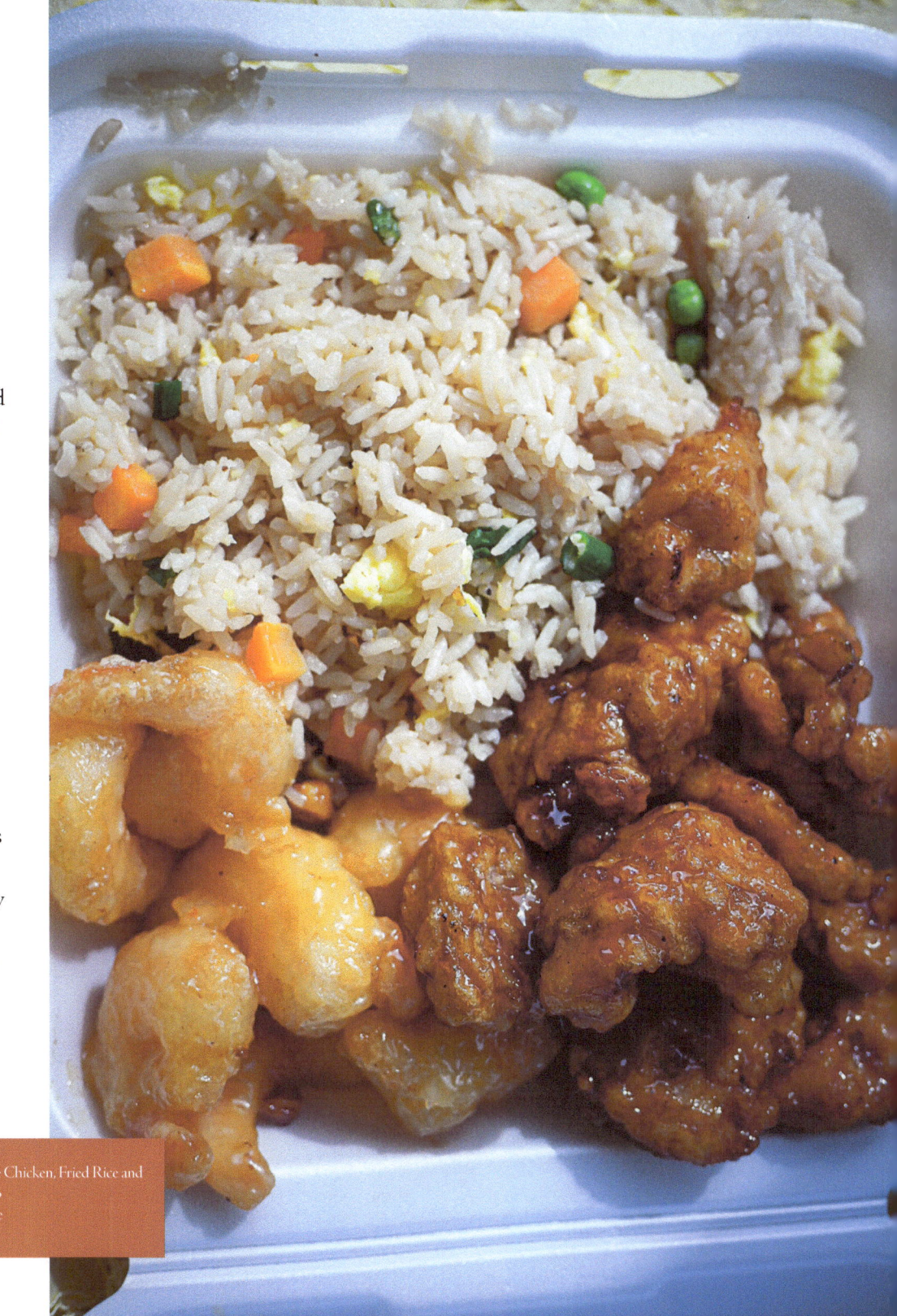

Panda Express' Orange Chicken, Fried Rice and Honey Walnut Shrimp
Photo by Maria Weyne

POPULAR DISHES

Some of the most popular Chinese food dishes in America are dishes such as General Tso's chicken and orange chicken.

On the journey to find the origins of one of the top served dishes in American Chinese restaurants, General Tso's chicken, the documentary, The Search for General Tso, concludes that the dish is not from China. It was created by a Taiwanese chef who adjusted a version of Hunan cuisine for the American palate.

Orange chicken, also inspired by the Hunan Province in China, is a completely American invention and to the surprise of many, it was invented by Panda Express. It was invented over 30 years ago by then-executive chef Andy Kao at one of Panda Express's locations in Hawaii. The idea was to modify a bone-in chicken dish that was popular, according to National Public Radio. In 2017 alone, NPR says that Panda Express has sold 80 million pounds of orange chicken.

Journalist Jennifer 8. Lee, author of The Fortune Cookie Chronicles and producer of The Search For General Tso says that General Tso's chicken and orange chicken are "Americanized mutations of sweet and sour dishes found in China." Although these dishes are not native to China and are even foreign to those living there, many restaurants choose to add them to their menu to please their customers. Ng can attest to this.

After his grandfather retired, his father took over the restaurant and eventually added popular items like orange chicken to the menu, per their customers' suggestions. Even though his family believes many of these popular dishes are American concepts, Ng recalls that "people ordered what was familiar to them." His family valued the community that they were a part of and stated that "the voice of the community was the top priority for them."

CHINESE FOOD AS A GATEWAY INTO CHINESE CULTURE

Ng reflected on how Americans have a very limited view of Chinese cuisine. He points out that we often associate Chinese food with affordability or "cheapness." According to Beth Lew-Williams, an assistant professor at Princeton specializing in Asian American history, this is due to the fact that Chinese laborers worked for low wages as new immigrants during the construction of the transcontinental railroad. Chinese people as a whole, over time, became associated with cheapness and that idea bled into their food production.

On the other hand, certain European cuisines such as French cuisine are more expensive because of their reputation. If Chinese food is a gateway into how we view Chinese people and culture, Ng wonders "How big of a voice is food when it comes to how people treat me, or how people treat the culture or how people think about the culture? And why is that?"

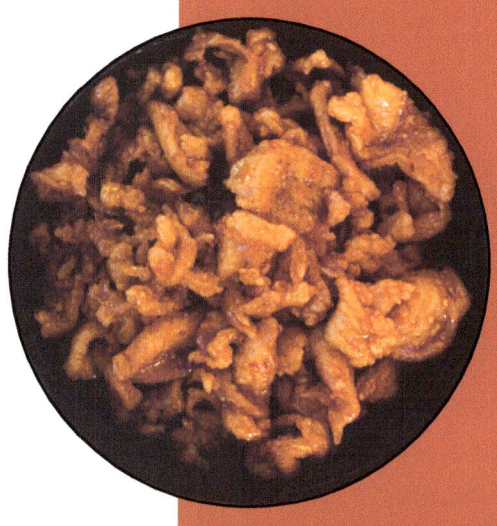

Full Moon House's Orange Chicken bowl
Photo by María Weyne

46

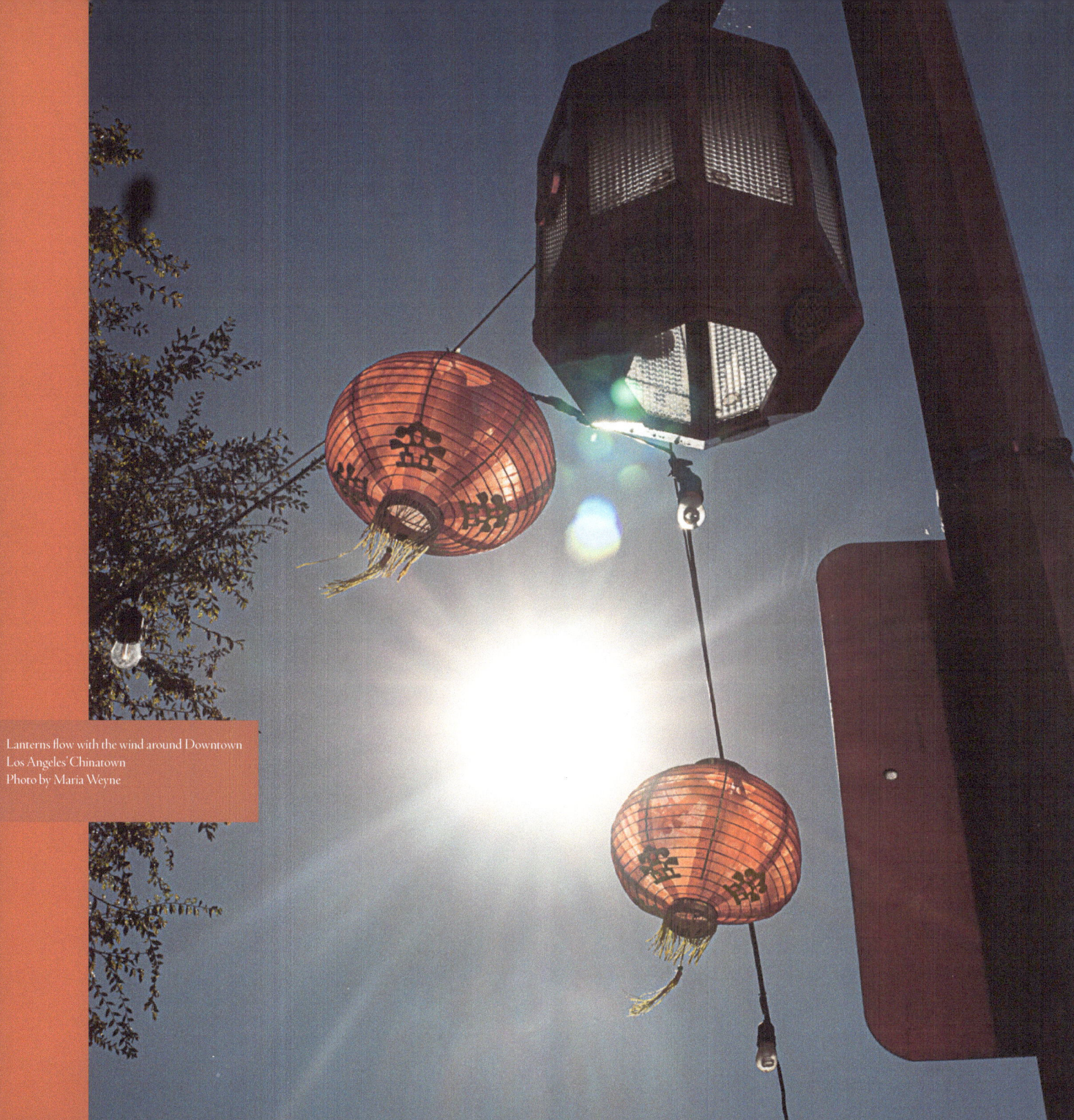

Lanterns flow with the wind around Downtown
Los Angeles' Chinatown
Photo by Maria Weyne

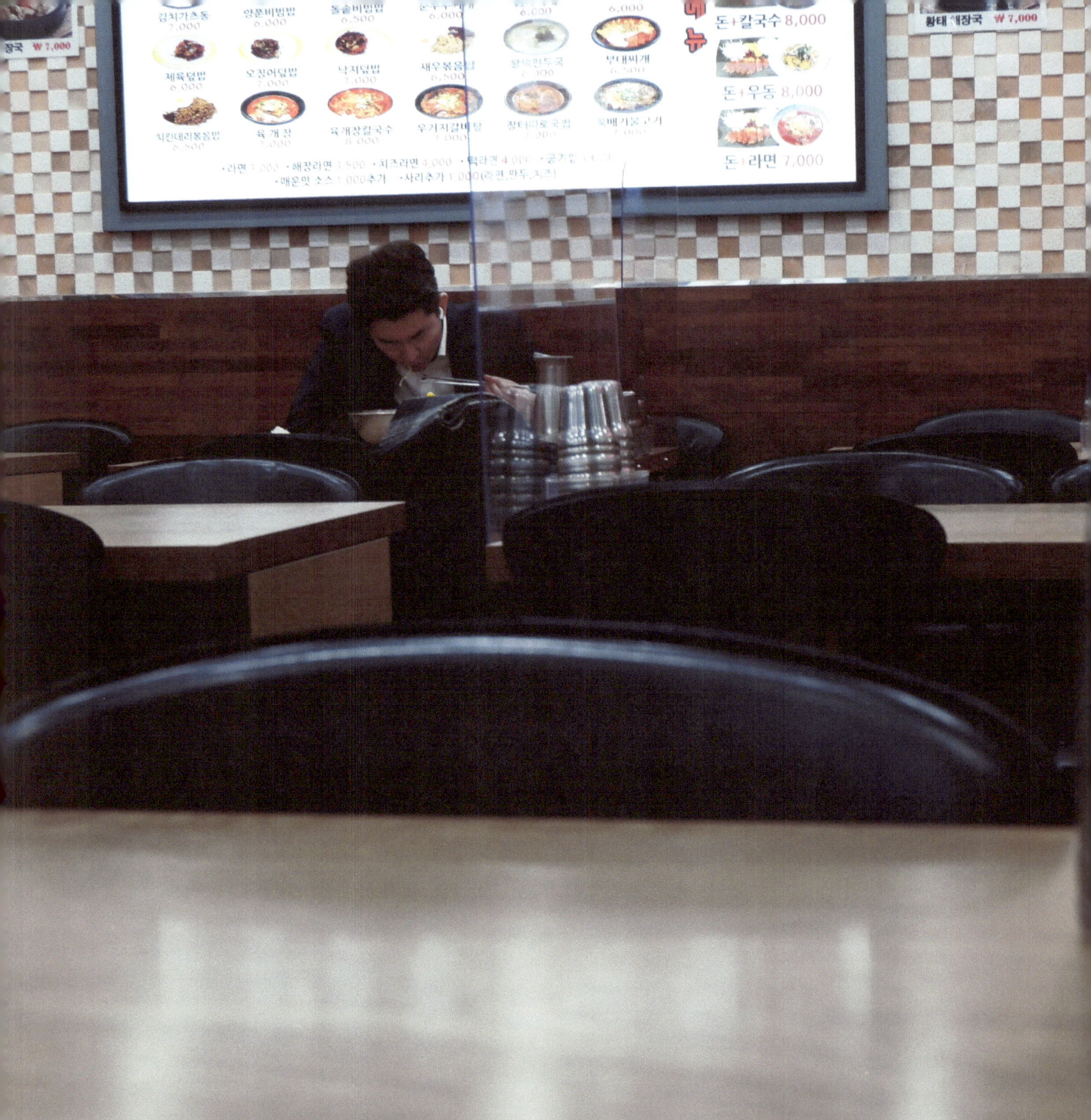

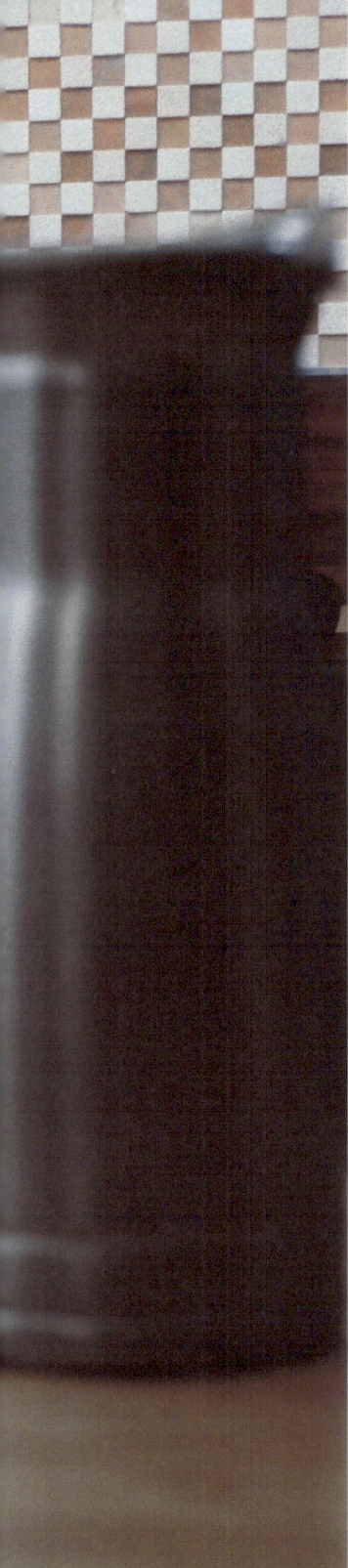

4. Korean Restaurants: Wading through a Pandemic with Family

Photo Essay by Hannah Dilanchyan and Micah Kim

For several months during the COVID-19 situation, a sole customer in the restaurant has been the exact repesentation for Korean family restaurants, Da Rae and Arisu Korean BBQ. With the help of each other as family, the two restaurants are still running with great pride and passion.

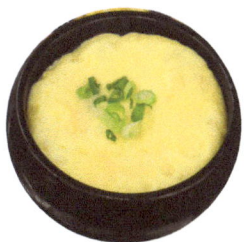

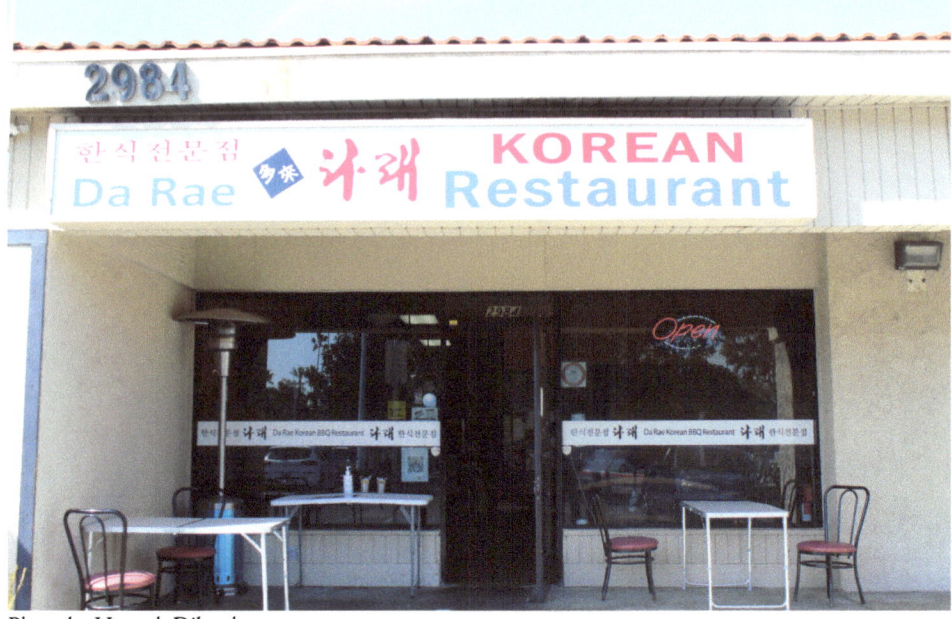

Photo by Hannah Dilanchyan

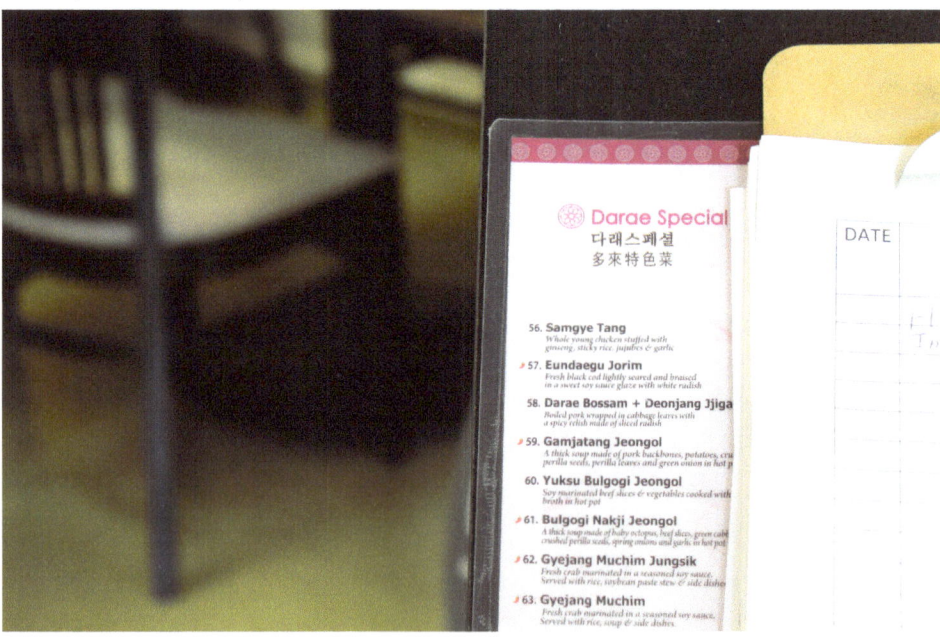

Photo by Hannah Dilanchyan

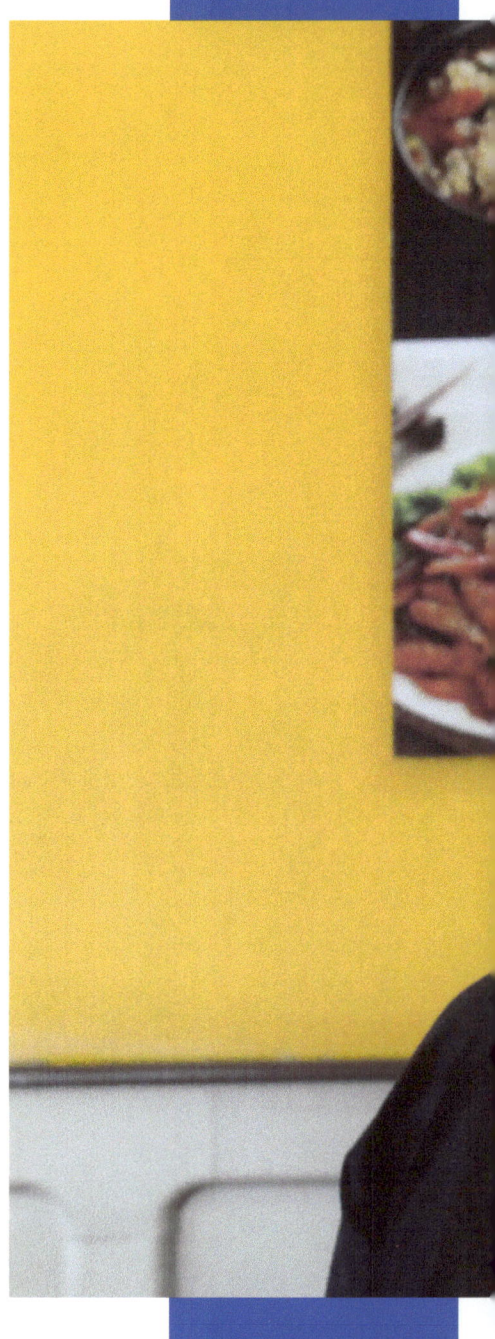

(Top) Due to the COVID-19 situation, sudden closures and harsh restrictions have forced Korean family owned restuarant like Da Rae--in Fullerton, California--to endure many changes. (Bottom) The restaurant has still been serving traditional Korean meals despite abrupt changes.

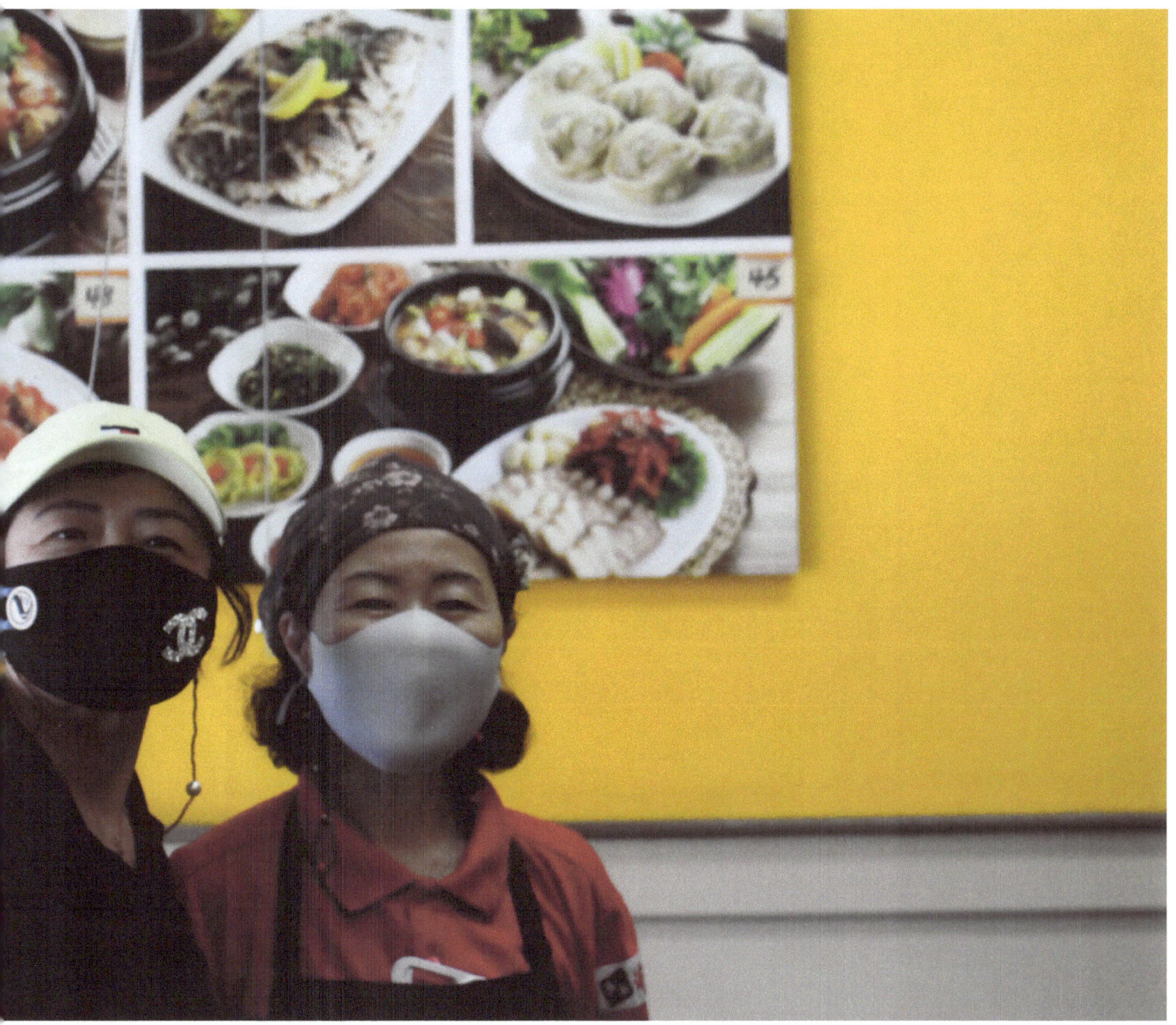

Photo by Hannah Dilanchyan

Owned by two sisters (right) Aeran Lee and (left) Eunmi Lee, Da Rae has suffered a 30% drop in income over the past year as they have struggled to keep their livelihood--their restaurant--alive. Despite these struggles, the two sisters expressed that giving up the restaurant was never a choice. Through their many years of serving, Da Rae had become too much of a commonality within their lives. According to Eunmi Lee, wearing masks has become a literal barrier from her and her customers.

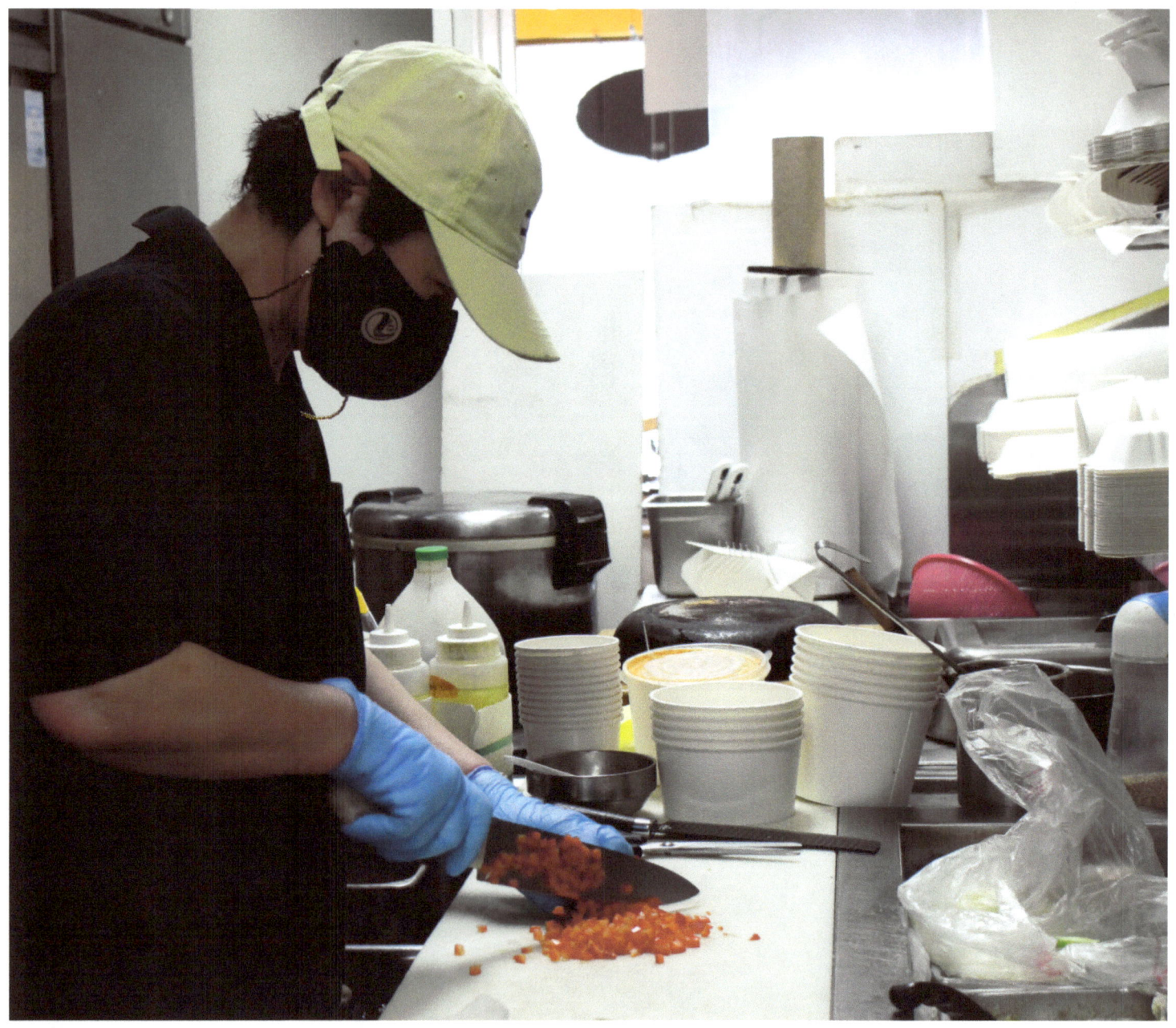

Photo by Micah Kim

Even through these new changes, the work never ends for co-owner-chef Aeran Lee, who is commited to keeping her restaurant alive and thriving regardless of the difficulties they've sustained from the pandemic. Preparing ingredients must be taken extra care of, according to Aeran Lee.

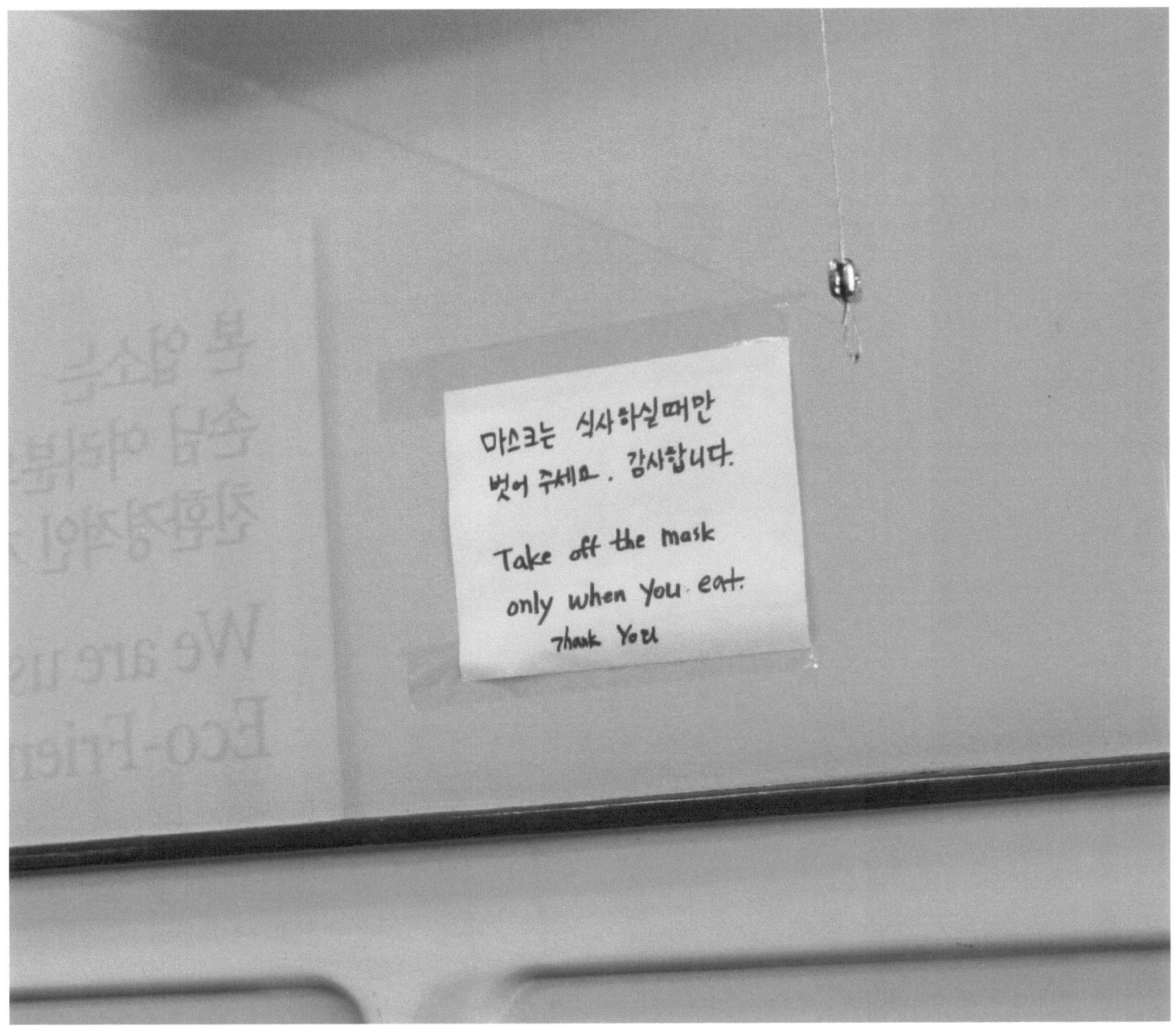

Photo by Hannah Dilanchyan

While indoor dining for Da Rae has re-opened, masks are still required for both workers and patrons. The owners of Da Rae add a handwritten reminder to keep the mask on until it's time to eat. Safety measures like this keep the restaurant safe and clear to remain open.

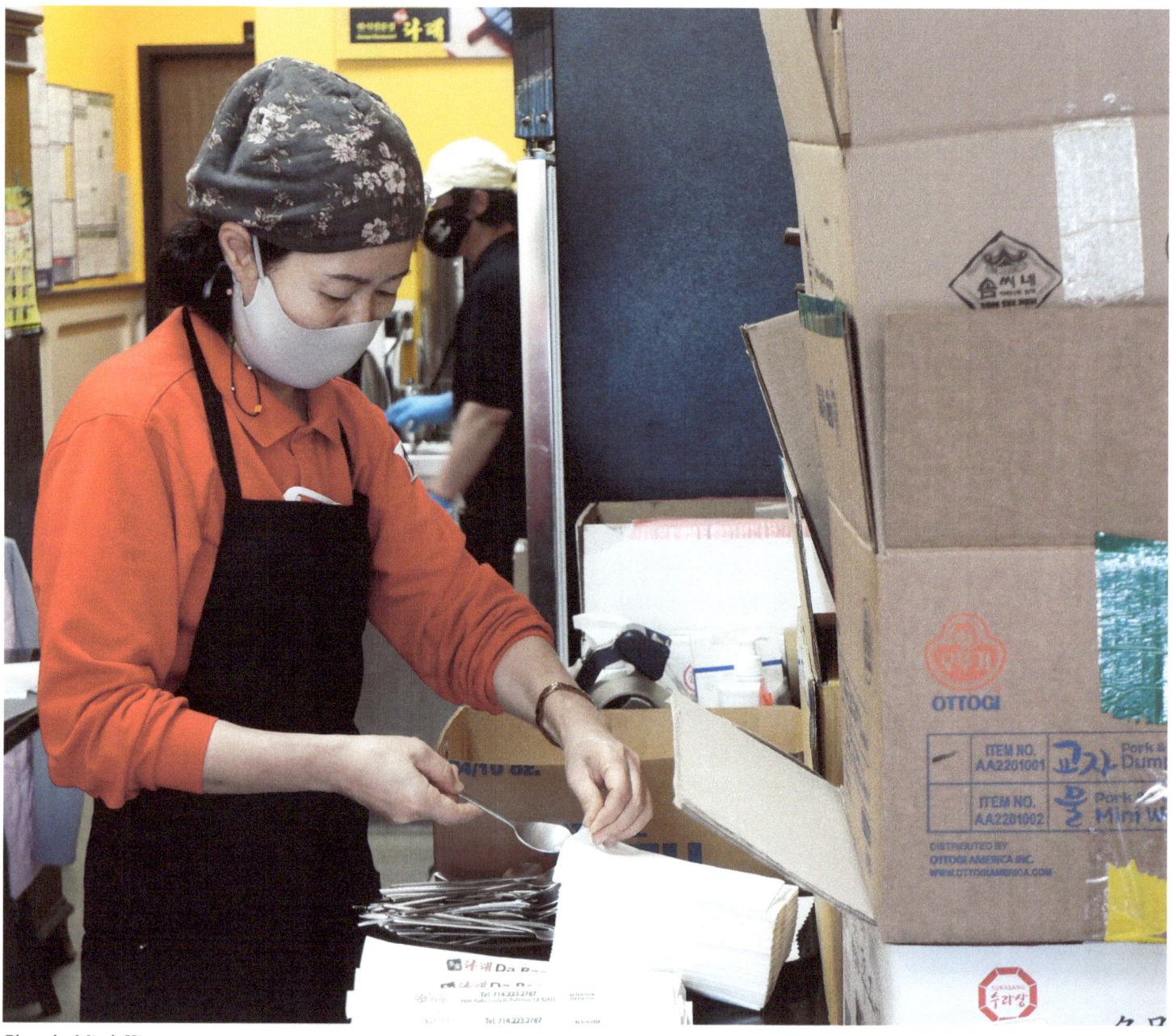

Photo by Micah Kim

Eunmi Lee, co-owner of De Rae Korean Restaurant, is usually in charge of preparing prepares for the coming dinner rush by arranging utensils for patrons in the empty dining room.

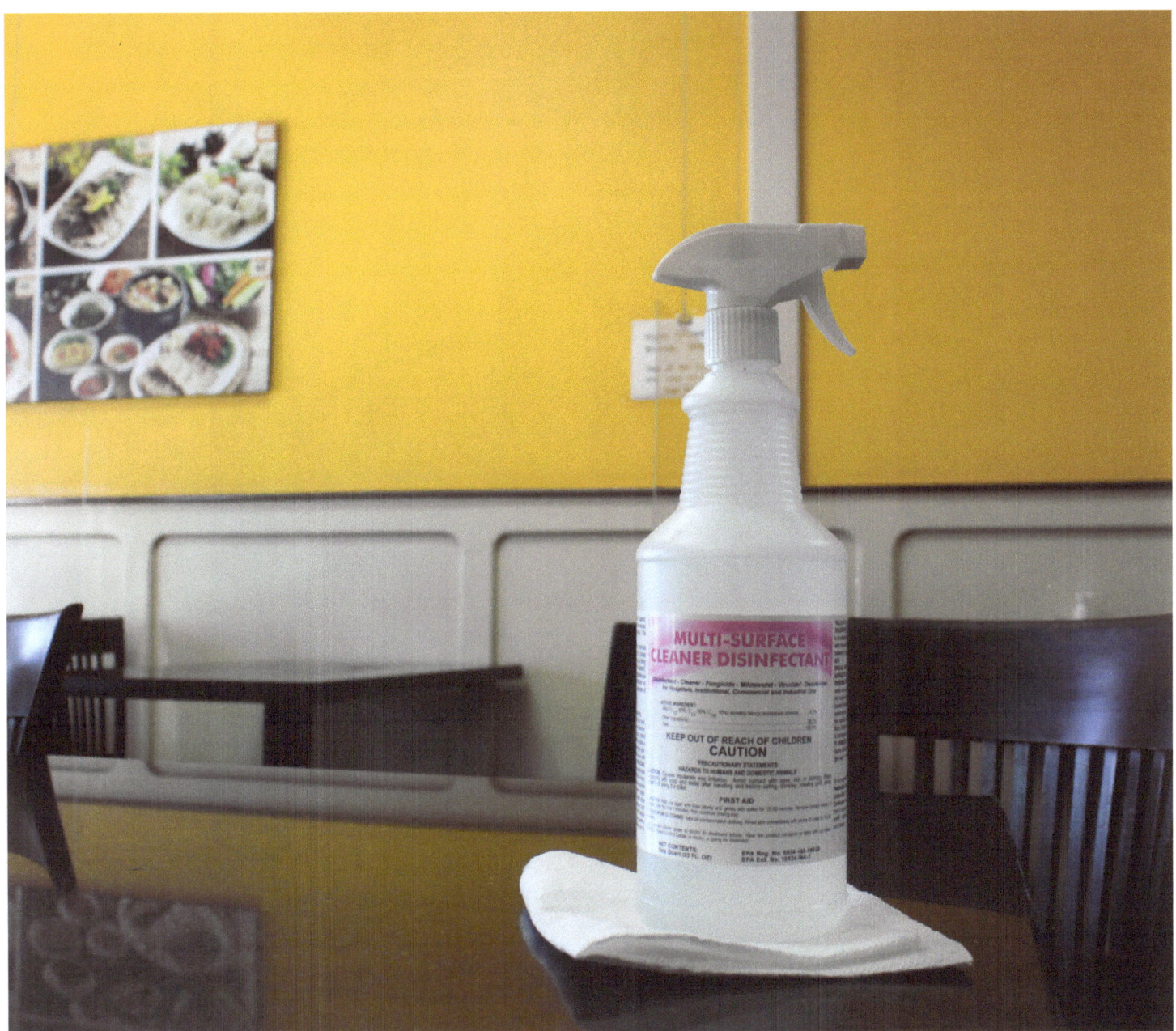

Photo by Micah Kim

Bottles of disinfectant reveal Da Rae's priority for safety as the owners hustle to ensure their guests are served in a tasty and safe manner, even amidst a lingering pandmic.

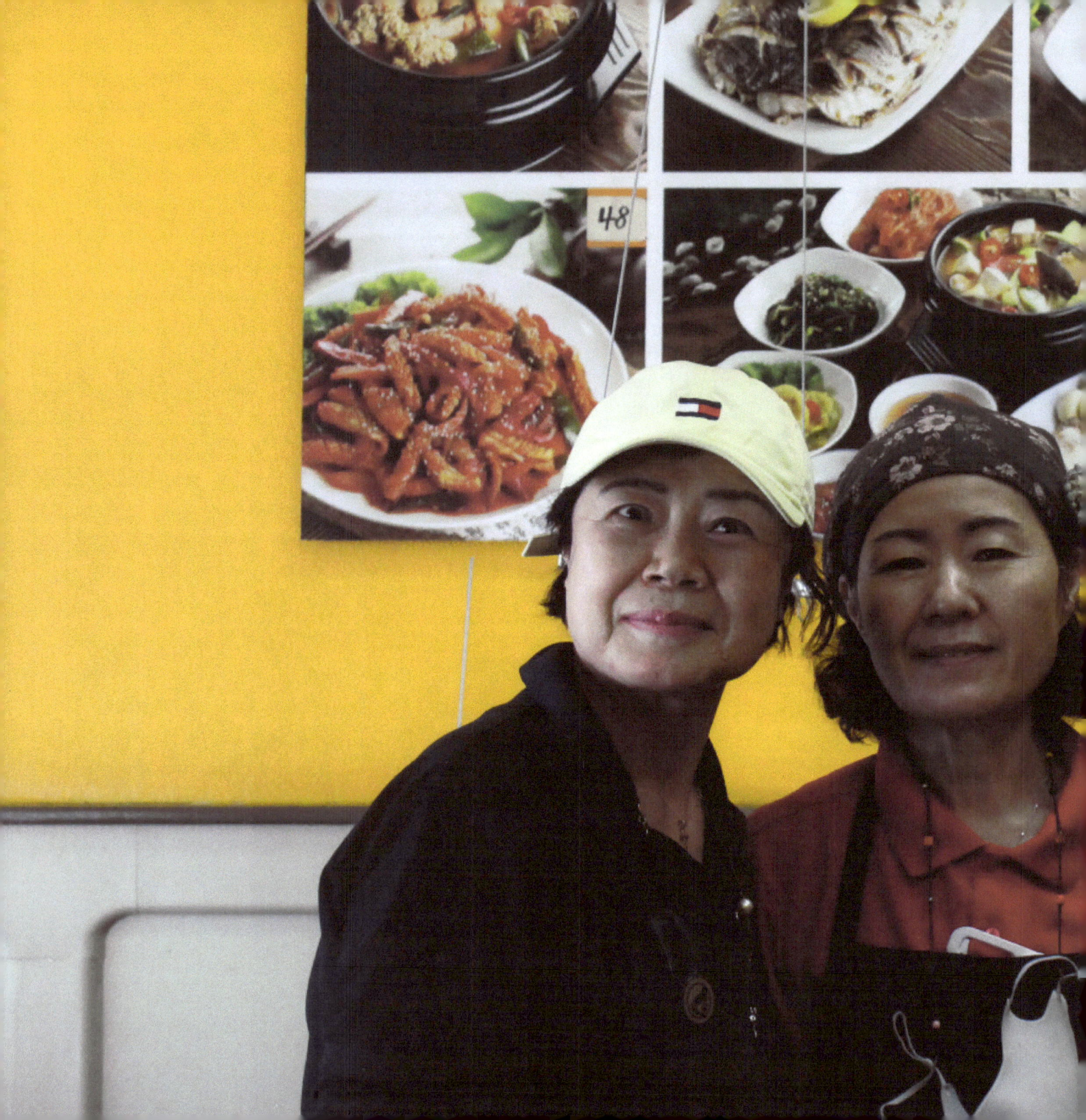

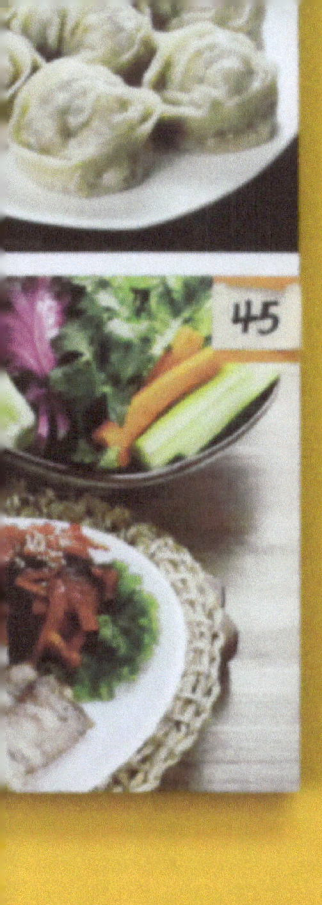

With their masks off, the two sisters beam with pride as they work tirelessly to keep their restaurant thriving six days a week throughout a long-lasting pandemic. As a family, they have overcome many difficulties; difficulties which range from pandemic-sized to family-sized. According to Aeran Lee, her sister has been th reason why she could continue through these recent hardships.

Photo by Hannah Dilanchyan

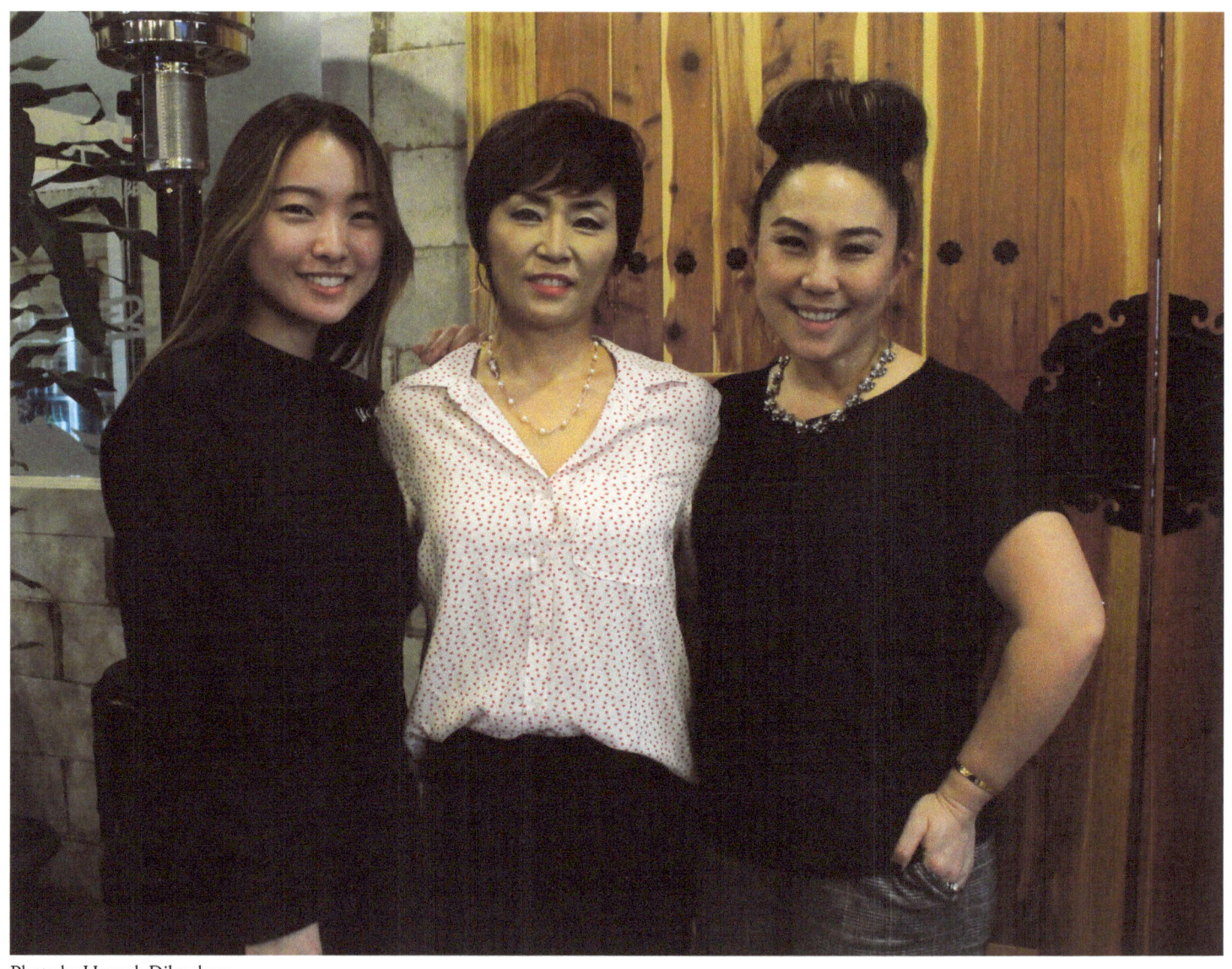

Photo by Hannah Dilanchyan

In Buena Park, California, another Korean restaurant run by mother-daughter trio Jasmine Kim, Michelle Kim, and Iris Jhueng (left to right) pour in countless hours to help ensure their family business prospers during the pandemic. They stand inside their beloved restaurant, Arisu Korean BBQ.

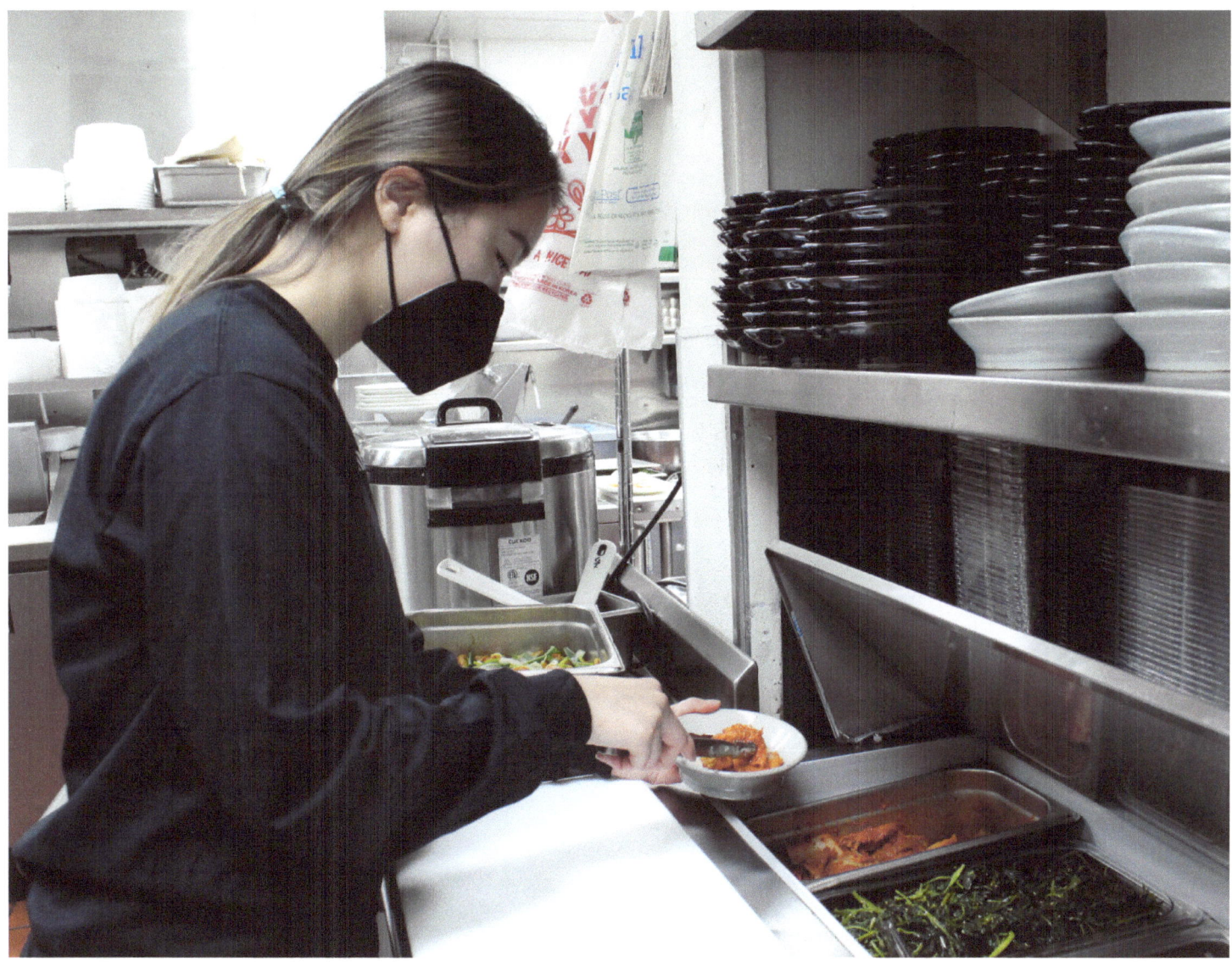

Photo by Hannah Dilanchyan

Every BBQ meal is offered with an abudance of delicious side dishes. Jasmine Kim helps prepare one of the various side dishes served at her mother's restaurant.

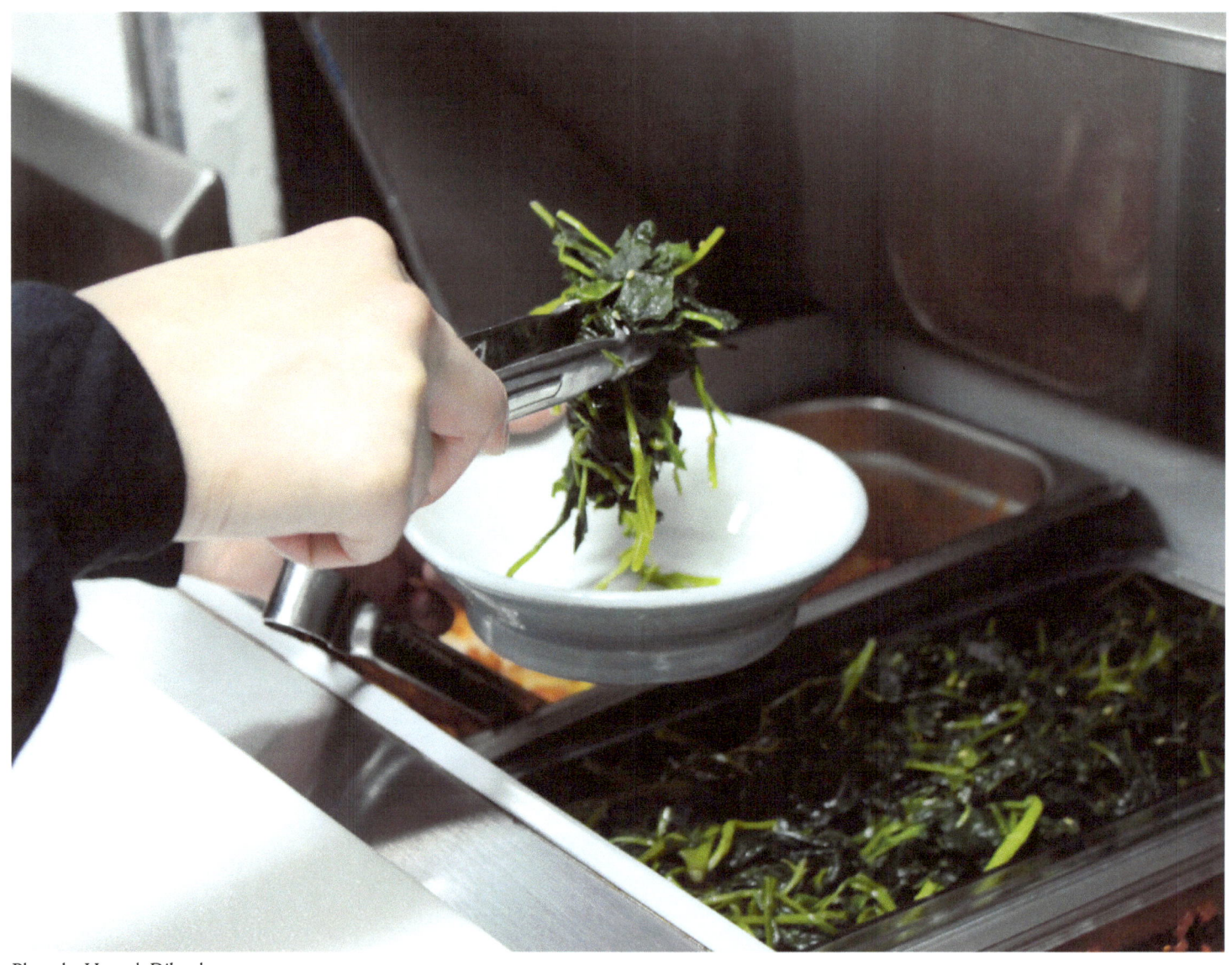

Photo by Hannah Dilanchyan

Jasmine Kim shows one of Arisu's side dishes, which are as essential as the main course. The restaurant takes pride in the many options they have available for their guests to enjoy-- a great example of their generous and warm spirit.

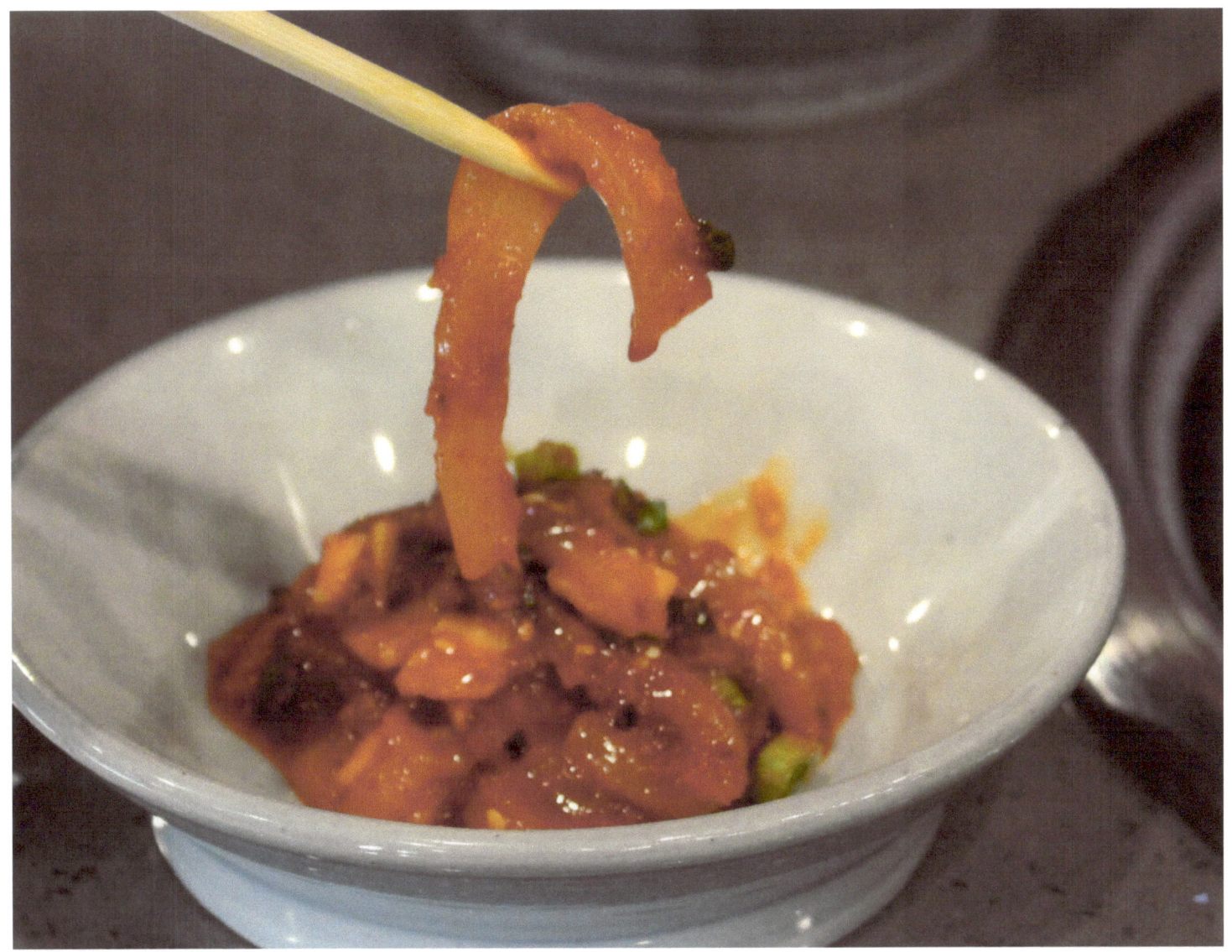

Photo by Hannah Dilanchyan

One of the best parts of a family-owned restaurant is being able to work together as a family and spend time together, Jasmine Kim explained while preparing a meal for their guests. The hardest? Finding other family members to watch each other's children while they work.

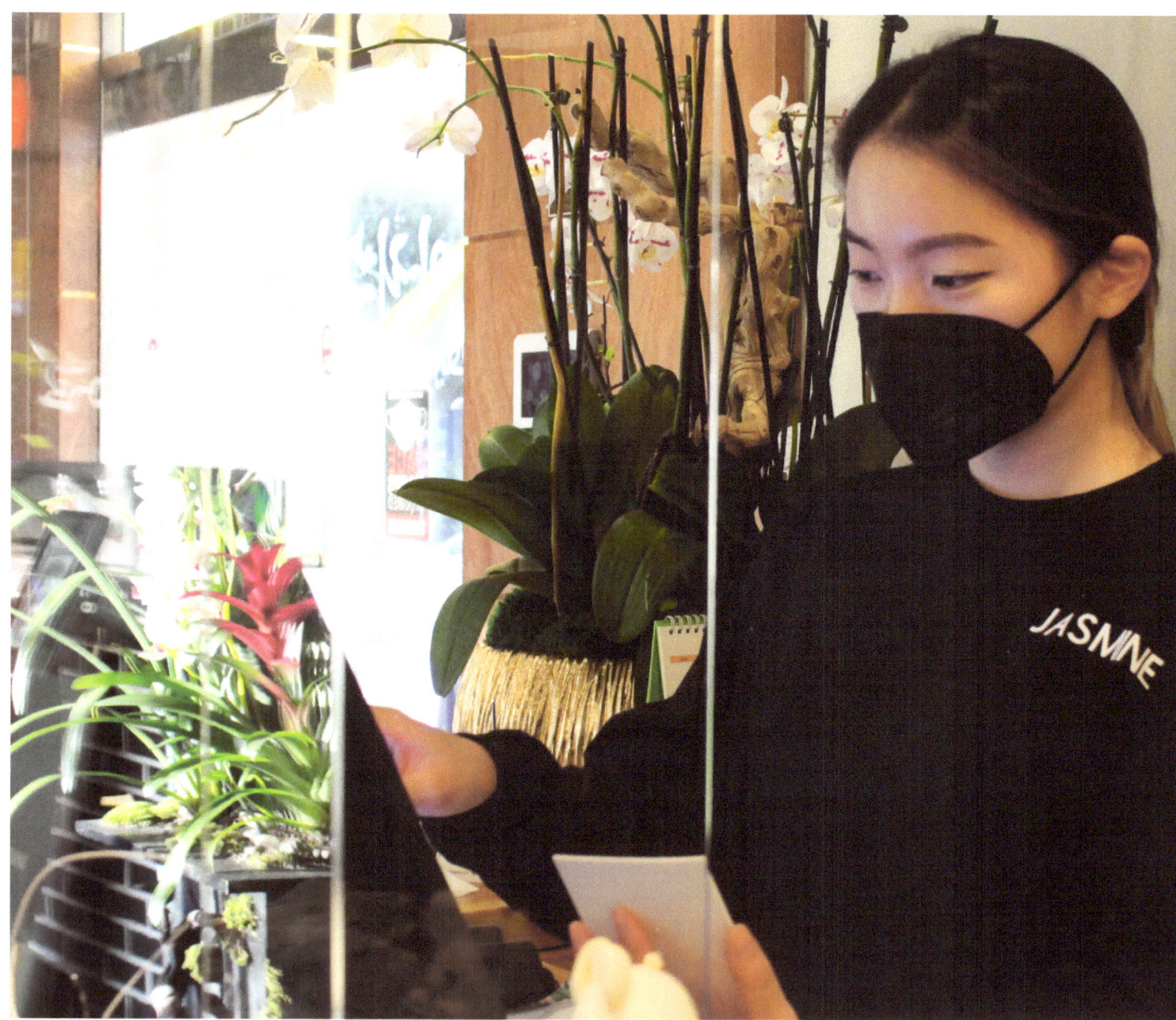

Photo by Hannah Dilanchyan

As a college student, Jasmine Kim splits time between classes at California State University of Fullerton, completing homework, spending time with friends and working at the restaurant. Behind the counter, Jasmine Kim greets guests, makes reservations, and answers calls, welcoming people ready for an authentic Korean meal; as many changes are evident as a result of the pandemic, including glass shields and face masks.

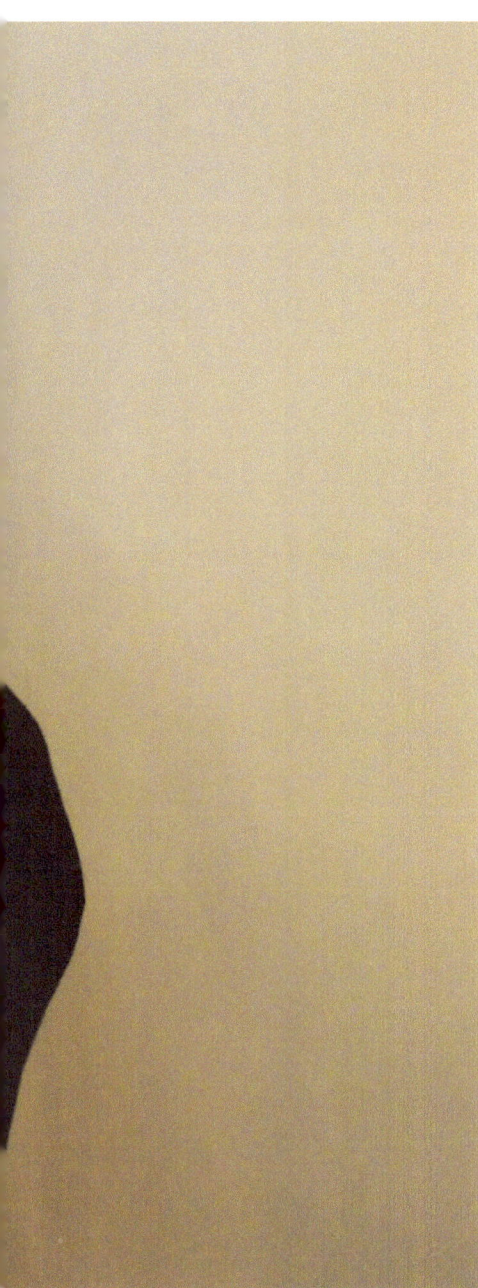

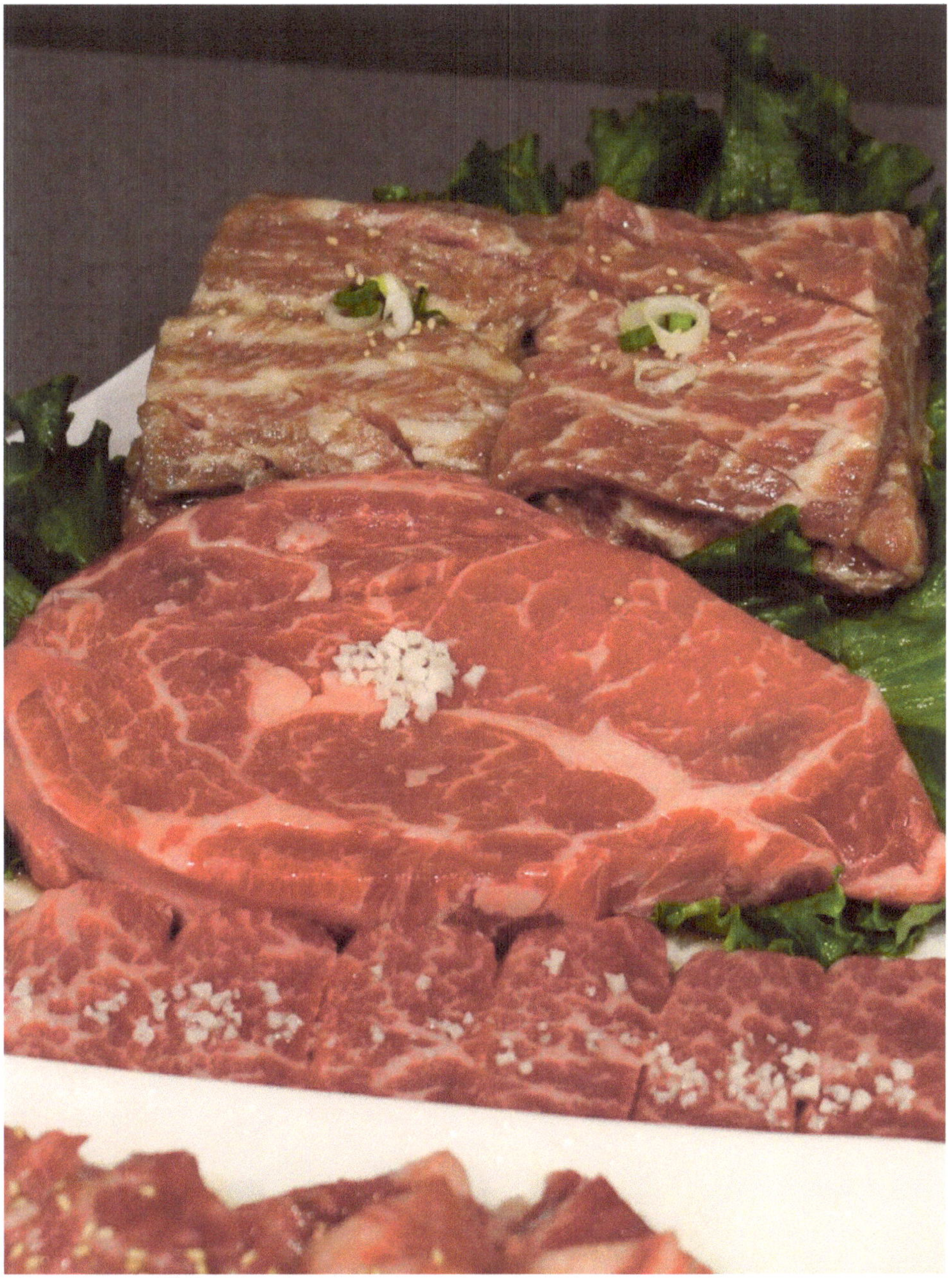

Photo by Hannah Dilanchyan

Korean BBQ is a popular choice among American diners. From the fresh, bold flavors to refreshing soju, it's no wonder that Korean cuisine is on many people's Friday night radar.

63

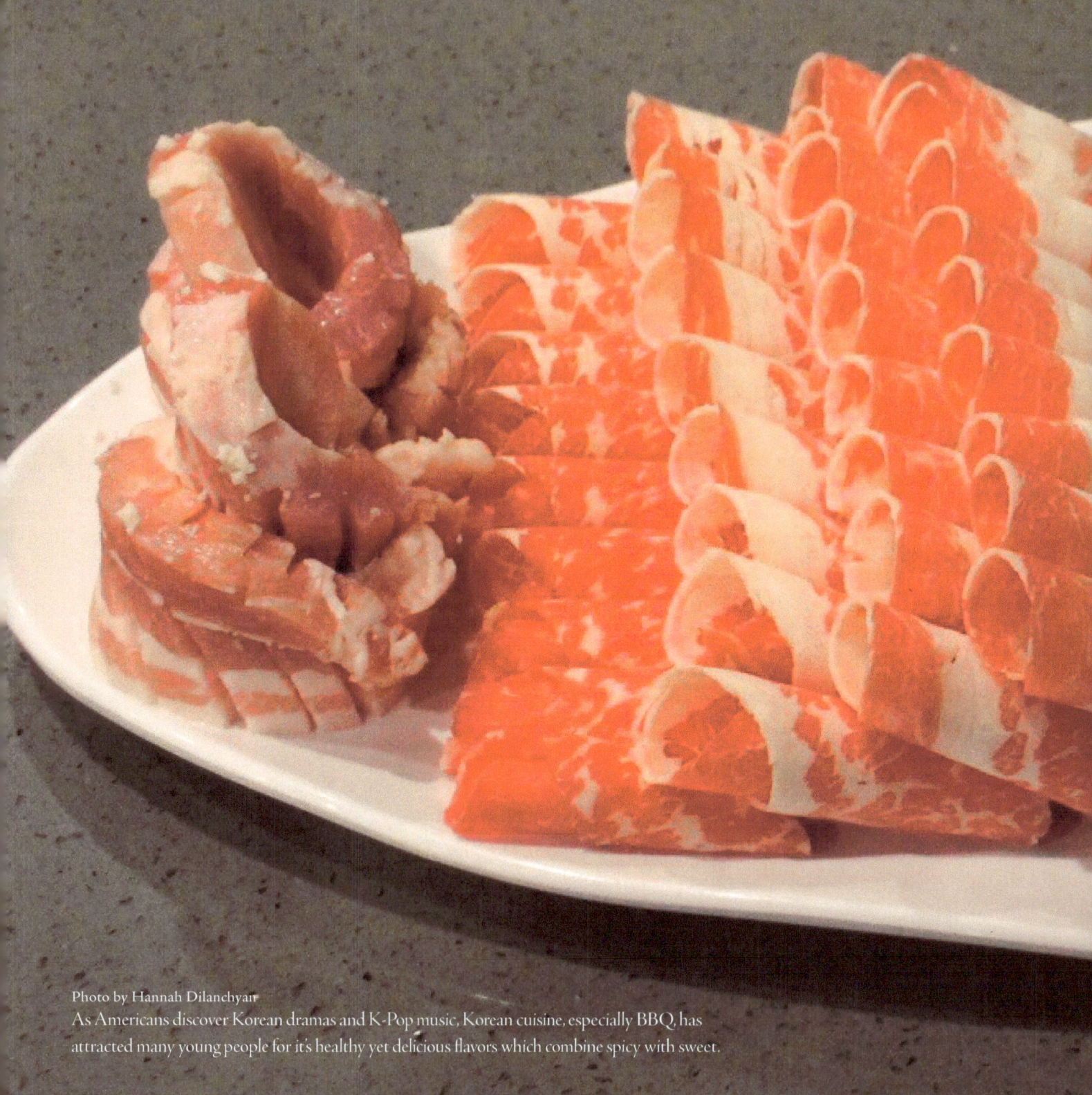

Photo by Hannah Dilanchyan
As Americans discover Korean dramas and K-Pop music, Korean cuisine, especially BBQ, has attracted many young people for it's healthy yet delicious flavors which combine spicy with sweet.

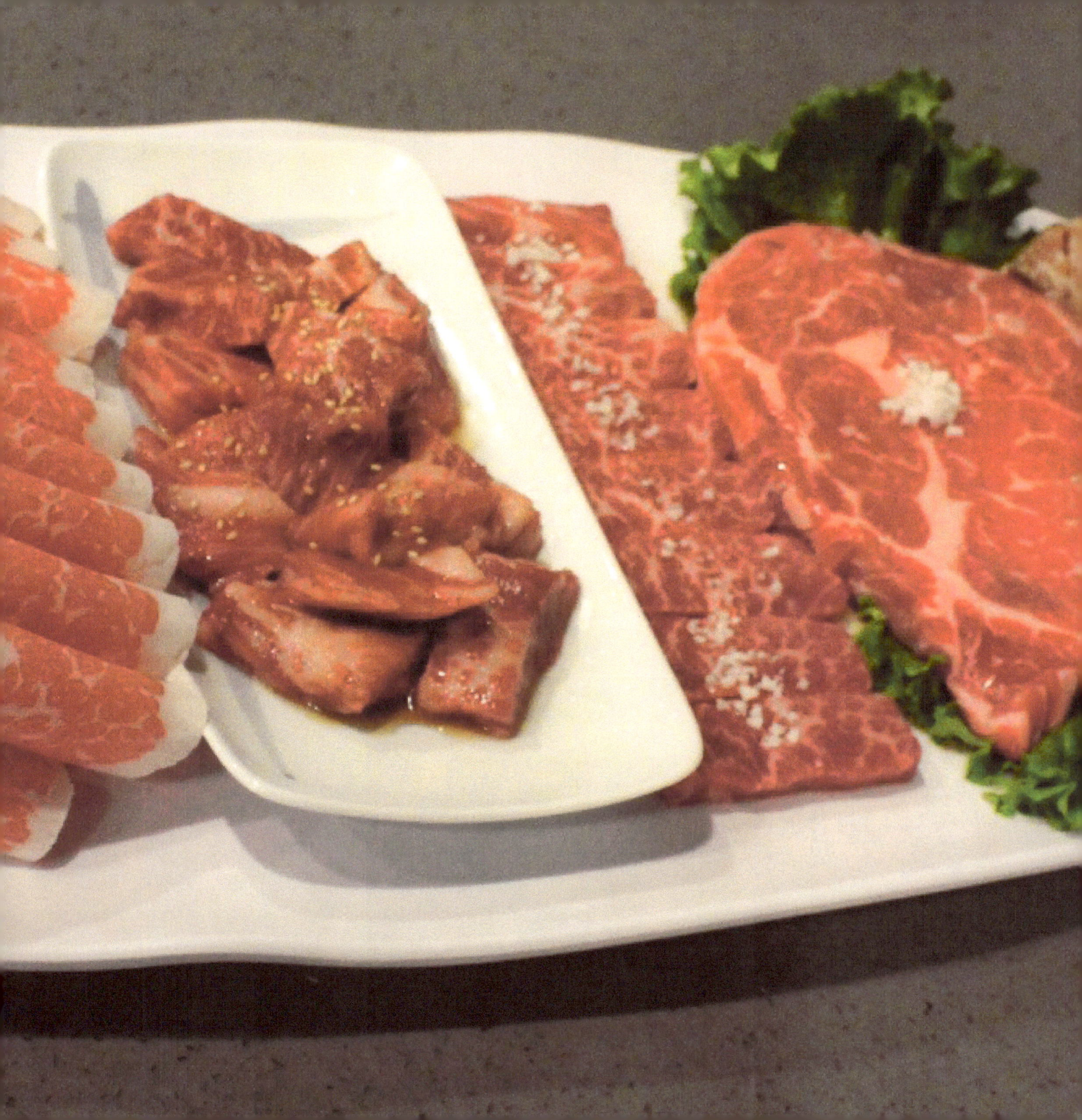

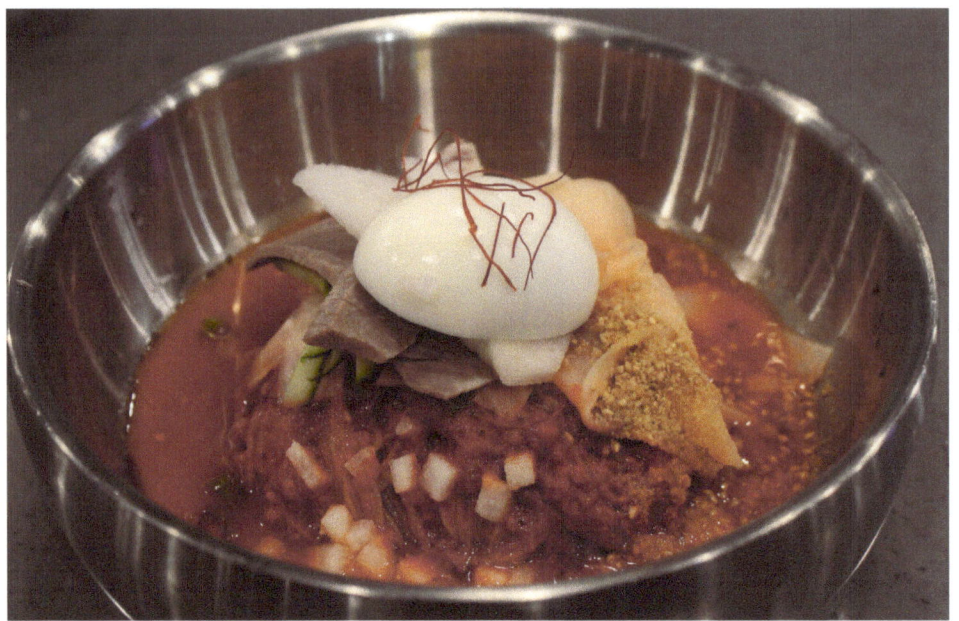

Photo by Hannah Dilanchyan

Spicy buckwheat noodle soup is a unique and colorful dish.

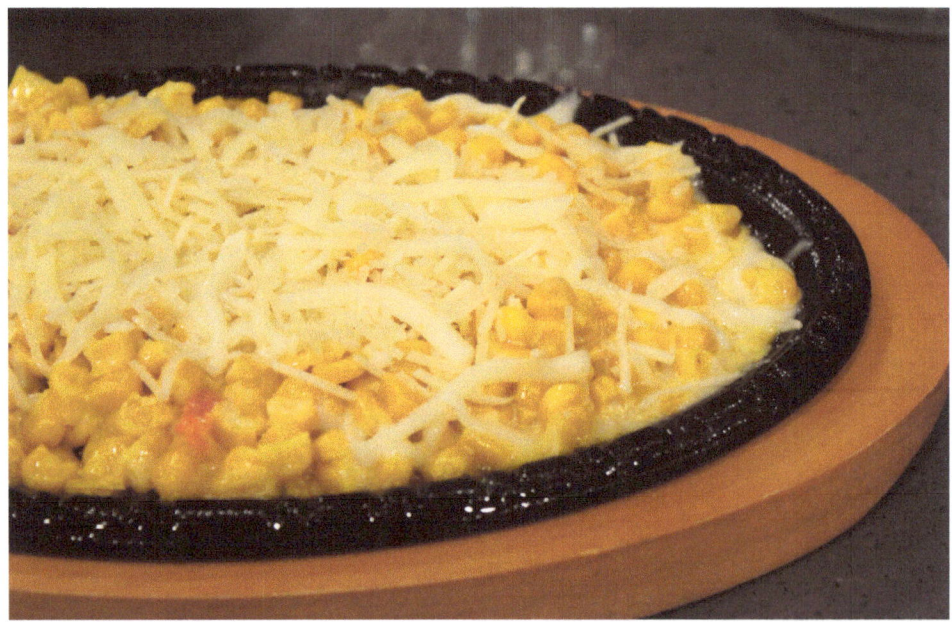

Photo by Hannah Dilanchyan

A delicious combination of corn and cheese is a popular part of Korean BBQ restaurants.

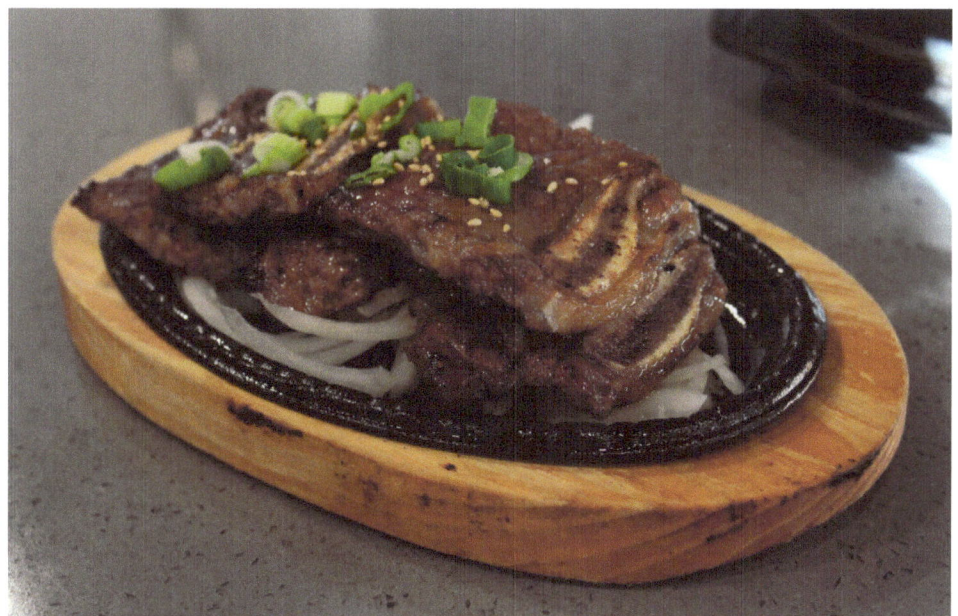

Korean BBQ offered on a plate of onions.

Photo by Hannah Dilanchyan

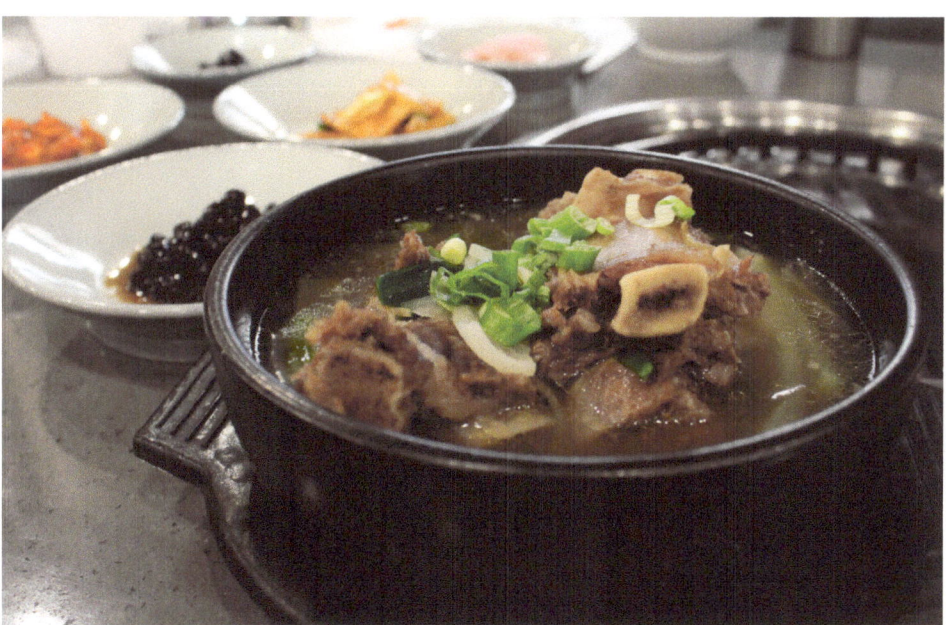

Made with beef short ribs, cabbage, and Korean soybean paste, this stew brings warmth to diners.

Photo by Hannah Dilanchyan

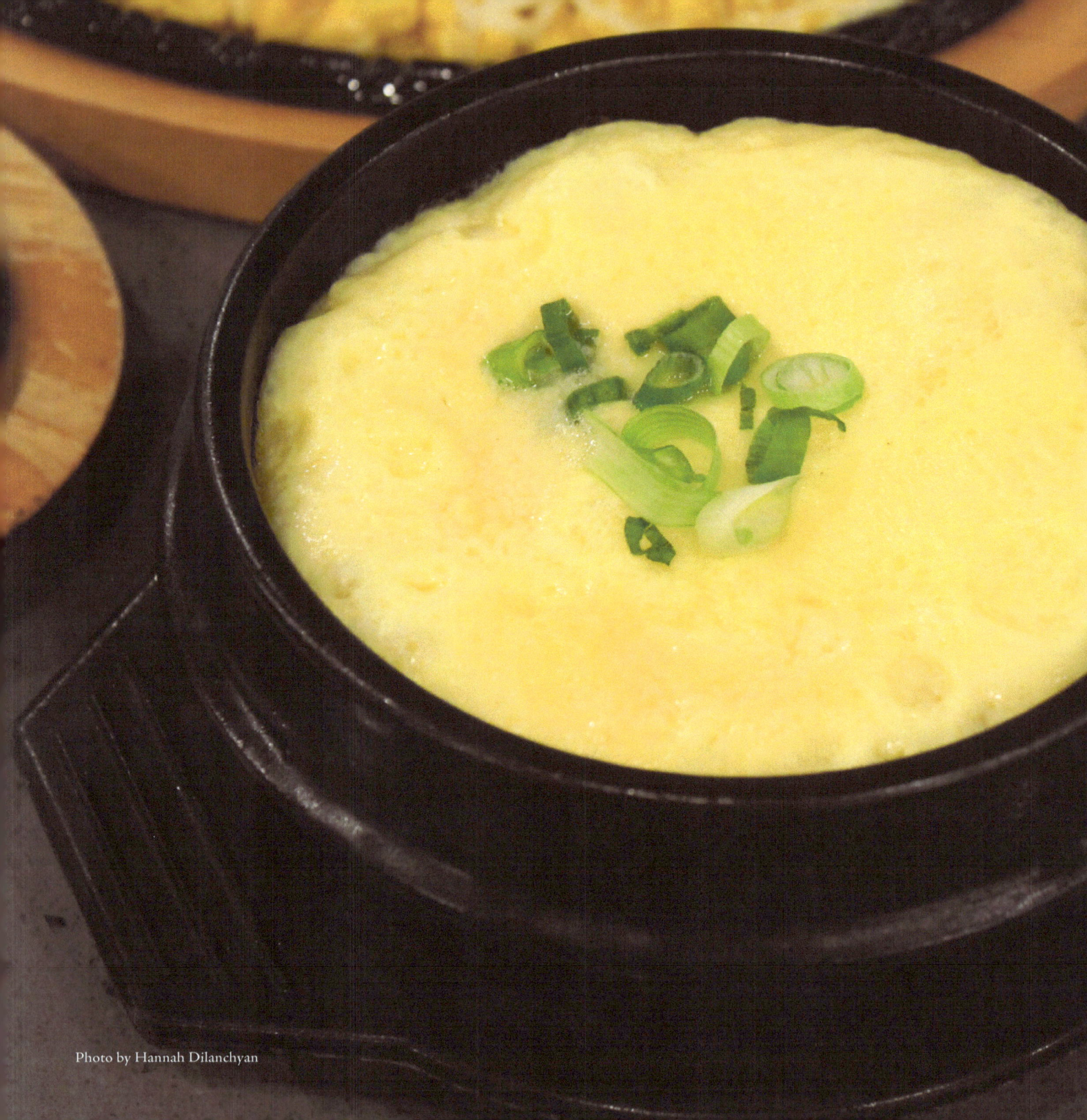

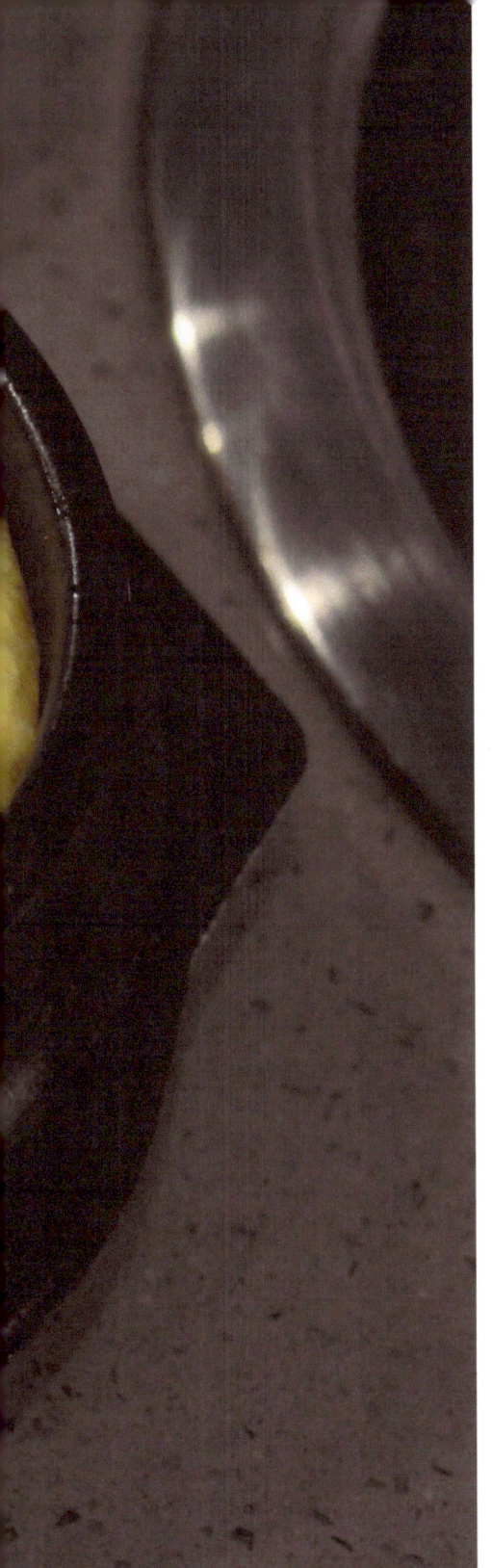

Comfort food, like this soup, are a part of the
Korean BBQ menu. Even a pandemic can't
stop the nostalgia that comes from enjoying
a warm meal while supporting a small, family-owned business.

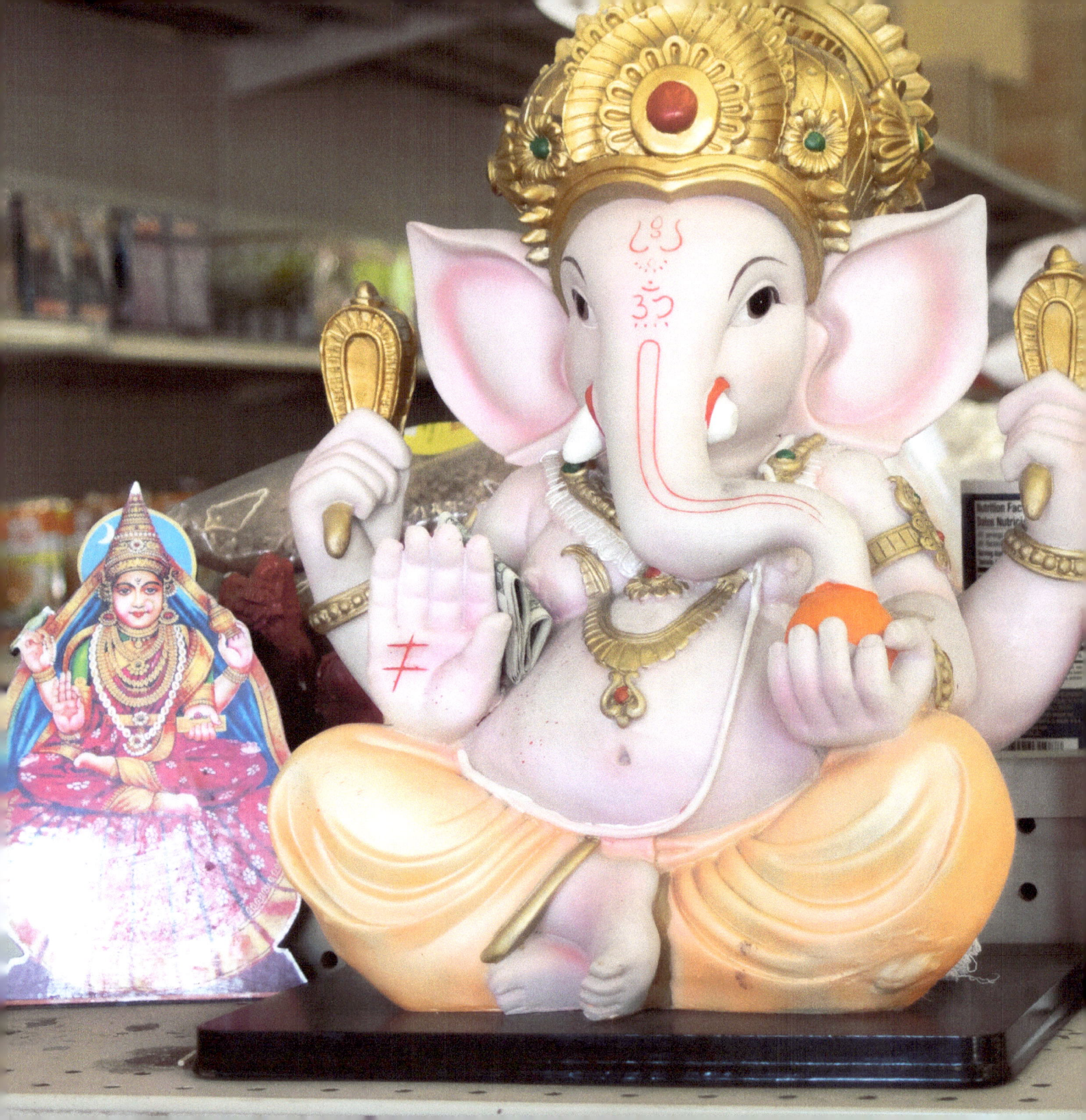

5. Indian Food and Religious Experience

By: Zachary Devane and Natalie Willis

Religion is a point of pride that is deeply embedded in the history of India. With a population of over 1 billion, the country located in Southeast Asia does not conform to any single religion, region, or diet. Instead, it is a mirror of the people it has encountered.

Social traditions and the foods of India go hand in hand as ideas of hospitality are closely tied to serving guests. Indian food is also closely tied to religious practices. Altogether spicy, rich, fragrant, electric and diverse, Indian food is addictive to the palette. The dishes provide comfort and joy to anyone lucky enough to taste the authentic cuisine. Unlike many Western meals, each Indian dish is purposefully created to provide a unique taste that does not overlap into other flavors. Spices are integral to food preparation and are used to enhance every dish.

"I don't like bland food. I can't stand mashed potatoes, I need to have some sort of spice in there and that just comes from eating a lot of Indian food over the years," said Udayvir Birdi, a sophomore from University of California, Los Angeles.

> "A great introduction to cultures is their cuisine. It not only reflects their evolution, but also their beliefs and traditions." -Vikas Khanna

Photo by: Corrie Myhr
Small statue of Hindu god, Ganesh

To Birdi, Indian food is more than just a flavourful meal, it holds an emotional weight that connects him to his culture and brings him close to his family. As a former Sikh, Birdi recalls the communal meal, Langar, shared by all who come to the Sikh temple or gurdwara. Langar has become an integral part of the Sikh religion because it is an expression of the equality of humankind and it strengthens the community. Birdi has since become agnostic, a person who claims neither faith nor disbelief in God, but he still enjoys the community of meals shared with his family. For many Indian Americans like Birdi, food connects them to their culture and family no matter where they are.

"It's definitely been one of those things where I've been able to relate back to my culture," Birdi said. "Especially after moving from India when I was seven and coming to the States. It's been one of those few anchors to my culture."

Family culture is one of the most important aspects of life to Indian people, and eating meals together is a significant social event. Birdi cherishes every meal with his family especially now that he is separated from them in college. The universal connection of food relates to all religions and regions in India and provides comfort to many Indian migrants to America.

RELIGION AND A GLOBAL PANDEMIC

The practices of all religions have undergone profound changes due to the COVID-19 pandemic. Because religious gatherings can be hotbeds for spreading the virus, many places of worship have been closed leading to a lack of community and shared meals.

Religious institutions have also had to adjust their services involving food to an online format. According to a survey from Pew Research[1], more Americans say that the pandemic has strengthened their religious faith. Almost half of the American adults surveyed say that their religious faith has not changed much while 28% of respondents say they have become more religious. The average Indian, however, places more significance on religion than other cultures psychoanalyst Ashok Nagpal explained in an interview for the Hindustan Times[2].

"For us, religion is a sociocultural encounter and to be able be to replicate old habits maintained through institutions like the family is to be able to draw on inner recesses, and keep hope and faith alive. In times like these, it's a force that releases new meanings and rituals," Nagpal said.

According to the Pew Research survey, family relationships have also been strengthened as the pandemic has brought with it an opportunity to get back to what matters. For Vivy Mathews, a Christian who grew up in India and has since moved to Southern California, and her family, it has been a time to share home cooked meals together once again. Both her sons are home for the first time since they were in high school, and the shared experience around the dinner table is wonderful.

Photo by: Natalie Willis
Hindu Temple of Kern County, like many places of worship, was closed due to COVID-19

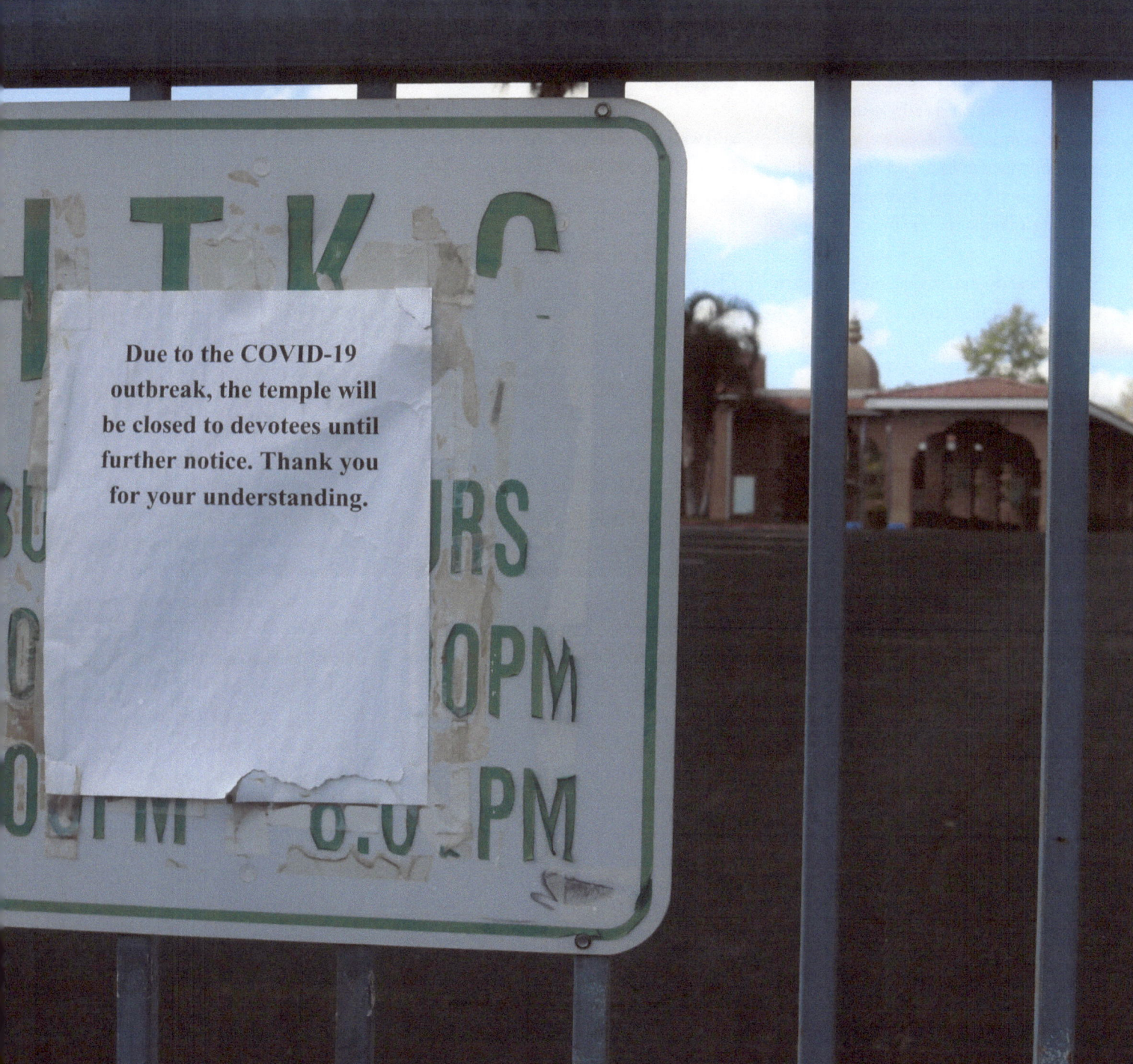

WHAT CAN HINDUS EAT?

The major religions of India – Hinduism, Buddhism, Jainism, Sikhism and Islam – all have particular dietary restrictions and specialities. 94% of the world's Hindu population lives in India, according to the Pew Research Center[3], which has had a sweeping influence on the Indian cuisine.

As the most dominant religion, Hinduism has had a profound impact on Indian cooking and food habits. The main concept of the Hindu religion orders respect for every living thing, which has contributed to the prevalence of vegetarianism in India. While some Hindus choose to adhere to the religion's dietary restrictions in varying degrees, such as refraining from beef and pork but consuming other meats, devout Hindus believe in the harmony of all living creatures. Spiritual development in Hinduism is closely tied to maintaining a proper diet.

The Hindu dietary code, according to Minority Nurse magazine[4], is divided into three categories that take into account food's effect on the body and mind.
1. Tamasic food categorizes leftover, spoiled, or other impure food which the Hindus believe correlates to emotions of anger, greed and jealousy.

2. The next category, Rajestic, includes meat, eggs, fish, spices, peppers, and other spicy or pungent foods believed to produce strong emotions such as passion and restlessness.

3. Lastly, the most desirable food category, Sattvic, includes fruits, vegetables, nuts and whole grains all of which are believed to purify the mind and "increase one's magnetism."

Most Hindus that immigrate to the United States have held onto their food traditions as a way to relate back to their culture. According to Stephen R. Warner and Judith G. Wittner's chronicle study on religion and immigration in America, Gathering in Diaspora: Religious Communities and the New Immigration, "Asserting pride in their Hindu Indian heritage has also been their way of claiming a position for themselves at the American multicultural table."[5]

Although nearly all Asian-American Hindus trace their heritage back to India, according to the Pew Research Center, only about 51% of Indian Americans consider themselves Hindu. As a result, many Indian restaurants in America do not conform to the vegetarian lifestyle of the Hindu religion.

To Hindus, food is spiritually connected to an individual's walk of life. There is meaning and significance behind every meal to emphasize connection with each other and India. The Upanishads, a series of sacred Hindu written works, emphasize the importance of food, relating it to the meaning of existence. There are between 180-200 Upanishads but the most popular 13 are separated into the four Vedas, translated as "knowledge." This Sanskrit literature places food far above a mere means of sustenance. Instead, it shifts from the Hindu gods consuming sacrificial food to the association of food to the birth of the universe.
According to Jennifer B. Saunders' sociology journal 'I don't eat meat': Discourse on food among transnational Hindus, "At the cosmological level, food unites the particular with the universal—it gives life and connects all living beings with the cosmos."[6]

In the Upanishads, the supreme existence or ultimate reality, is Brahman. That is, food is god. Some Hindus believe that food is a manifestation of the Brahman and is actually part of the ultimate reality of existence according to R.S. Khare's book The Eternal Food: Gastronomic Ideas and Experiences of Hindus and Buddhists.[7] Furthermore, to Hindus food is the necessary aid to humans until the exchange between the self, body and world ceases and Brahman is realized.

Photo by: Corrie Myhr

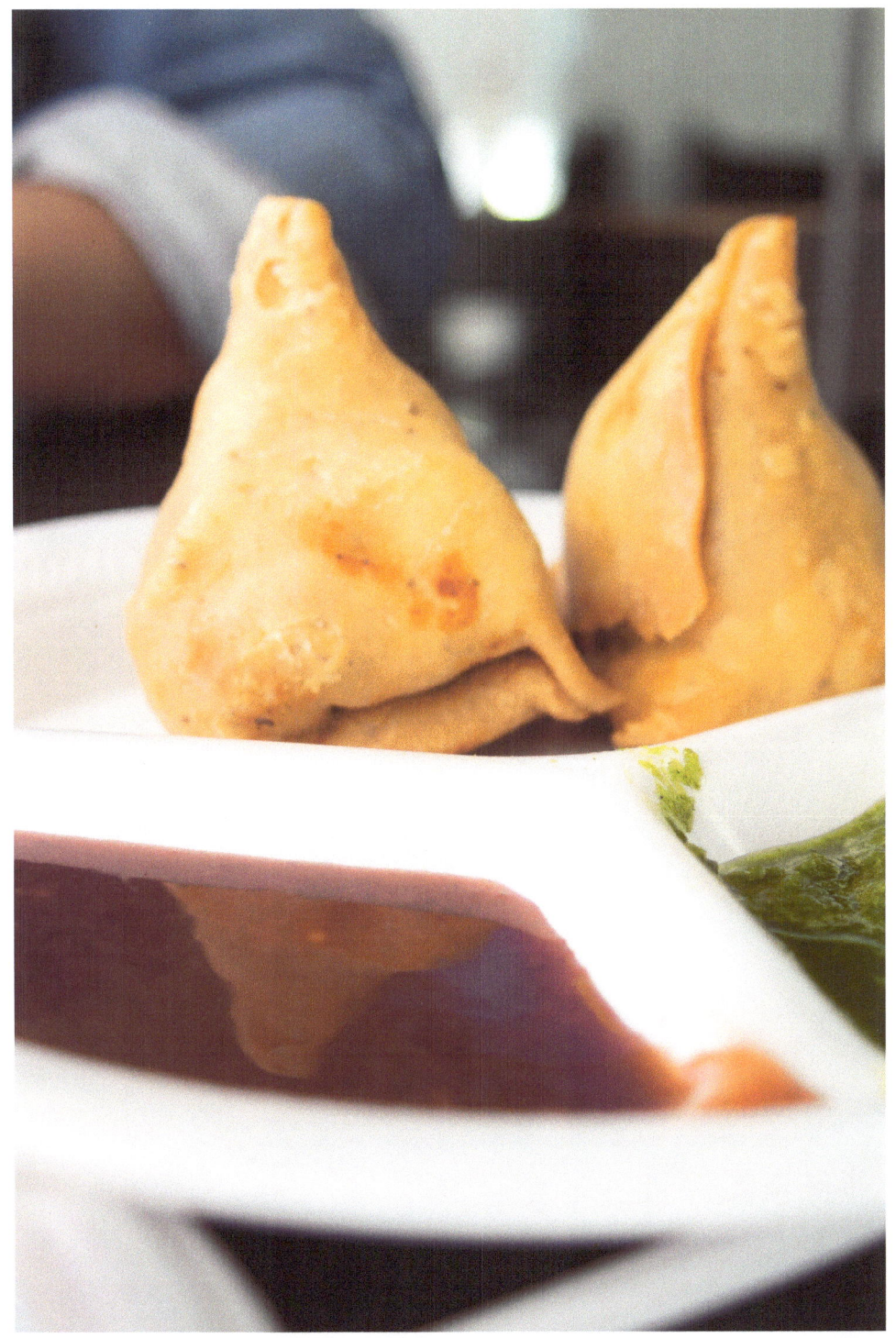

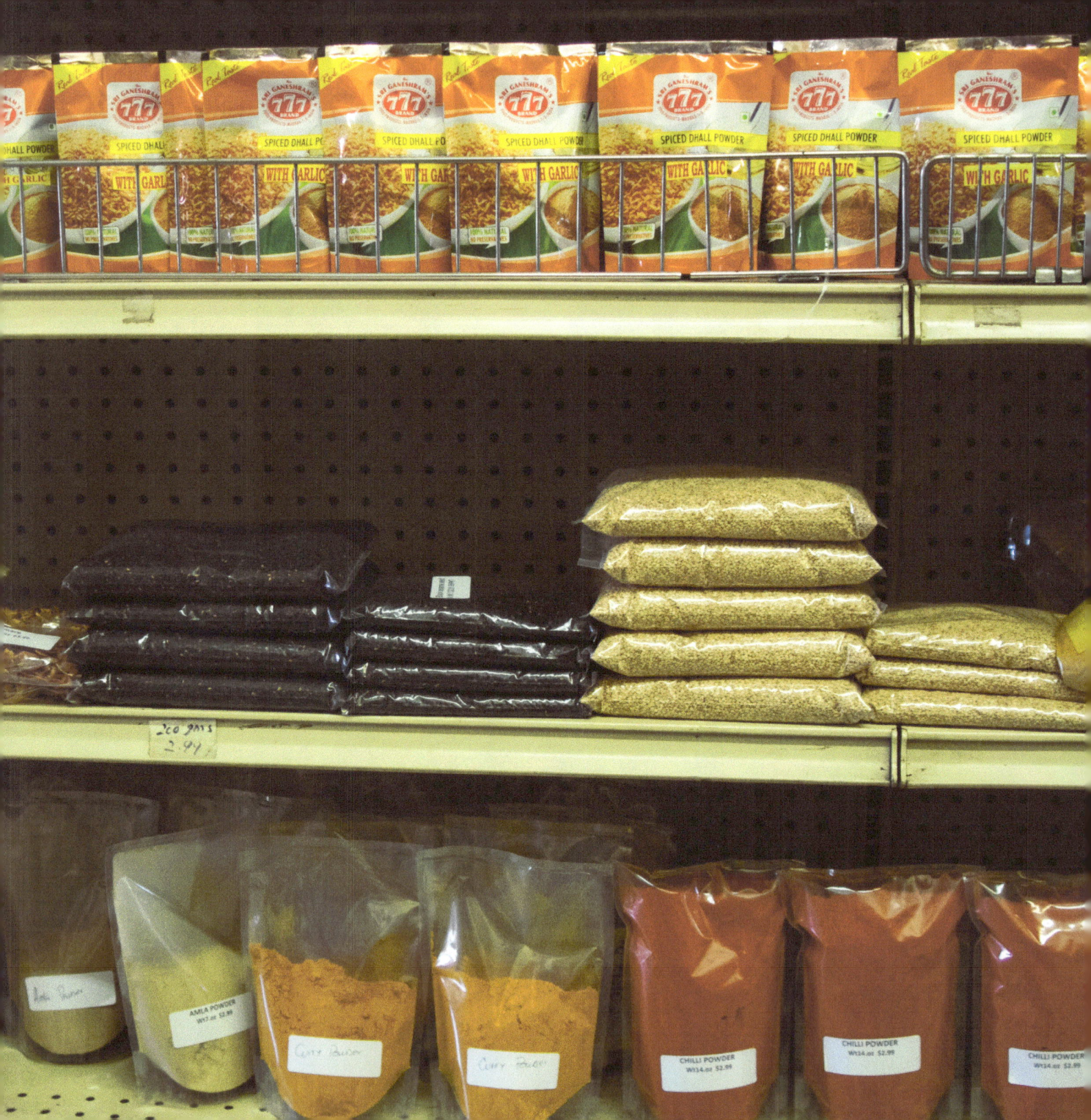

ISLAMIC FOOD PRACTICES AND THE SIGNIFICANCE OF HALAL

The second largest religion in India, Islam, established by Muslim rule in India about the time of the Timurid Dynasty, has greatly influenced dishes and food preparation in northern India. Currently, India has the second largest Muslim population in the world.

According to Food Culture in India[8] by Colleen Taylor Sen, a reference of the history of Indian cuisine, Islam has far fewer dietary restrictions than Hinduism. However, the restrictions they do adhere to come from the religious texts of the Qur'an and Sunnah. While Muslims are not vegetarian, they must adhere to the Islamic method when slaughtering animals—halal. When they are preparing meat permitted by halal, they must first handle the animals with kindness and kill them quickly to mitigate suffering. In order for food to be considered halal or pure, the name of the Muslim god, Allah, must be invoked as the animal is killed. While most meat such as lamb, beef, goat, chicken and fish are considered halal, any product containing pork is forbidden as are all types of alcohol.

Halal, the lawful dietary standard for food preparation and its opposite, unlawful preparation haram are universal terms that are applied to all aspects of life. These include food products, meat products, cosmetics, personal care products, food ingredients, pharmaceuticals and any item that will come in contact with food.

The emphasis on the importance of halal products is growing and moving into the mainstream market. According to Kambiz Heidarzadeh Hanzaee and Mohammad Reza Ramezani's journal, Intention to Halal Products in the World Markets,[9] the global halal market is worth roughly $150 billion a year and the halal food industry is expected to grow exponentially at a 2.9% annual rate. Required by religion to ensure the products they use are halal, Muslims are also encouraged to shy away from commodities that are doubted.

"It is estimated that 70% of Muslims worldwide follow halal standards and the Global Halal Market was $12 billion in 1999. It increased to $150 billion in 2001 and currently is reported as $580 billion," Ramezani explained.

Today, Muslims are asserting their presence at a social, economic and political level by pushing for halal-verified food products. They can be assured of the credibility of a halal product when a reliable institute issues a halal certificate to suppliers.

Photo by: Corrie Myhr
Traditional Indian spices and ingredients found in store.

CHRISTIAN FOOD CULTURE AND HOSPITALITY

Food tradition in Christianity is largely centered around the Lord's Supper, where according to the Christian scriptures, Jesus broke bread and drank wine with his disciples prior to his crucifixion. In remembrance of this act, Christians around the world, including India, partake in this event now referred to as Holy Communion.

Through this event of remembrance, Christians not only become one with Christ by eating bread and drinking wine, they gain a sense of community. By sharing what Chrsitians refer to as "the body of Christ" they unite themselves into one body, centered around the ceremonial bread and wine.

The integration of communion among Evangelical and Pentecostal Christian in India has been adapted in regard to the culture and surrounding environment. According to Paul M. Collins' examination of the relationship between the Christian message and cultures in his book Christian Inculturation in India,[10] the worshipping Chrsitian community in South India has adapted the Lord's Supper by supplementing the bread with coconuts.

"The coconut can also be symbolic of His body being broken and His blood shed for each of us. By using the coconut instead of traditional bread and juice, Hindus understand Christ's sacrificial act in a new way," Collins explained.

Innovations such as this in the new Evangelical and Pentecostal church traditions demonstrate a somewhat distinct practice with other Christian traditions in India.

For most Christians in India, the lack of religious-based dietary restrictions set them apart from the majority of the population. The exclusions included in Hindu and Muslim tradition do not carry over in the minority Christian sphere of India.

An inclusion of all types of meats and animal-based food, like eggs, is common for the Christians in India. Cake, for example, is a delicacy due to the use of eggs in baking— and during holidays like Christmas, the cakes and desserts made in Christian households are often not found anywhere else in the country.

"Christians prepared certain dishes that the non-Christians never prepared in their homes," said Mathews. "For some reason, cakes were all made by Christians, and the Hindus enjoyed when we shared that with them."

Christians had to be aware of the food traditions of their Muslim and Hindu counterparts. A common Hindu practice of worship, called puja, involves food being offered to the gods and returned to the worshippers, according to Hinduism in India: The Early Period.[11] The food, or prasada, would then be shared amongst the community—something Christians did not often take part in.

"I was always uncomfortable when somebody brought me something that was from puja," said Mathews. "There were times where I said 'we don't eat food offered to the [Hindu god].'"

Furthermore, Christian households, like the Mathews, also had to be cognizant of the tradition of others in their communities. Often times, separate or "clean" utensils would be used when Hindu or Muslim friends came over out of respect for their meatless diet.

SEPARATED BY RELIGION, CONNECTED THROUGH FOOD

To many Indian Americans, food provides a sense of familiarity and connects them to their culture. Regardless of religion, the emotional significance of food has the distinct ability to nourish the soul. For Birdi, it has brought him closer with his family and links him to his culture. He recalls spending countless hours watching his grandma preparing Indian food and teaching him about his culture.

Mathews grew to understand the importance of hospitality from her mother, who always had guests in mind. It was common that loved ones or friends would visit the house unexpectedly, and so Mathews' mom would have undoubtedly had food or candy ready to receive them with. It was not meant to impress those visiting, but rather to make them feel at home.

Although religion in India is a dividing factor among its huge populations, the traditions that hold them together are all centered around the way they engage with food. The ideals of hospitality and care for others is a part of Indian culture that is cemented by the sharing of food.

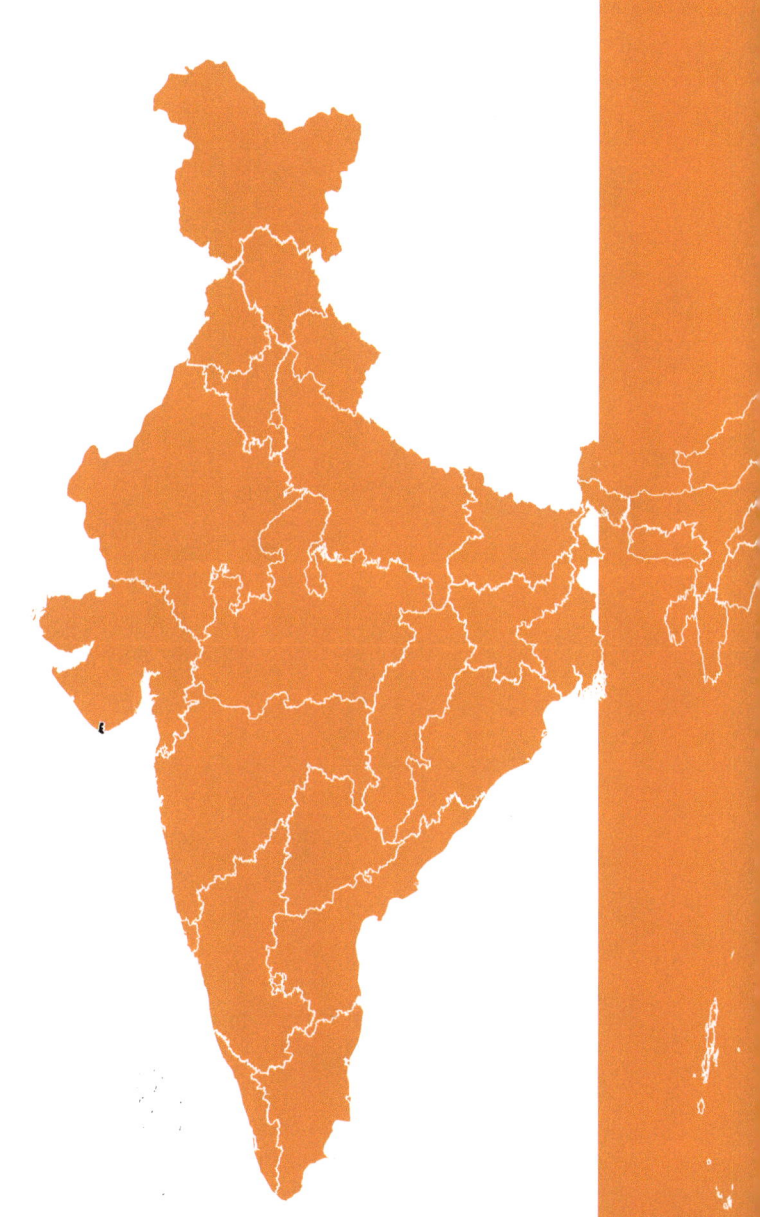

REFERENCES

[1]Pew Research Center. (2021, January 29). How covid-19 has strengthened religious faith.

[2]Ghosh , P. (2020, July 22). Holding onto faith in the middle of the pandemic. Hindustan Times.

[3]Majumdar, S. (2020, May 31). 5 facts about religion in India. Pew Research Center.

[4]Hindu Dietary Practices: Feeding the Body, Mind and Soul. Minority Nurse. (2019, November 26).

[5]Warner, R., & Wittner, J. (Eds.). (1998). Gatherings In Diaspora: Religious Communities and the New Immigration. Temple University Press.

[6]Saunders, J. B. (2007). 'I don't eat meat.' Contributions to Indian Sociology, 41(2), 203–223.

[7]Khare, R. S. (1992). The Eternal food: Gastronomic ideas and experiences of Hindus and Buddhists. Albany: State University of New York Press.

[8]Sen, C. T. (2004). Food culture in India. Greenwood Press.

[9]Hanzaee , K. H., & Ramezani, M. R. (2011, May 5). Intention To Halal Products In The World Markets. Academia.edu.

[10]Collins, P. M. (2007). Christian inculturation in India. Aldershot: Ashgate.

[11]Bailey, Greg, and Geoffrey A. Oddie. Hinduism in India: The Early Period. New Delhi: Sage, 2017.

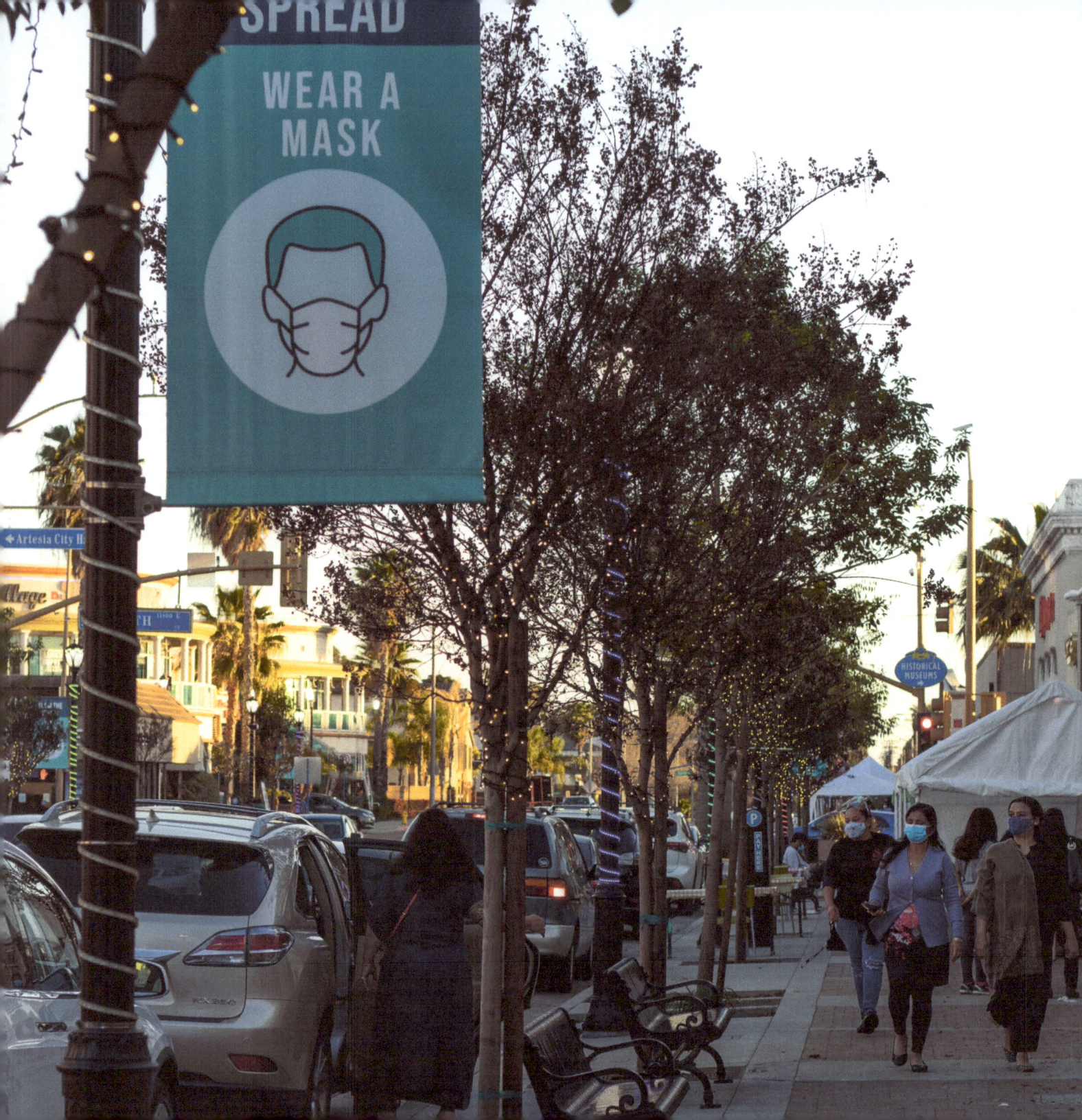

6. Little India: A Cultural Landmark

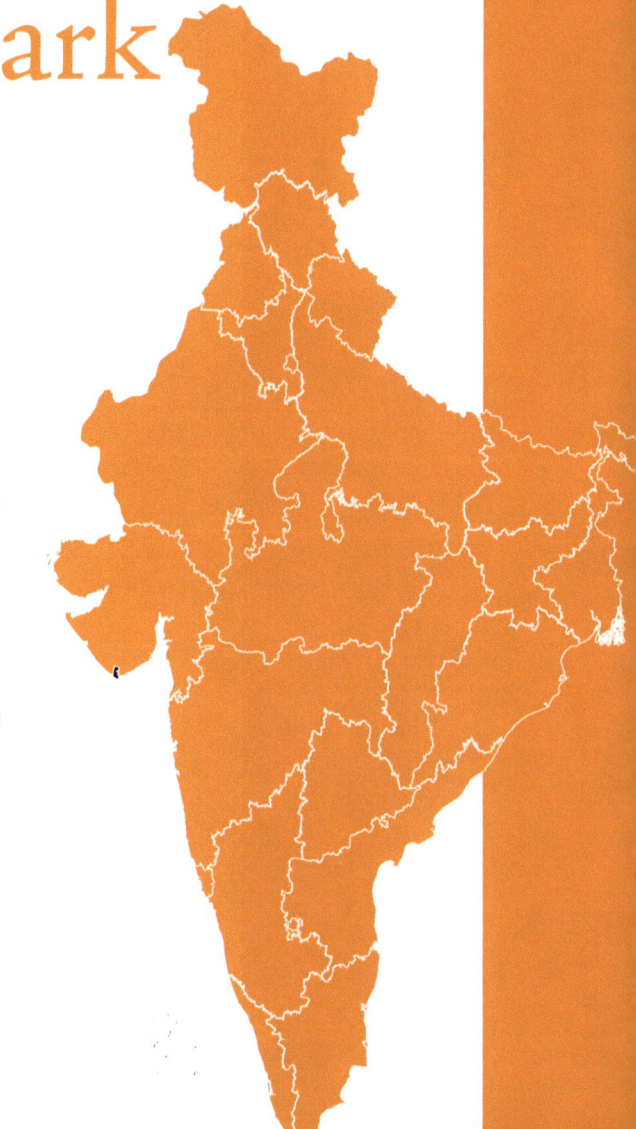

By: Vanessa Morales and Corrie Myhr

"Little India" located on the middle three blocks on Pioneer in Artesia, Southern California extends beyond just Indian foods, markets, and clothing stores. This strip on Pioneer represents home away from home. The first Indian store that popped up in Artesia was in 1970 when Balkishan Lahoti established an Indian grocery store.

"The seeds for what would become Little India were planted in 1971 when Balkishan Lahoti, a Cerritos resident, began selling spices and foods out of an Artesia garage. Lahoti later moved his business to Bellflower, but other Indian merchants began setting up shop on Pioneer to cater to the large Indian population in Cerritos, which borders Artesia on three sides," said former Los Angeles Times reporter, Jessica Lee. [1]

According to the LA History Archive[2], in 1994 Ramesh Mahajan, Founder and President of the Little India Chamber of Commerce had suggested that signs be placed on Pioneer, from 184th street and extends until 188th street, to welcome consumers to "Little India."

"Feels like you're on a street of Bombay, today's Mumbai, a lot of the streets— the way the shops are designed— I feel like I'm back home," Said Caryl Jones who grew up in Bombay and later moved to the U.S. in her mid-20s.

Photo by: Corrie Myhr
Situated in the Southern Californian city of Artesia, Pioneer
Boulevard hosts the center stage of Little India.

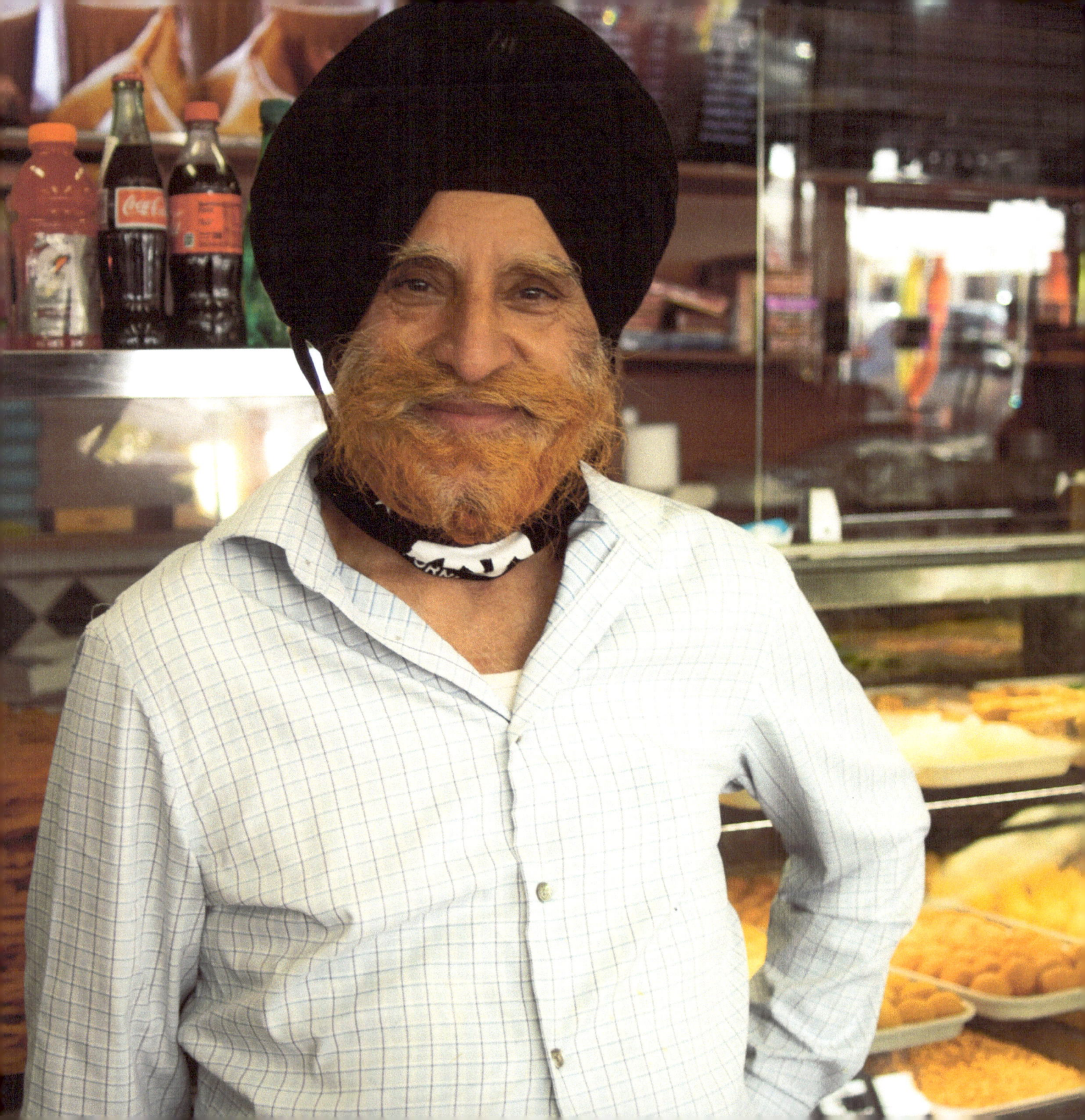

AMBALA SWEETS & SNACKS

What makes Ambala so authentic is Paramjit Singh, owner of Ambala Sweets and Snacks.

Uncle, a term native Hindu people use to refer to any older gentleman and one that many call Paramjit Singh, helps each customer as if they are his own family. He stacks up the sweets and snacks, he offers them a cup of chai, each customer accepts whatever Singh offers– none are left empty-handed or dissatisfied.

"Paramjit is like a landmark," said a local customer waiting in line.

His personal and uniquely fostered relationships with each customer are created the minute you step into the shop. His hospitality, the lingering of each customer's visit, his patience with each customer provide the special ambiance created and has been kept for the past 40 years.

Ambala is a northern city in the Haryana state of India, majorly known for cotton, grain, and sugar trade it was no surprise that Singh, having been from Ambala, was closely associated with the snacks and sweets largely accustomed by those who live in this district.

Singh opened his doors in 1979 back when there were only a handful of Indian markets in Artesia. Coming from Ambala himself he brought his childhood home to his new home in California. Uniquely sharing his experience of what makes Indian sweets and snacks so special to him and how he can extend it to us. We are provided with a glimmer, an inkling, of his home 7,675 miles away to just our backyard.

Singh had first started to trade his own baked goods for businessmen back in India. He told about customers who would demand traditional Indian dishes from him in return for groceries. He then began to sell his products on Pioneer Boulevard along with a couple of other markets– a decision that would lead to his success story of a business that has lasted 40 years. Singh sat down to explain how each snack and sweet has a specialty to them. He creates each food with a specialty that cannot be found anywhere else.

"With every customer who can come back [for more] we want to make happy," Singh said.

On their menu, there are a few snacks such as samosa, Aloo Tikki, paneer pakora, pani poori, and Dahi Sev Puri just to name a few. Trays full of sweets are displayed at the front counter where they serve jalebi, gulab jamun, pinni dal, cham cham, milk cakes, balushahi, and almond burfi among others.

"I like these sweets, personally, and that's why people come near and far away to buy from here," Singh said.

This array of snacks and sweets each contribute to the nostalgia customers may feel having roots in India. Singh makes an effort to serve each and every customer, he has even gone so far as to provide free meals to those who could not afford it. His generous nature and unique hospitality character each lend a perfect hand in being an owner of a food market.

Ambala is a unique experience, one that feels quite at home, even if one has never delved into the culture. It felt natural to gravitate towards Singh as he generously provided every customer with food and drink, never allowing one to sit in dissatisfaction.

"What I get from God, I spread to all my customers," Singh said.

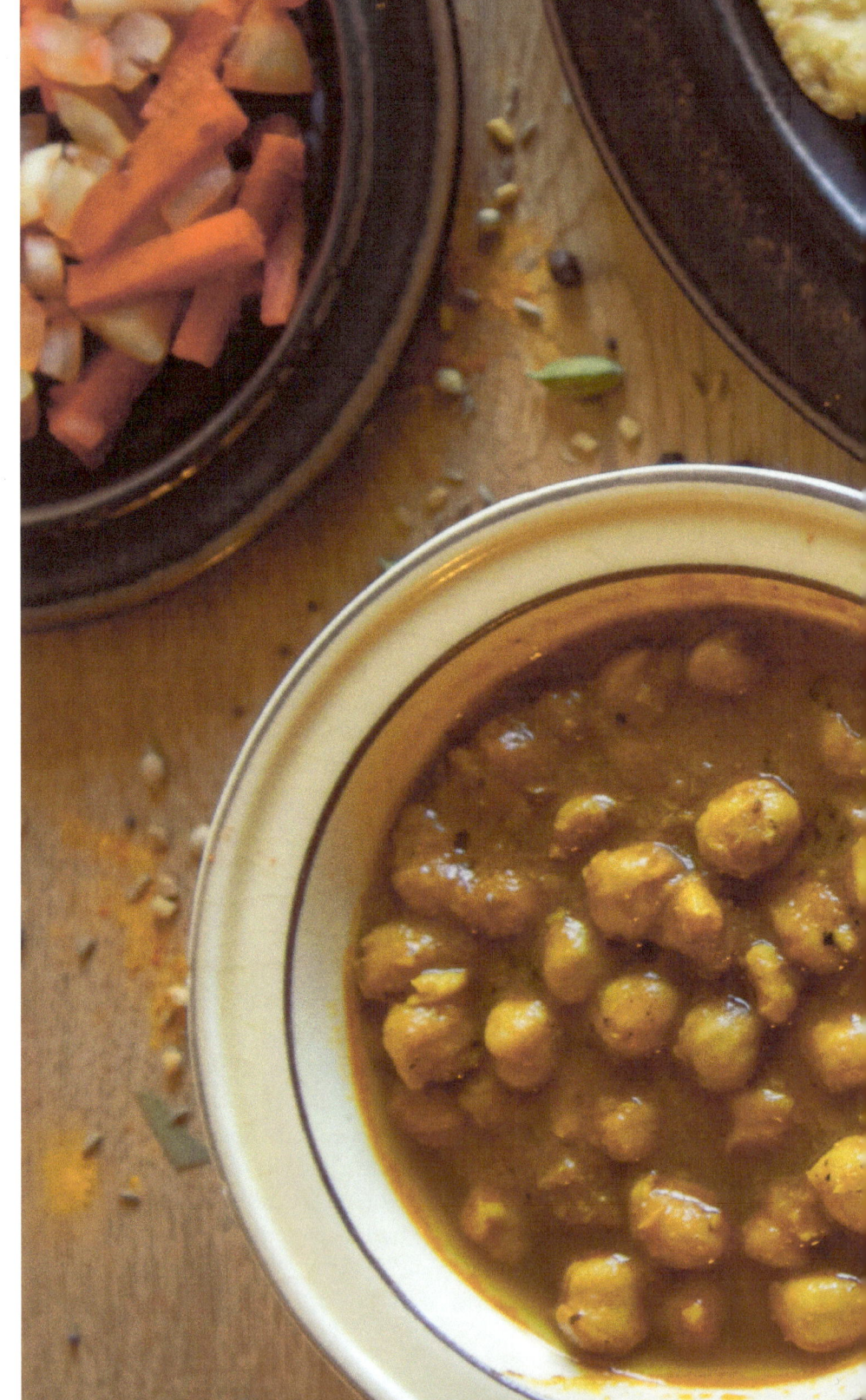

Photo by: Corrie Myhr
Chole bhature served with pickles is one of the many
dishes customers come to enjoy.

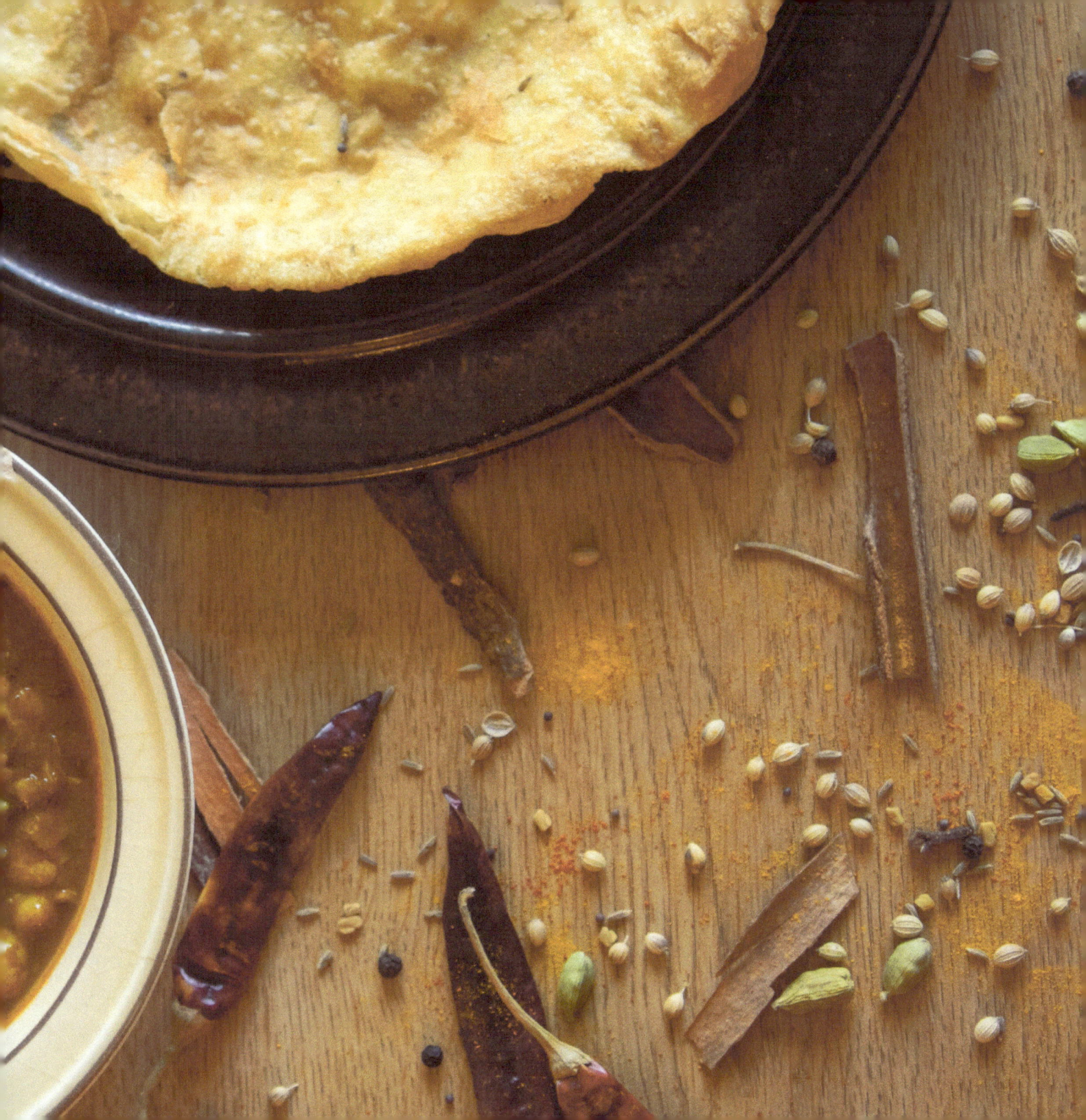

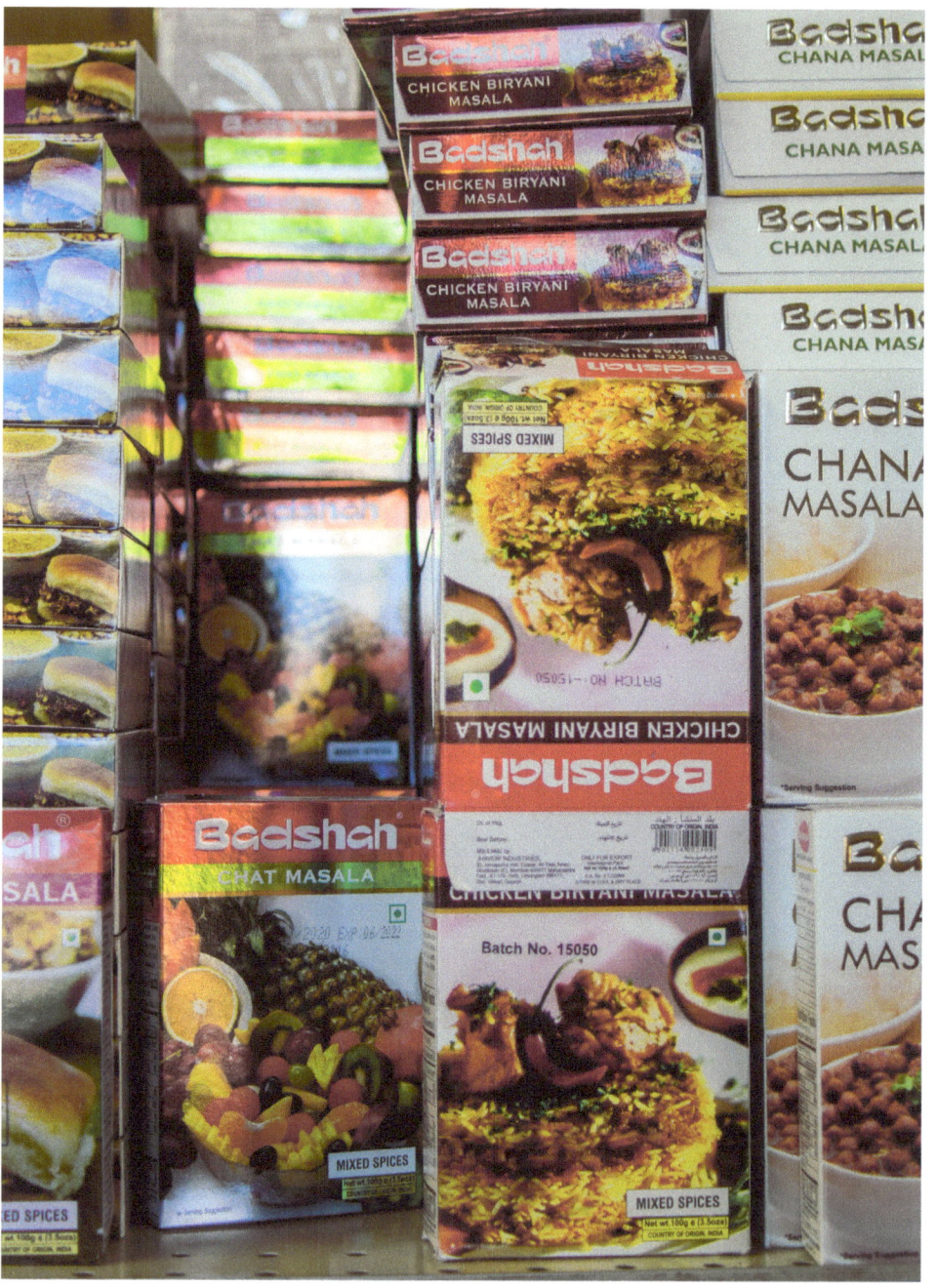

Photo by: Corrie Myhr
Several shelves contain pre-packaged spice boxes for staple Indian dishes to be made at home.

GROCERY STORES

Shelves littered with bags of rice, spices, lentils, and the various boxed easy-to-make dinners.

Scents of chili powders, different fragrant spices, vibrant oranges, yellows, and greens accenting the surroundings of the stores, shoppers barely looking at the labels as they shove bags of food into their carts or balance them in their arms– this is a typical Indian market.

Grocery stores including Rasa Indian Grocery, Saruti Cash and Carry, Indo Lanka Cash and Carry are among the few authentic Indian markets. Amidst the spices, boxed foods, and packaged lentils there are images of Hindu gods; a subtle protective imagery over those who enter the stores.

"It's like if you walk[ed] into [a] Middle Eastern store, you see a bunch of different things, right? So you'll see vegetables, the regular grocery canned food or regular food," Shara said.

One unique visit is Rasa Indian Grocery with its short shelves stocked with varying ingredients and packaged goods. This grocery store first opened its doors in 2005 and continues to serve customers authentic vegan groceries. This store sticks true to Hindu traditions and does not serve meat or fish.

Why should visitors shop here? Well, "we have special Indian groceries, items to be used by Hindus, only items you can buy from Indian groceries," said Sridher Aiyer, CEO of Aiyer's Inc, owner of Rasa Indian Grocery.

Shara notices the difference between American traditional experiences and that of Indian grocery shopping, most shoppers in "Little India" have a specific agenda. Grocery lists are a must to grab and go. Whether it's due to the pandemic that has hit our globe or is just in typical Indian fashion, most shoppers spent little time roaming the grocery store aisles like most Americans tend to do.

Along Pioneer sit half a dozen grocery stores, each possessing their own style of shelves stocked with relatively the same products but housing their own unique experiences. Walking into one of the grocery stores you are immediately hit with the scents of spices, the shelves carry bags on top of bags neatly stocked for easy access to grab and go.

"My favorite spot is the Pioneer Cash and Carry. That feels more like a small store, I like their groceries, they're fresh and

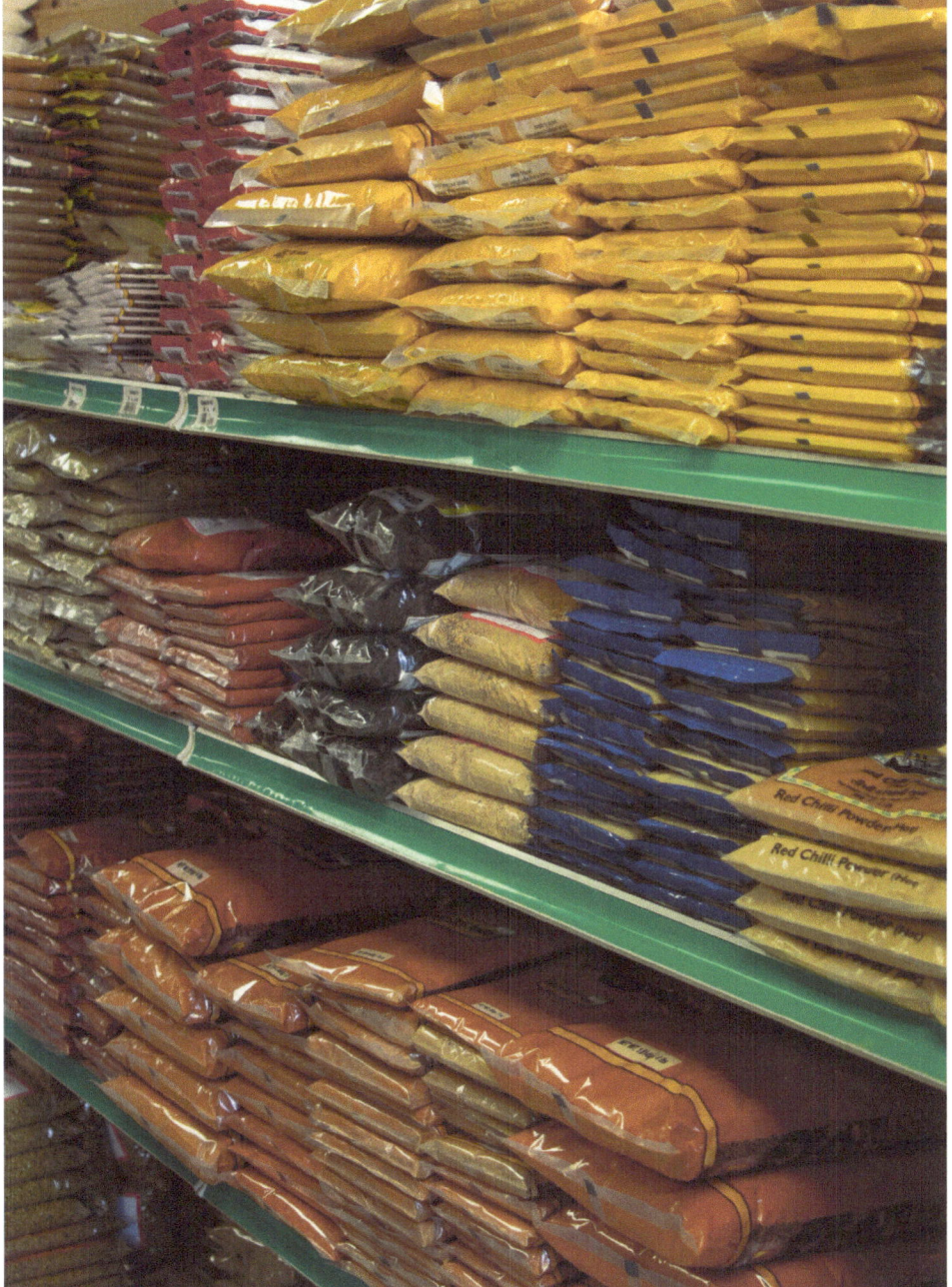

Photo by: Corrie Myhr
Bags of assorted and specialized spices are piled on shelves for customers to purchase.

the spices– there's a lot of variety," Shara explains.

From Shara's experience, it was as if those who came to shop for Indian groceries had traveled afar in order to find the exact product that is used in traditional Indian dishes. They shop here to authenticate their meals because it is worth it, because it is comforting, and because it is familiar.

Grocery stores across America cater to many different tastes to fit different cultures, but none are quite true to their authenticity. It is important to many immigrant families that their cultures are represented by means of authentic cuisine ingredients. There is nothing more true to the nostalgic feel of home than the food made with ingredients that are authentic.

Ambala Cash and Carry is one of the more popular grocery stores in Little India. Customers find that most ingredients and groceries are fresh and hold true to the Indian culture.

"Every now and then we like to go for the whole day. Go shop, eat, the whole strip, going down and back up, it's very fun," Shara said.

For Shara, Little India is an all-day event, each store calls to be peeked inside, to find any kind of spice or food. The markets and restaurants aid a hungry customer and you can't help but to step into the inviting environment and the welcoming atmosphere.

REFERENCES

1. The LA History Archive. (n.d.). Retrieved March 29, 2021, from http://lahistoryarchive.org/resources/Pioneer_Project/timeline.html
2. The LA History Archive. (n.d.). Retrieved March 29, 2021, from http://lahistoryarchive.org/resources/Pioneer_Project/timeline.html

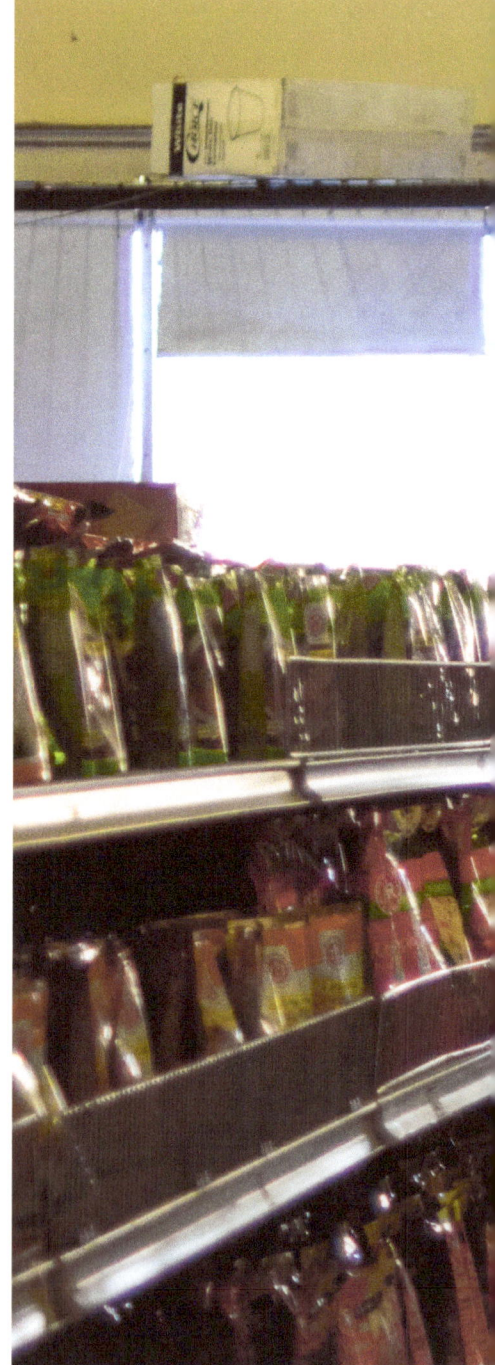

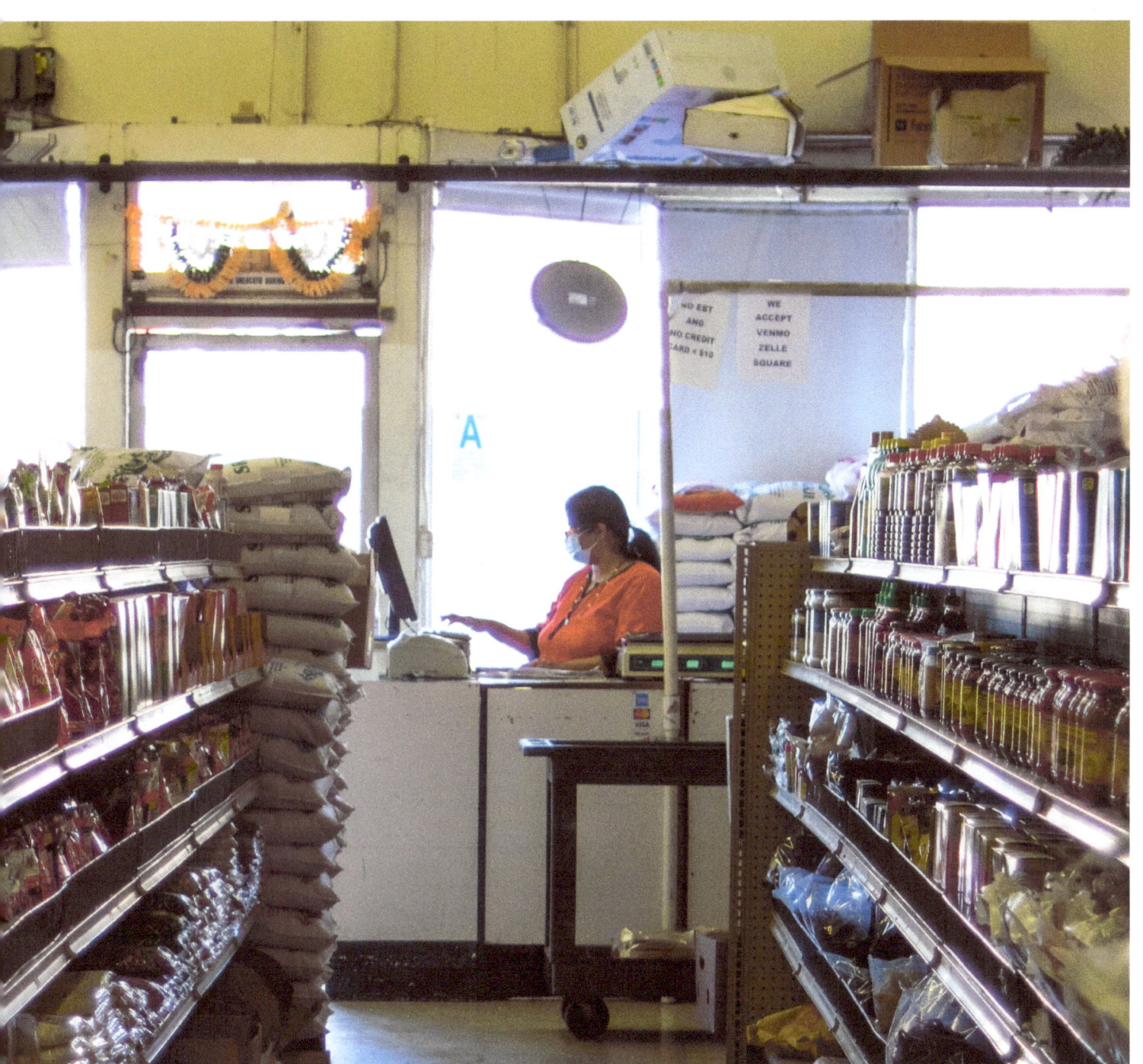

Photo by: Corrie Myher
A grocery store owner sits by the cash register preparing for the next customer.

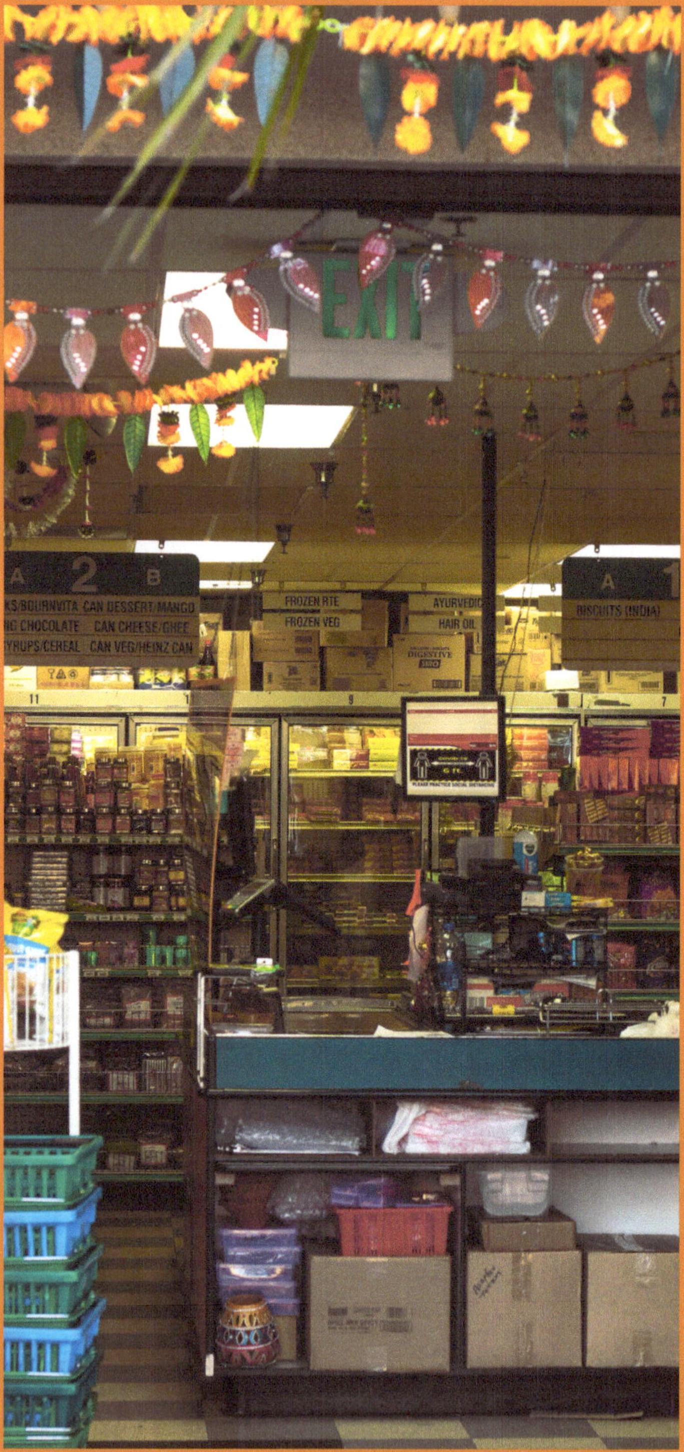
EXIT
A 2 B
CAN DESSERT MANGO
CAN CHEESE/GHEE
CAN VEG/HEINZ CAN
FROZEN RTE
FROZEN VEG
AYURVEDIC
HAIR OIL
A
BISCUITS (INDIA)
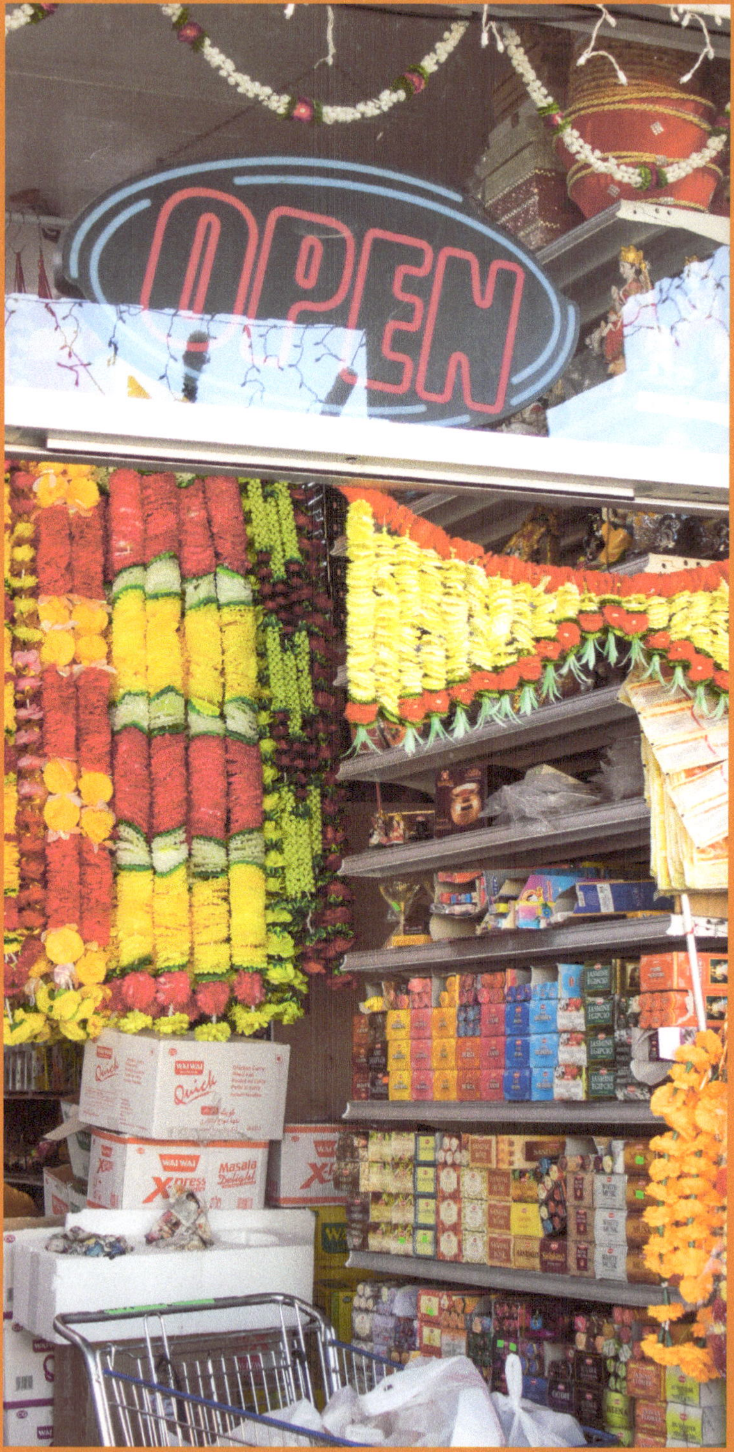
OPEN
WAI WAI
Quick
Masala Delight
Xpress

Photos and essay by: Corrie Myhr

Something about the storefront sends an open invitation to those visiting

Little India.

Maybe it's the display of vibrant colors or the frenzy of many searching to find the missing ingredient for dinner. Maybe it's the draw towards something that feels familiar.

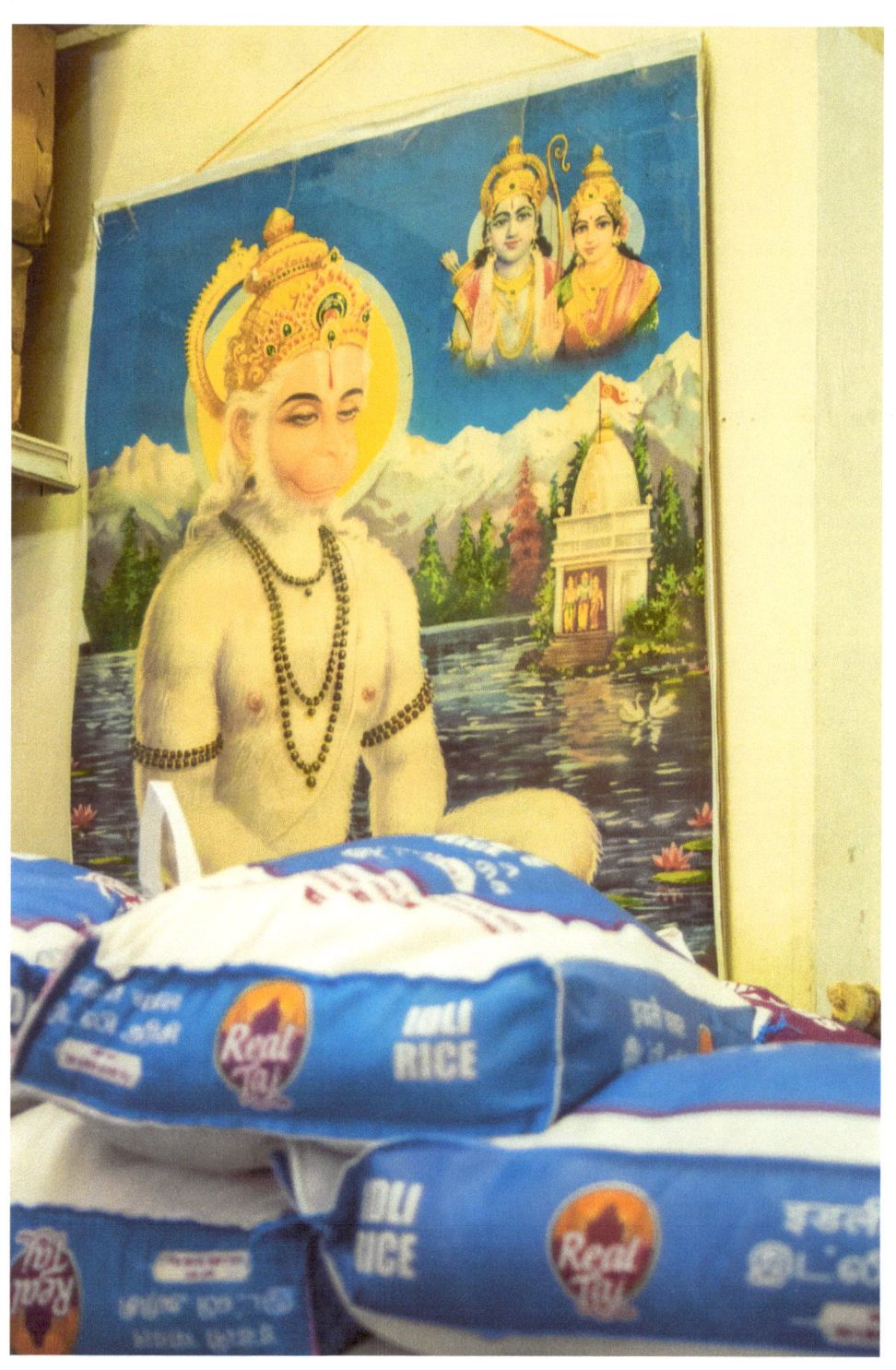

As shoppers step inside, their eyes land on Hindu gods that adorn the store's ambiance. Some are hung up on walls, while others sit on shelves.

They're a
reminder that
religion and
food share
many stories.

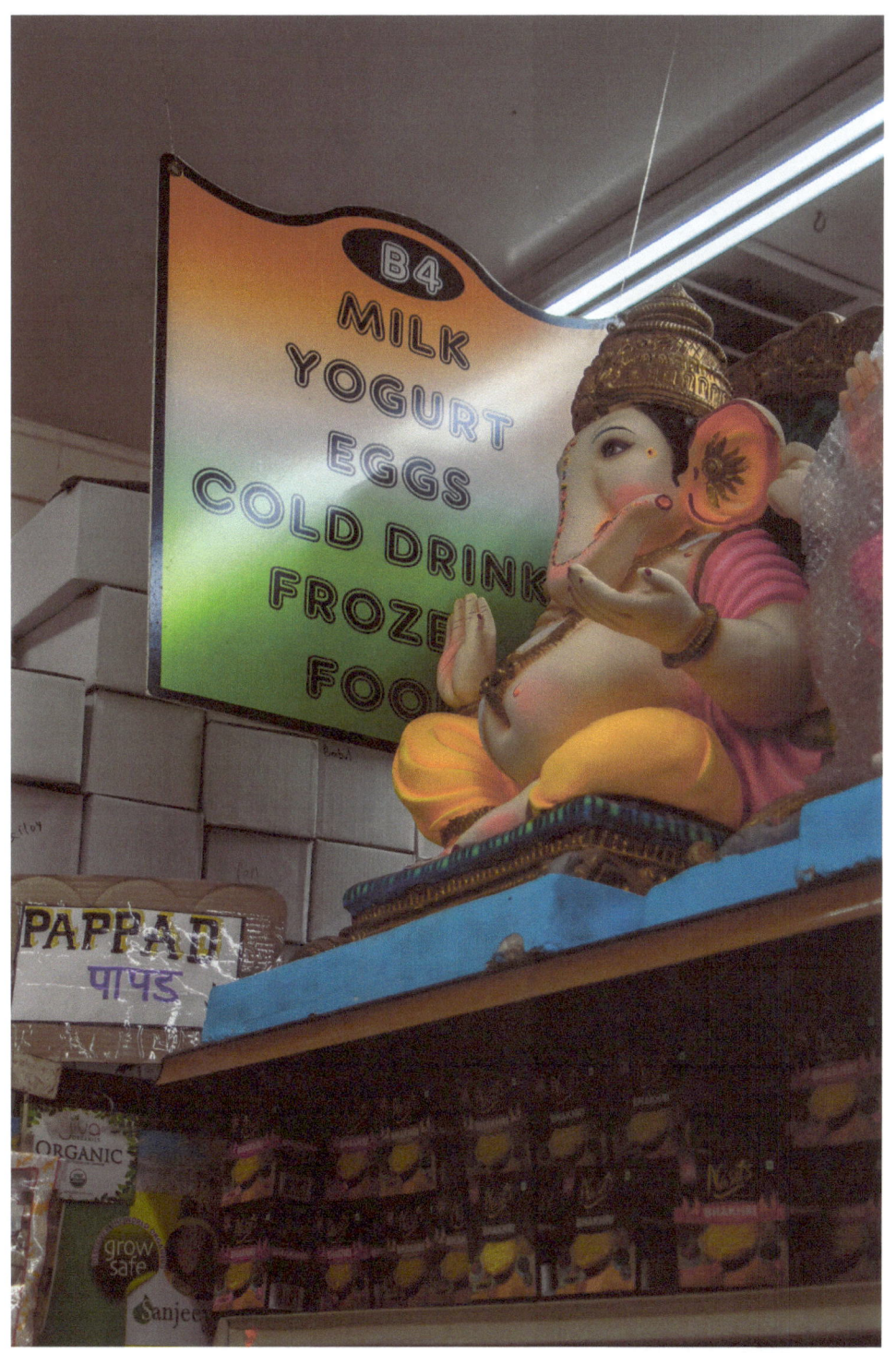

The aisles are full of signs hanging from the ceiling and labeled foods that not everyone in this country can read. Shoppers don't mind that the aisles are tight. They dance around each other as they continue on their mission.

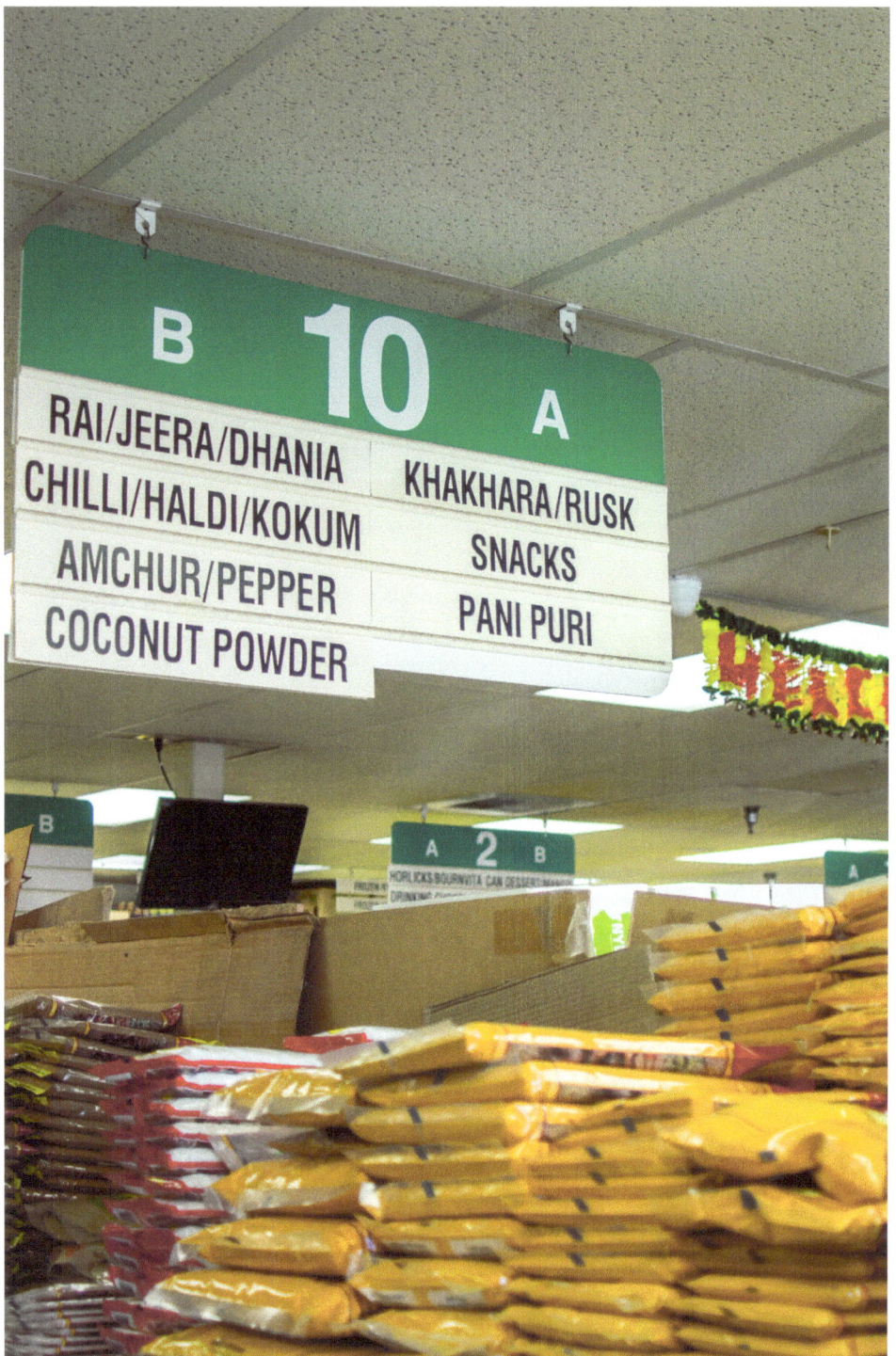

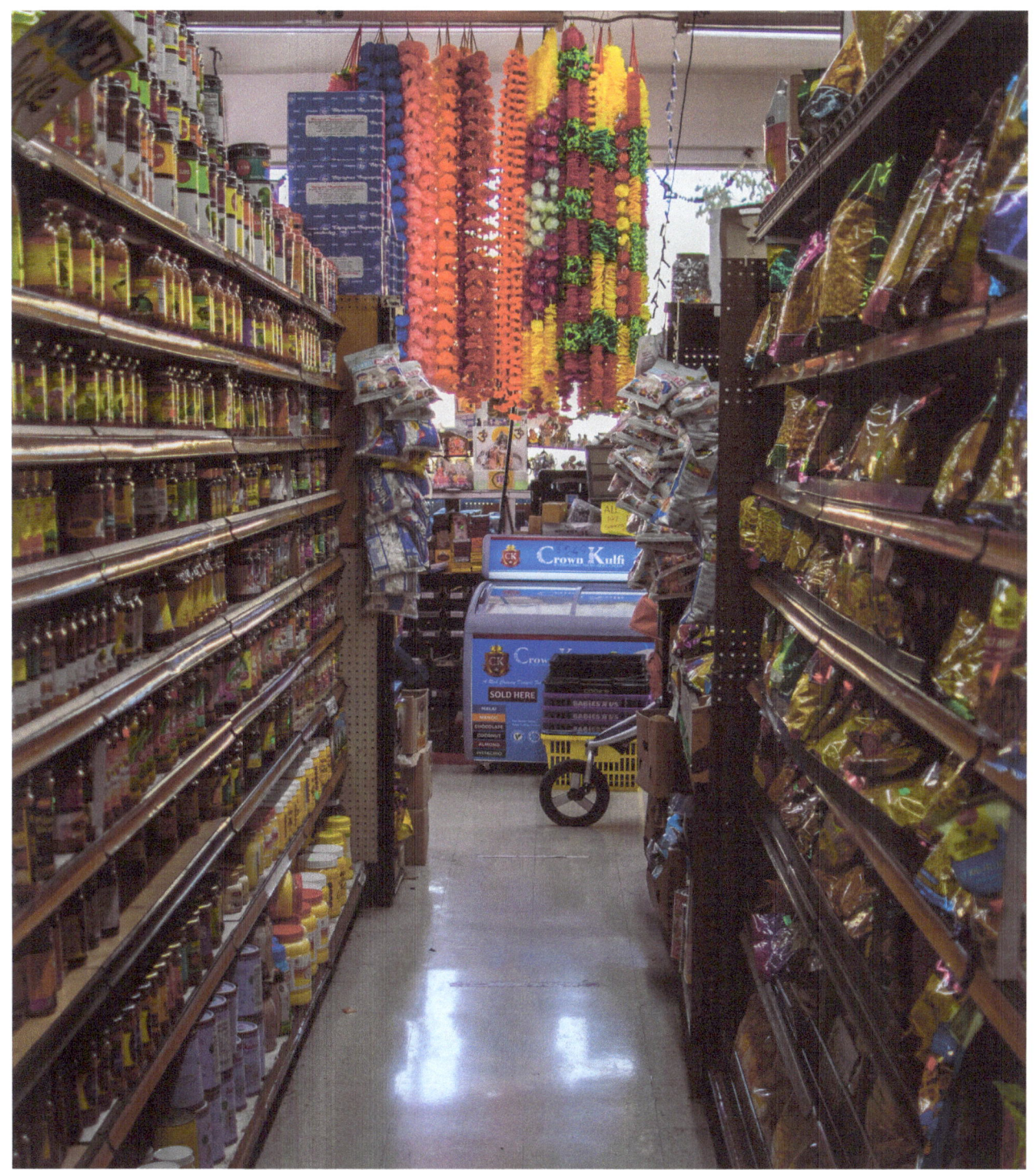

Four blocks away English is being spoken in the Denny's and Yum Yum Donuts that line the street. Here, a variety of South Asian languages fill the room. Each unique, they land on everyone's ears in musical harmony.

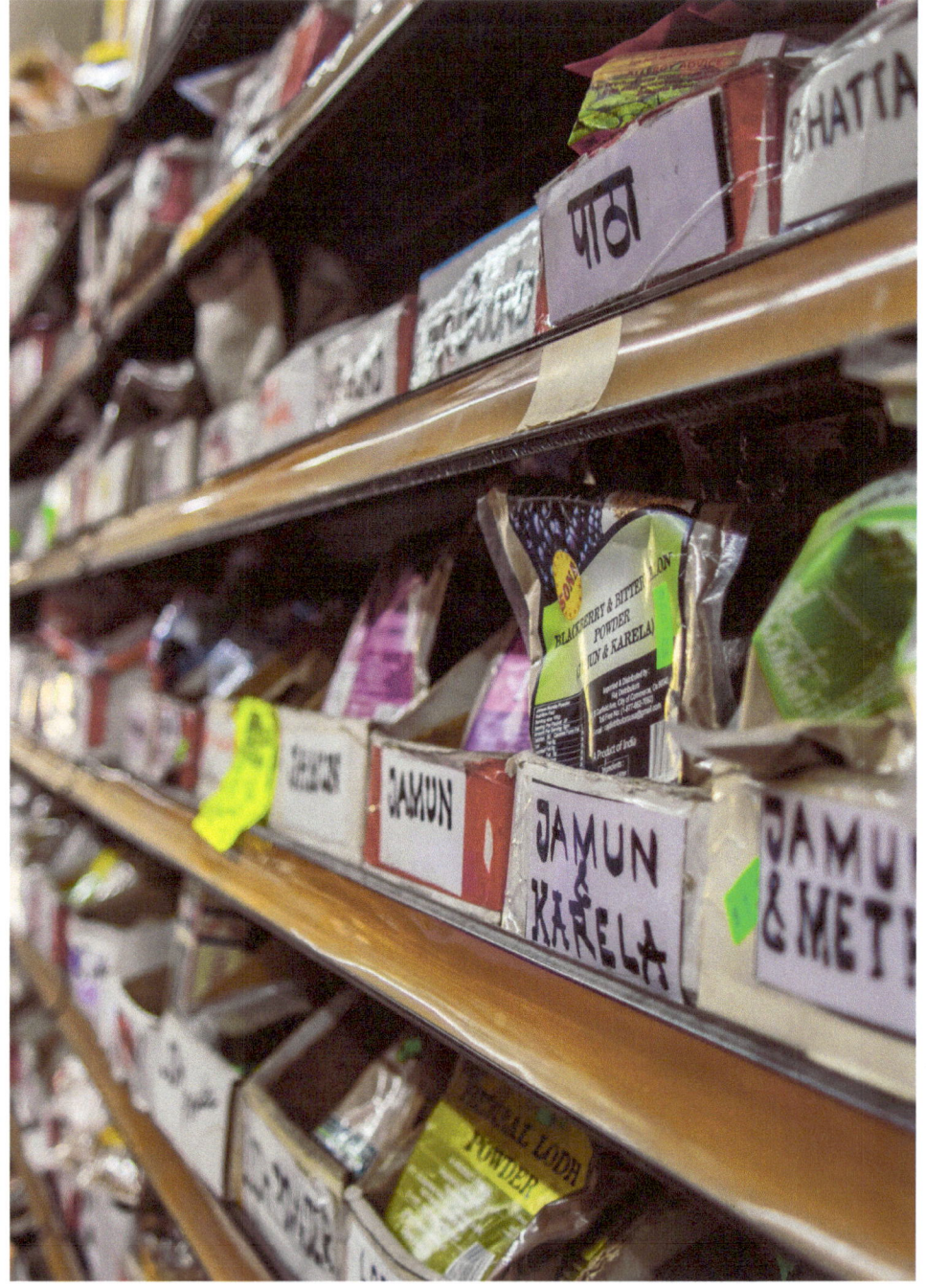

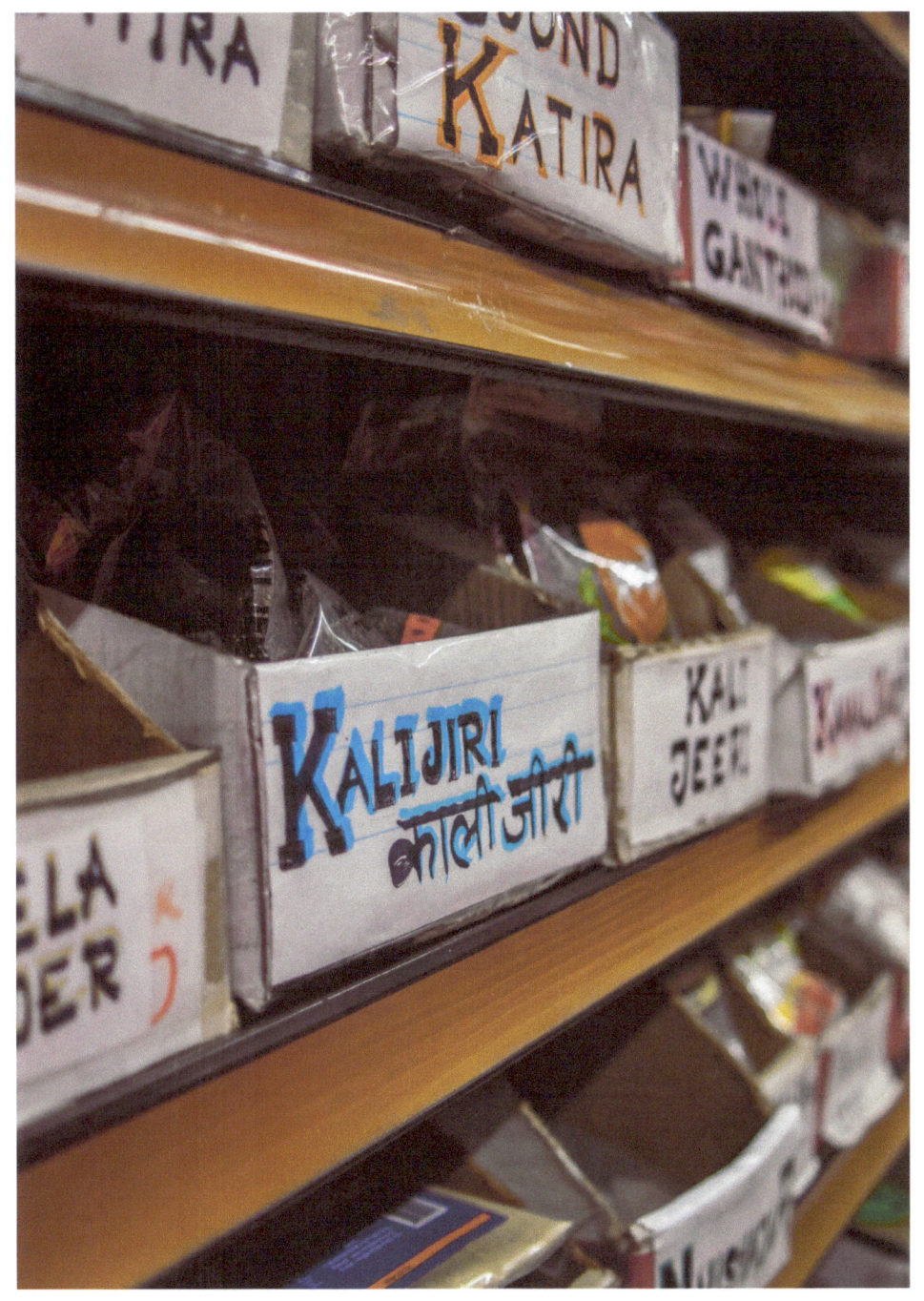

As shoppers fill their carts, they are hit with the complex aromas of cardamom, garam masala, saffron, cumin, and the list goes on. These are the smells of their childhood.

Some shoppers might even
close their eyes and picture standing
in their family's kitchen.
Perhaps memories of holidays,
family gatherings, and everyday life
are brought to mind.
When they open their eyes
to the narrow grocery aisles,
there is one thing they know.

THIS IS HOME

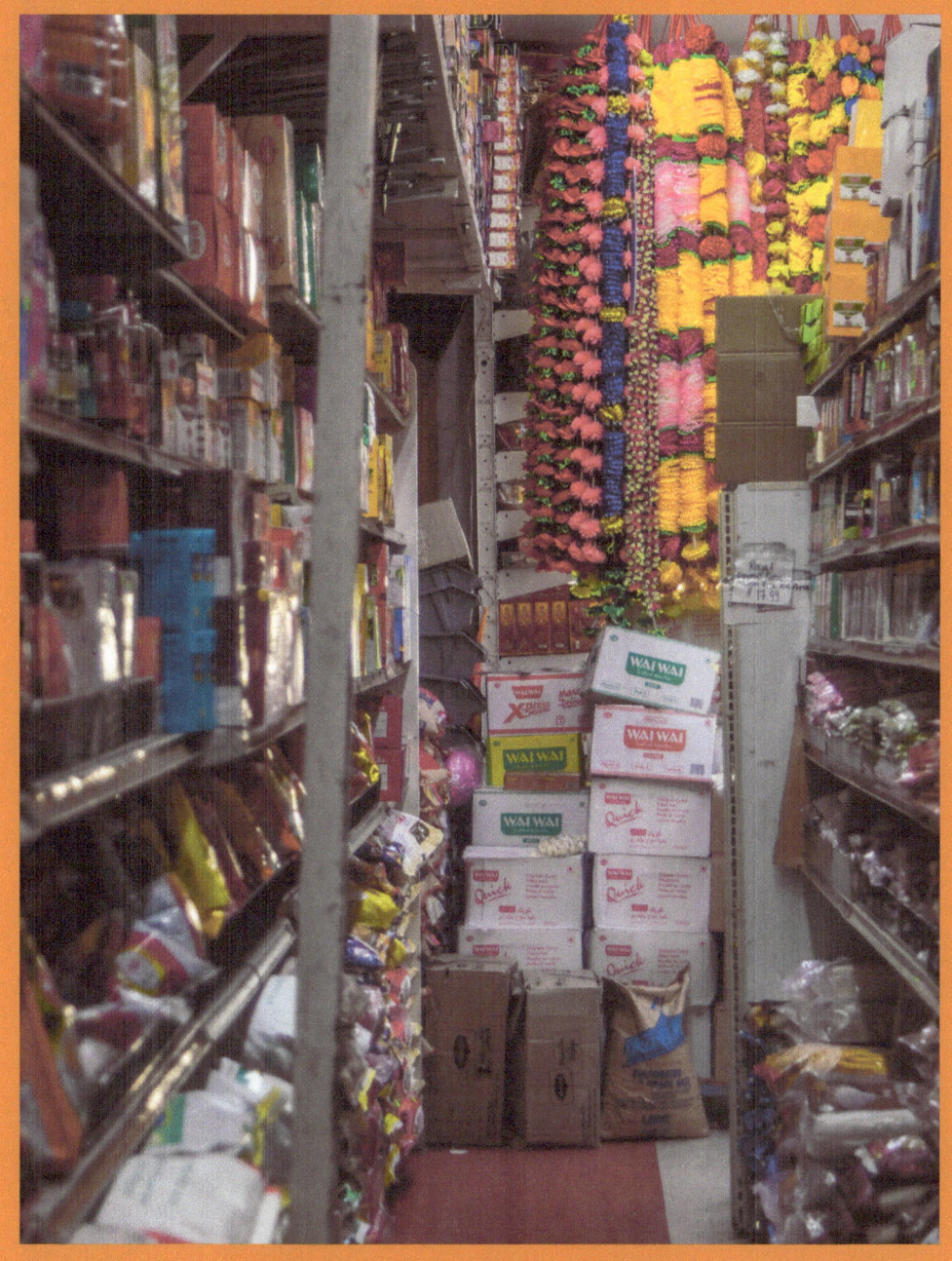

AWAY FROM HOME.

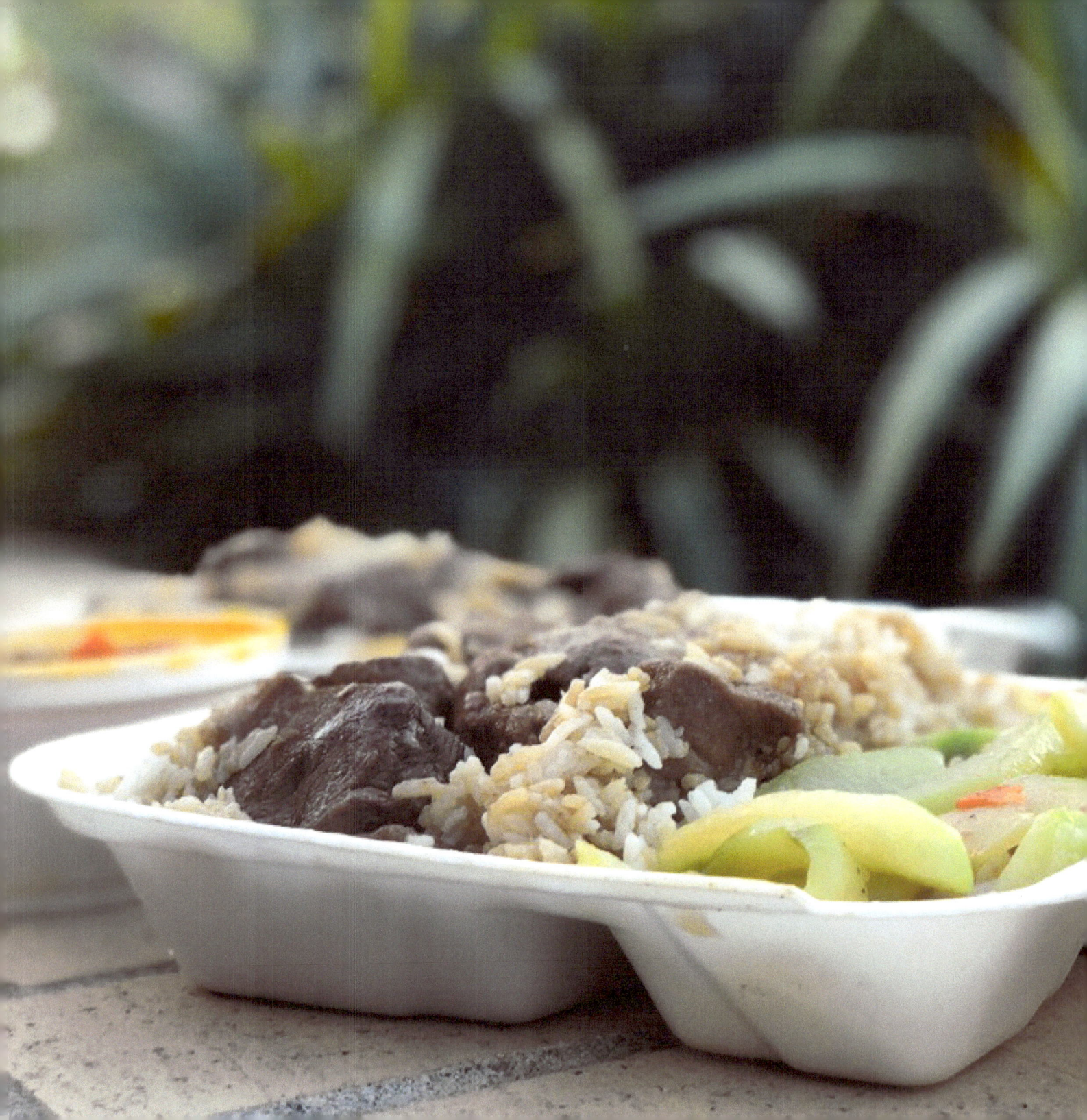

7. Filipino Food, Culture and Education

By: Briana Byus and Grace Morales

Off of the 15 freeway in Fontana, California, in the corner of an eclectic shopping center, the Manila Wok & Grill stands out next to the muted tones of the injury law firm and the dry cleaning business it sits between. Vibrant signage designed with the royal blue, crimson and white of the Philippine flag is displayed on the windows to show the meals that are offered to customers. As you step through the entrance, the buzz of machinery and the whir of a lively kitchen strikes you as you see co-owner Belen Ang Hao hurriedly stirring a pot of meat at the grill.

This chapter looks at Filipino culture in the US through the eyes of middle-aged Filipino American Manila Wok & Grill co-owner Gilbert Ang and Filipino American college students. A 2017 Pew Research Center article, Key facts about Asian Americans, a diverse and growing population, reports that

"Identity is the history that has gone into bone and blood and reshaped the flesh. Identity is not what we were but what we have become..."

-Nick Joaquín

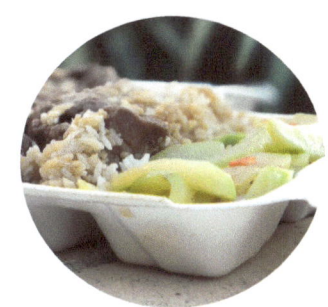

Filipino Americans account for 19% of the Asian American population, which is the third-highest demographic of Asian Americans in the US. Yet, according to the book Filipino Americans: Transformation and Identity by Maria Root, there is still a haze over other groups' understanding of Filipino culture. Although family life and holidays will be touched on, this chapter will primarily focus on the cultural perspective of food, education and career success.

GILBERT ANG'S BACKGROUND

Manila, the capital city of the Philippines, is known for its vivacious museums, theaters, and restaurants. In high demand by both locals and tourists to the area is also the distinctly sour tang found in dishes like adobo and sinigang. 25 years ago, Ang, who grew up in the Philippines, brought the vibrance of Manila with him to the United States and it eventually became the namesake of his and his sister's restaurant, Manila Wok & Grill. As a young boy, Ang and his siblings watched excitedly as their mother made sweet adobo in the kitchen of their home in the Philippines. "I would say most of my dishes are passed down from my mom. My mom's a great cook," Ang said. Filipino food is often known for its use of white vinegar but by removing the vinegar from her adobo recipe, Ang's mother highlighted the sweetness of the meat. Ang's family recipes are not the only things that have equipped him to own a restaurant. Ang attended the Philippine School of Business Administration before moving to the U.S. to enter into what he calls "the land of better opportunities." Ang also spent between 15 and 20 years working in sales before his sister, Belen Ang Hao, proposed a sharp career pivot: opening a restaurant together. "We had a passion for cooking so why not try it out?" Ang said. The siblings received encouragement and support from their family in the process of opening their business and solidified their out-of-the-blue decision to open a restaurant with their grand opening on July 29, 2010.

DISTINCT FILIPINO DISHES

Upon entering the Manila Wok & Grill and approaching the glass case that displays meats and vegetables, you may either feel completely at home or suddenly lost as to what to order. Ang said that roughly 75%-80% of his customers have connections to Filipino culture and are familiar with the foods in front of them but for the other 20%, some explanation may be required.

Adobo and steamed rice are paired to bring a burst of sour flavor and make one of the best-known Filipino dishes. "It's a very popular dish. For me, anytime I see it anywhere I'm like 'oh must be Filipino.'" Ang said. Adobo is a vinegar-based sauce that goes over meat and can also be made with soy sauce, according to 'Adobo: The History of A National Favorite' on Pepper.ph, a Filipino food blog based in Makati, Philippines. The different combinations of sauces and seasonings create a savory experience that is perfectly complemented by white rice.

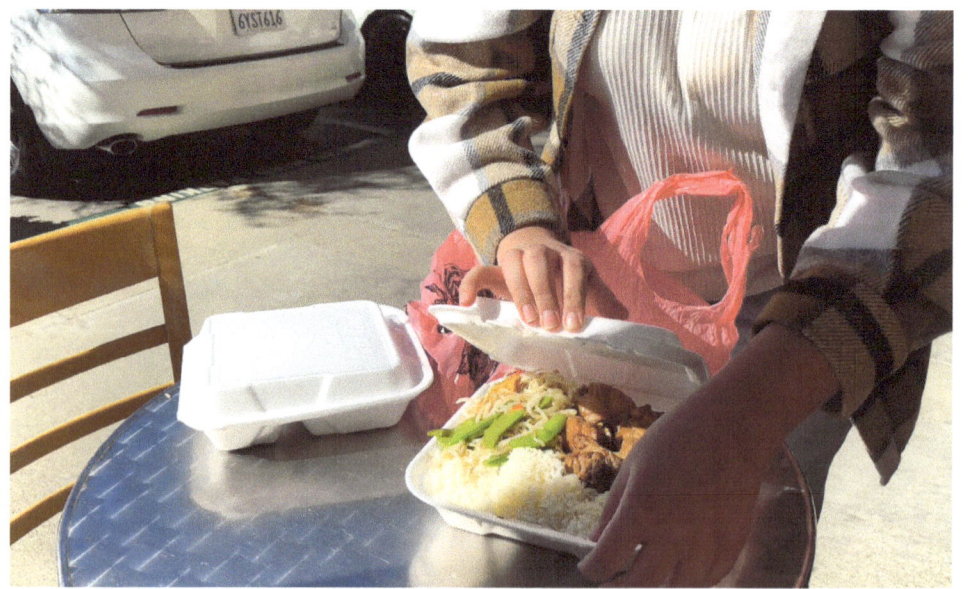

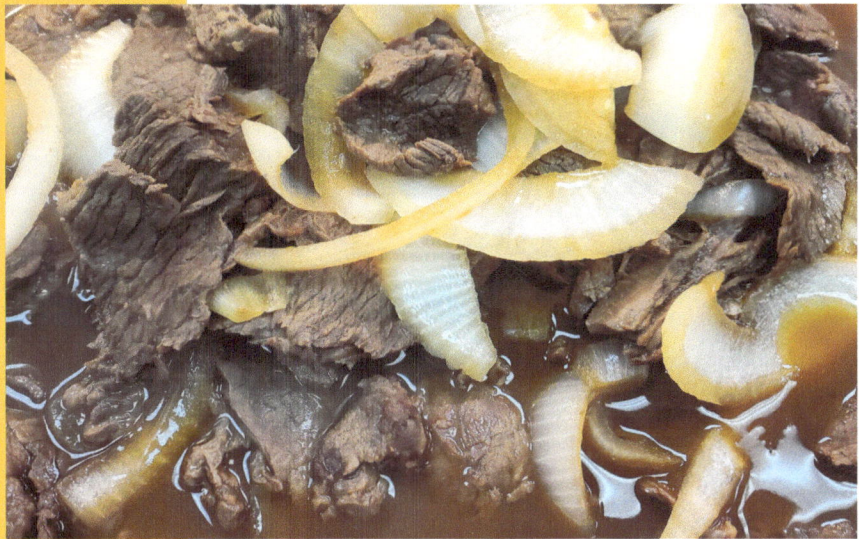

Bistek- Photo By: Gilbert Ang

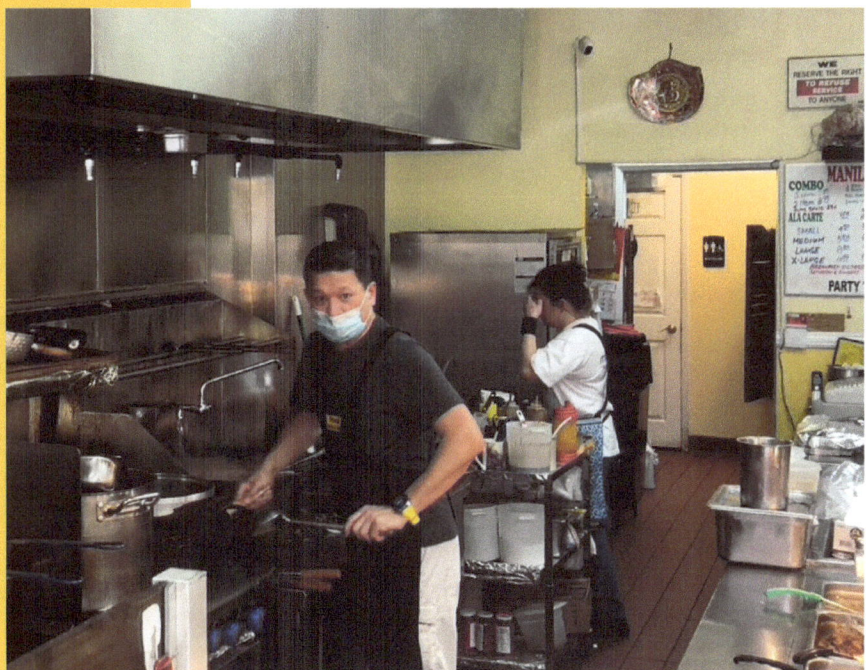

Gilbert Ang (left) and Belen Ang Hao (right) cooking in Manila Wok & Grill

Photo By: Briana Byus

Another notable dish in the Philippines is pancit. This entrée is believed to have been introduced centuries ago by a Chinese merchant and was adopted into the Filipino culture, according to a Pepper.ph article. It is found at a variety of gatherings but is most commonly seen at birthday parties because the long noodles signify a long and prosperous life. It can be made in various forms depending on the region.

Thinly sliced sirloin and onions make up another favorite Filipino dish named bistek (beefsteak). This dish is marinated and tenderized in soy sauce and lemon juice, which gives it a zesty flavor. Unlike pancit, which is mainly seen at gatherings like birthday parties, bistek is a dish that can be served at any time. Filipino food offers the experience of captivating sour tastes and rich aromas. Each region of the Philippines has its own way of preparing dishes but the range in diverse flavors makes Filipino cuisine uniquely satisfying. "When I cook food, it's the way I want to taste my food. It's not according to the way it has to taste...Sometimes you don't like the original taste, so you change it a little bit," Ang said.

MADE WITH LOVE

Whether you are his mother on her birthday or you are a complete stranger, Ang assures without hesitation that he and his sister will prepare your food with love and passion. Ruthie Montesines, a student who grew up in Manila, said "we are one of the friendliest people in the world. We treat each other like a family."

Ang believes that love is the key, distinguishing ingredient that makes his food mouthwatering. "You've got to put your heart into it. Cooking is a passion...For me, that's the key. It's not all about following ingredients. Even if you follow them to the tee, it doesn't come out right," Ang said while considering the idea of making food without love.

As a father and a businessman, he recalls the warmth associated with watching his mother make sweet adobo in his childhood. He and his sister now esteem their mother's old recipes by using them to cook with familial love in the kitchen of the Manila Wok & Grill.

Because of their personal connection to the dishes, they immediately recommend them to new customers.

EDUCATIONAL EXPECTATIONS

Statistics published by the Pew Research Center in 'Social & Demographic Trends: Asian Americans' show Asian Americans to be better educated and paid more than other American groups. These statistics certainly do not apply to everyone that they reference and do not focus on the Filipino American demographic specifically, however. "Asians

"Each region of the Philippines has its own way of preparing dishes but the range in diverse flavors makes Filipino cuisine uniquely satisfying."

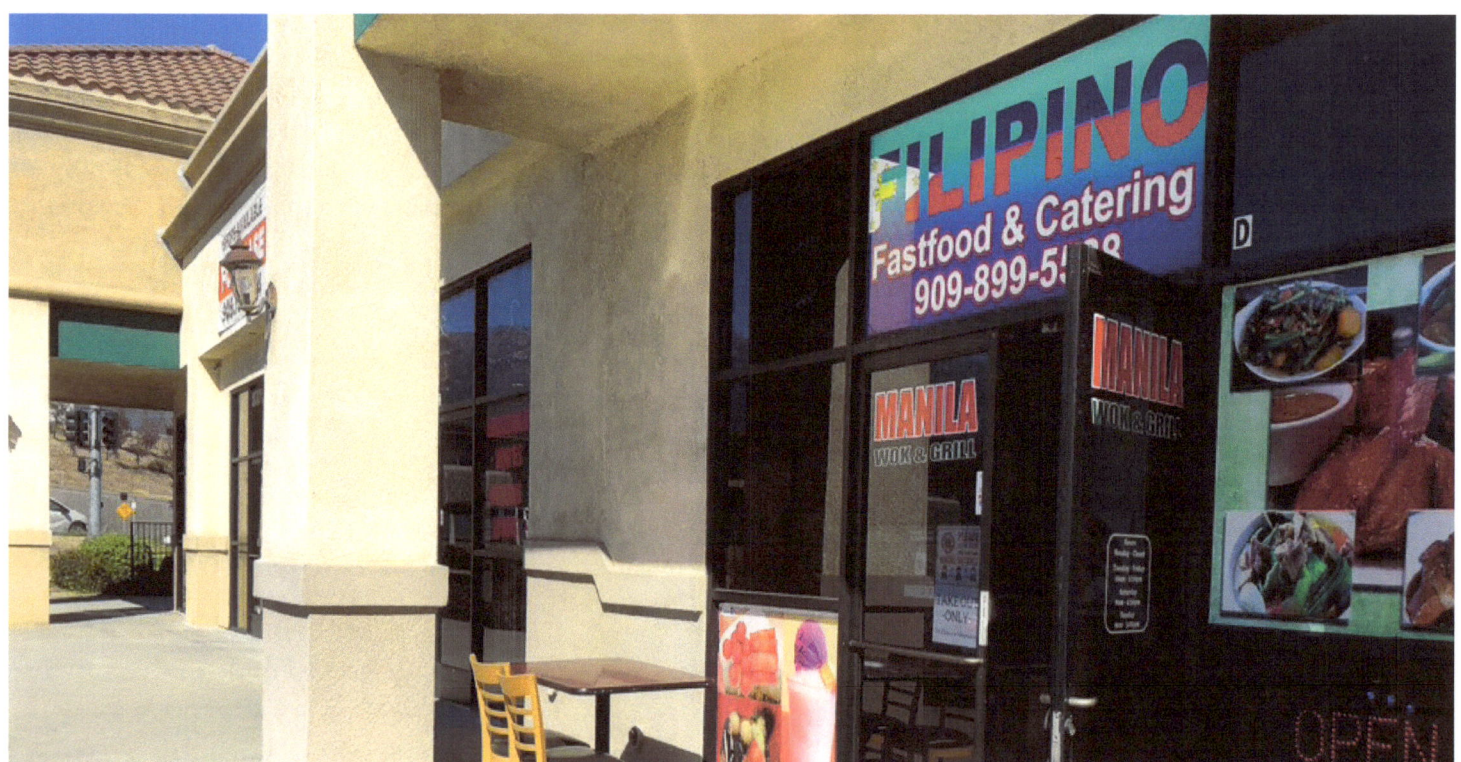

Manila Wok & Grill storefront. Photo By: Briana Byus

aren't a monolith...there are so many different cultures, and we come from so many different places," said Filipina Biola University Freshman Rachel Ramirez.

To understand the experience of Filipino Americans, it is important to know the historic relationship between the two countries. The United States colonized the Philippines from 1898 to 1946 until the country became independent. American influence on the islands did not cease at that time, though. In the book "The 'Other' Students: Filipino Americans, Education, and Power" by Dina C. Maramba and Rick Bonus, the control that the U.S. had on the Philippine education system, establishing American education policies in the country similar to those enforced upon Native Americans is discussed.

The American colonizers believed that English was the best language to teach the Western values that they wanted the Filipino children to learn. In the years since the Philippines became independent, the prevalence of American influence has continued. The 2000 Census of Population and Housing yielded that the Philippines has the fifth-highest English-speaking population. That is above the United Kingdom. Sophomore Biola student Ruthie Montesines, who grew up in the Philippines, said that through her private school experience, she "would definitely think that the PH education system is aligned to the U..S system." Though the education systems are similar, that does not mean that the educational values are the same.

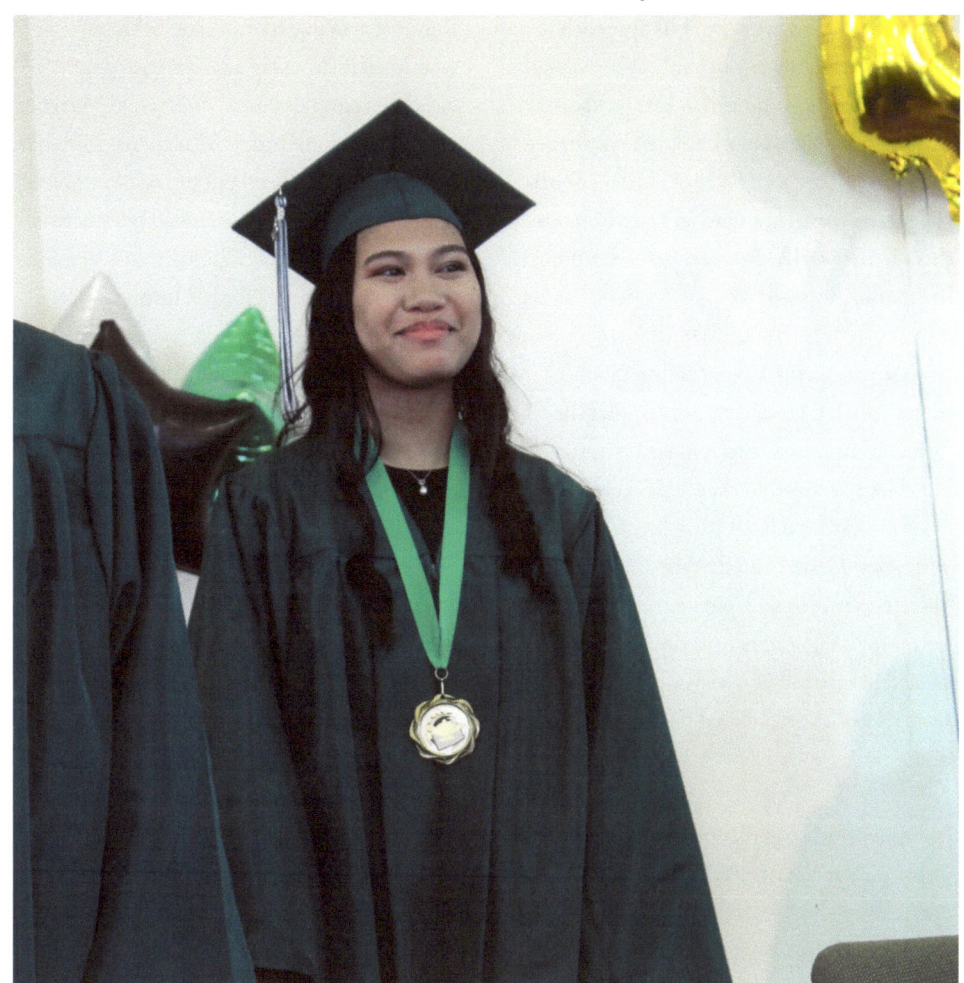

Rachel Ramirez graduating from high school in Hawaii. Photo courtesy of Rachel Ramirez

ResearchGate.net published "Filipinos in the U.S.: Historical, Social, and Educational Experiences" in 2016, showing that Filipino Americans statistically have higher educational achievements than other United States demographics. This, according to the article, is often connected to a desire to uplift one's family through career success. Montesines spoke to her own experience of getting a college degree as "mainly because it will help

me be successful in the future and at the same time help my own family that supported me all throughout my studies."

Ang explained that school was a priority for him but that he did not feel pressured to pursue a career in his field of study. After attending the Philippine School of Business Administration, he got a job in sales and used the organizational skills that he learned in college to inform his work. His approach to higher education was primarily focused on the value of a degree rather than his specific major, as he said that most work-related knowledge is learned on the job. "By the time you finish college, you don't know what's going on out there in the world...Pretty much everything is hands-on," Ang said.

In contrast, Victor Valley College Sophomore Cariah Claridad recounted that she felt tremendous pressure to remain at the top of her class and was told that to do so was "the most important part of [her] life." Claridad was raised in the United States and said that her experience as a Filipina American woman under the weight of educational pressures caused her to dive into self-improvement and simultaneously prohibited her from being her best.

Just as with any population demographic, individuals will have unique experiences and relationships with the world around them. People like journalism student Rachel Ramirez report a feeling of freedom from strict career expectations or limitations from their families while others work within the boundaries that they are provided. "My mom and her siblings are mostly all nurses, and my dad is an engineer, so majoring in journalism is a bit out of the norm for our family," Ramirez said. It is popular in the United States to follow your dreams but that is not necessarily the path to the happiest life.

Ramirez articulated moments when she wondered if choosing a career path would have been simpler if her parents had given her a clear direction. Ruthie Montesines said that her parents influenced but did not force her to pursue a career path that would be beneficial for herself and her family. She wants to mimic this type of guidance for her future children. Each person's perspective on education impacts not only themselves but also the generation that follows right behind them, as descendants often match their predecessors' footprints.

The National Center for Education Statistics released a study in 2018 called "First-Generation Students: College Access, Persistence, and Postbachelor's Outcome" revealing that the number of students enrolling in college correlates to their parents' level of education. When presented with the question, "how would you talk to your own children about education and career success," Ang responded that he would give them the same opportunity that he was presented by his parents: "I tell my kids, finish college and then you do whatever you want."

The deep love that Filipino people have toward one another extends into their desires for their children to find happiness and security through their career endeavors. The relational Filipino culture prioritizes "hard work and family a lot. When one member is going through something, we all try our best

to help," Ramirez said in appreciation of her heritage.

The gentle, masked smiles of Gilbert Ang and Belen Ang Hao when you walk into the Manila Wok & Grill, whether for the first or the hundredth time, mirror the hospitable warmth of the culture that their food pays homage to. As children, they wondered at their mother in the kitchen, mouths watering and hearts brimming with inspiration. Now when they celebrate holidays with their mother, dishes in-hand, they present her old recipes back to her.

"you've got to put your heart into it. Cooking is a passion...For me, that's the key. It's not all about following ingredients. Even if you follow them to the tee, it doesn't come out right."

- Gilbert Ang

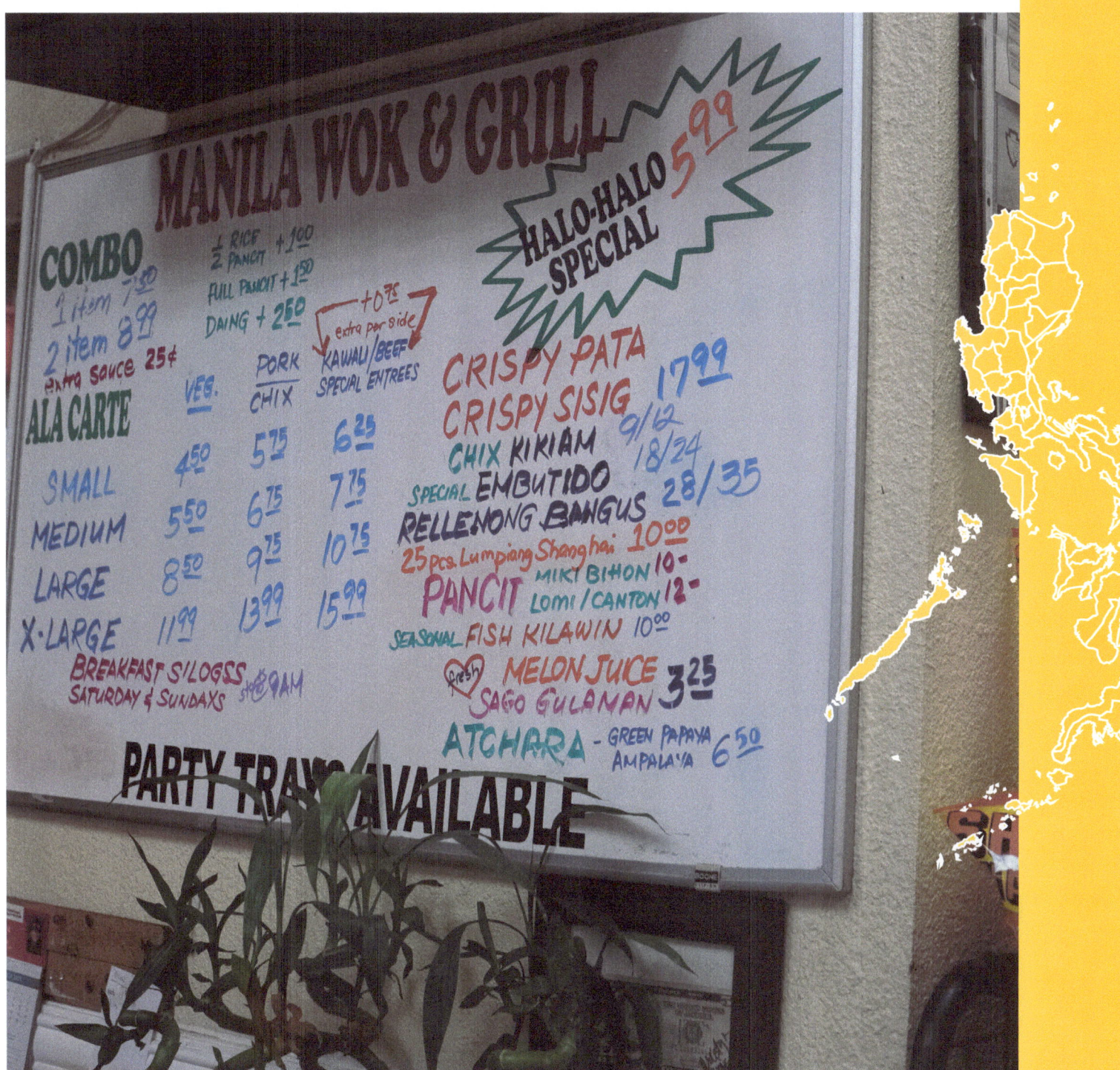

MANILA WOK & GRILL

HALO-HALO SPECIAL 5⁹⁹

COMBO
1 item 7⁵⁰
2 item 8⁹⁹
extra sauce 25¢

½ RICE +1⁰⁰
½ PANCIT +1⁰⁰
FULL PANCIT +1⁵⁰
DAING +2⁵⁰

+0⁷⁵ extra per side

ALA CARTE

	VEG.	PORK / CHIX	KAWALI/BEEF SPECIAL ENTREES
	4⁵⁰	5⁷⁵	6²⁵
SMALL			
MEDIUM	5⁵⁰	6⁷⁵	7⁷⁵
LARGE	8⁵⁰	9⁷⁵	10⁷⁵
X-LARGE	11⁹⁹	13⁹⁹	15⁹⁹

BREAKFAST SILOGSS
SATURDAY & SUNDAYS 5 to 9 AM

Special Entrees
CRISPY PATA
CRISPY SISIG 17⁹⁹
CHIX KIKIAM 9/12
SPECIAL EMBUTIDO 18/24
RELLENONG BANGUS 28/35
25 pcs. Lumpiang Shanghai 10⁰⁰

PANCIT
MIKI BIHON 10-
LOMI/CANTON 12-

SEASONAL FISH KILAWIN 10⁰⁰

fresh MELON JUICE
SAGO GULAMAN 3²⁵

ATCHARA - GREEN PAPAYA
AMPALAYA 6⁵⁰

PARTY TRAYS AVAILABLE

Manila Wok & Grill- Photo by: Maria Wayne

MENU

DUMPLINGS (6) pieces per order

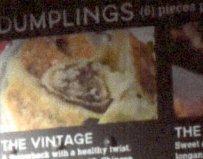
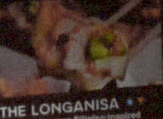
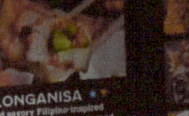

WAFFLE FRIES

THE VINTAGE
A turkey twist healthy ground turkey with Chinese chives and green onions dumpling

THE LONGANISA ★ ▼
Sweet and savory Filipino-inspired longanisa sausage dumplings, topped with grilled pork belly and jalapeño
9 5

PORK BELLY WAFFLE FRIES

WAFFLE FRIES

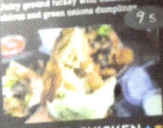
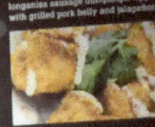
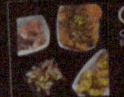

THE FRIED CHICKEN ★ ▼
Award-winning fried chicken and pepperjack cheese dumplings crusted with corn flakes and served with cilantro aioli, lime, and jalapeño
9 5

THE MAC
Deep-fried and crusted with Japanese panko. These Mac N Cheese dumplings are oozing with goodness and served with a side of cilantro aioli
9 5

COMB
CHOOSE (2) TW
CAN CHOOSE SAM

Dumplings (4)
Waffle fries (p
Rice dish (part

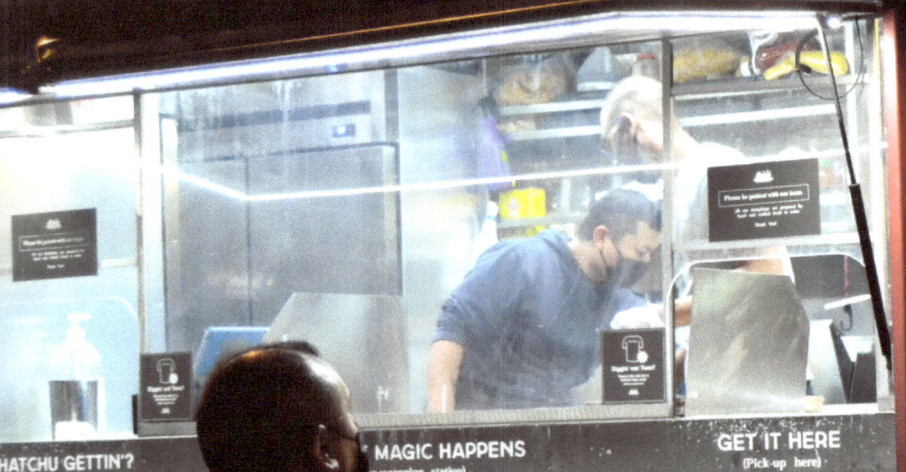

Please be patient with our team.

HATCHU GETTIN'?
(Order here)

MAGIC HAPPENS
g-wrapping station)

GET IT HERE
(Pick-up here)

E AS... ...SION DUMPLIN

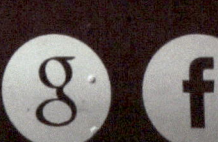

food network

BIG FOOD TRUCK TIP

WINNER
1st

ANDREW ZIMMERN'S FAVORITES
LONGANISA DUMPLINGS W/ PORK AND JALAPEÑO
CORN FLAKE FRIED CHICKEN DUMPLINGS
★ ★ ★ ★ ★

g f

WWW.MADDUMPLINGS
MADDUMPLINGS@GMAIL.COM
@MADDUMPLINGS

8. From Street Vendors to Food Trucks: Fusion and Food Culture

By: Andrea Basista and Caleb Jonker

Take centuries of cultural traditions, combine with a kitchen on four wheels, add some subjective innovation, put it on the streets and you've got the recipe for Asian-fusion food trucks. Food trucks have exploded in popularity in the United States over the last decade. Lorri Mealey[1], a small business blogger, suggests that after the 2008 recession, food trucks were on the rise as a low-cost alternative to traditional restaurants and created a pathway for culinary creativity. Because of people losing their jobs left and right, the situation created a new need, and there was swift adaptation. While many were figuratively pushed into the business of street food, it came with shocking benefits of, "wow, I can actually do this." Over ten years after the food truck revolution mobile kitchens have solidified themselves as innovative kitchens.

"I think of [street food] as the antidote to fast food; it's the clear alternative to the king, the clown and the colonel."

— Anthony Bourdain

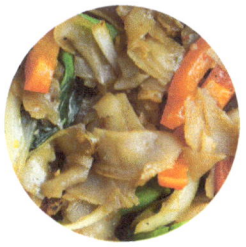

(Left)Photo By Andrea Basista

Mad Dumplings truck

Rachel Perkins[2], a blogger for Innovation in Food Transport, explains how the cost of starting a food truck is roughly $100,000-$175,000. But buying and starting up a restaurant? That is going to cost you over $500,000, a stark difference in financial ability.

Montre Liwirun[3], the head chef and owner at 8e8 Thai food truck added that renting a food truck, which costs around $2500 a month, saves the chef even more money. Yes, the numbers are a positive reason to invest in a food truck, but they are so much more than just a cheap escape.

STIGMA AND SAFETY

Some people may have hesitations about eating food from a truck. Without knowing better it is easy to associate uncleanliness with food trucks, but Liwirun explained that when it comes to health and safety food trucks are held to the same standards as any other restaurant.

In fact, Liwirun says that because of the mobile nature of the food trucks, they are often permitted and inspected in multiple counties and cities. Liwirun used Pasadena as an example. Though Pasadena is a part of Los Angeles County, Pasadena has their own health department. Liwirun must stay up to date with inspections and permits in Los Angeles County as well as under the Pasadena health department for his food truck 8e8 Thai Food, a fact that should help sway any remaining skeptics of food truck safety.

The stigma of dining at a food truck has drastically changed over the last decade. What was previously perceived as a grimy poor man's food is now a trendy gourmet party in a parking lot. The idea that food trucks produce only low-quality food just simply isn't true anymore. Dr. Bryan Moe[4], an assistant professor for communication studies at Biola University, is an expert on the rhetoric of food and social movements.

"[The assumption] that food from the street is bad food, they took that argument and raised it up and say that argument doesn't hold water anymore," Moe said.

Sidewalks and curbs double as benches, street lights work as dramatic lighting and the sound of the city acts as background music. It is an experience like no other, and it is always changing. The recession kick-started the revolution that is only improving.

THE PURSUIT FOR FUSION

The coolest part about food trucks? They have the ability to pull their culinary inspiration from all over the world and from a wide spectrum of cultures. Focusing in on Asian food trucks in particular, we see the beauty in having centuries of culinary tradition from all across Asia to draw on. Take the Indonesian food truck Stop Bye Cafe, for example. The Asian-fusion-inspired food truck was converted from a brick and mortar restaurant into a food truck in 2017 when they lost the lease on their building. Tom Tee and Justin Tulus have been the foundation of the Stop Bye Cafe and have created a family-run business inspired by travel.

Chef Tulus is from the Spice Island in Indonesia, but has spent the last six years in Los Angeles learning the art of Asian cuisine from well-respected celebrity chefs all around the city that taught him the importance of exploring beyond cooking.

"I left Indonesia to pursue my American dreams," Tulus said. "After I came to the USA, and I worked at Lukshon, which [was] my first fine dining restaurant experience and worked with a celebrity chef, it opened my eyes beyond that. So at that time I fell in love with cooking and chose [being a] chef as my career."

At the front of the organization is Tom Tee. He is the friendly face that greets all customers who come to their truck.
Tee has a background in education and is the businessman running the show with skills in management and customer service. Together, the two have served food to thousands of people across Los Angeles, spreading the journey through Indonesian fusion to people all across Southern California.

"In Asian culture, foods can bring people together to share stories and each other's company," Tee said, speaking on the faithful following they have found over the last few years. "They are our loyal customers. When someone greets you by name after they first

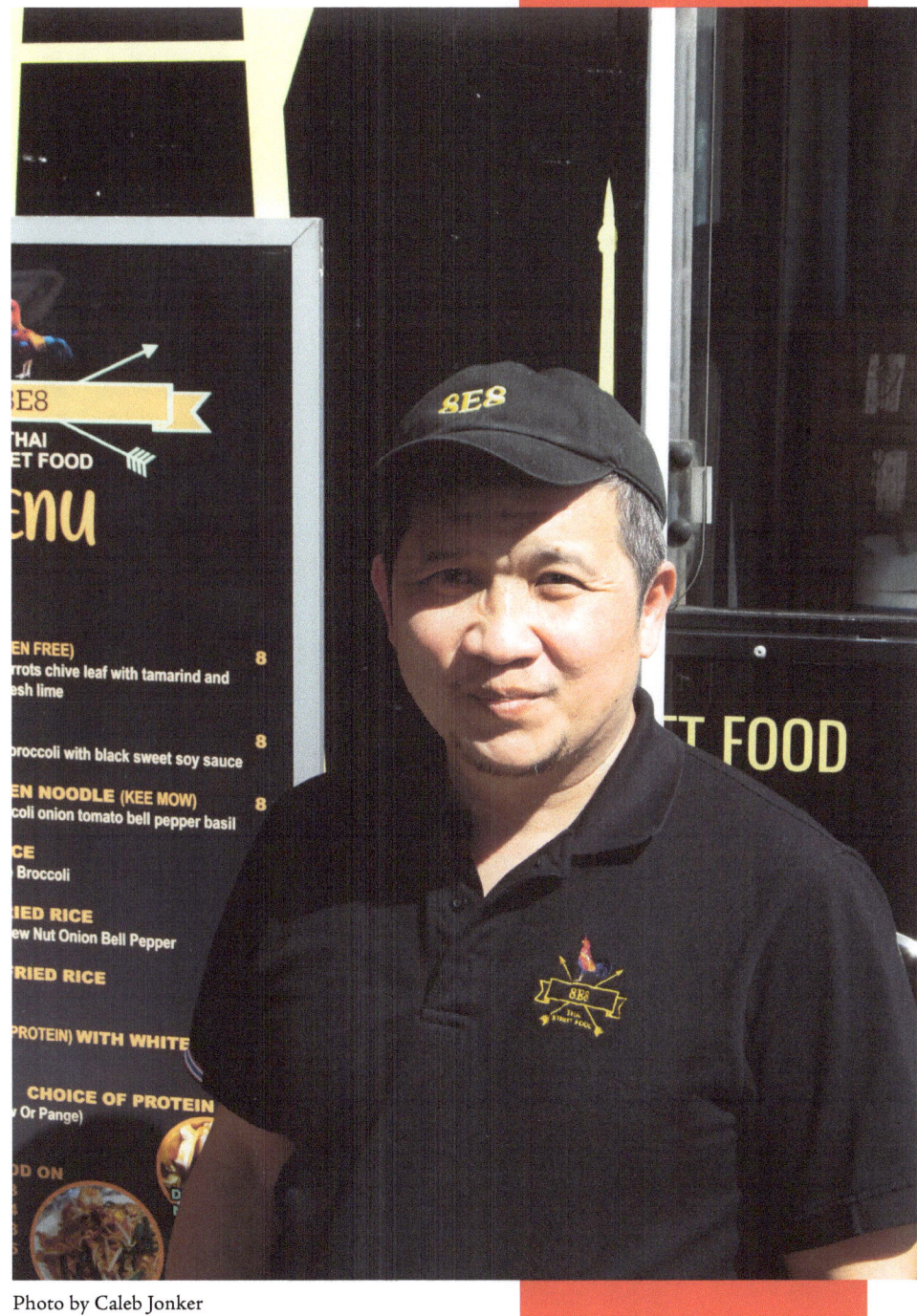

Photo by Caleb Jonker

Montre Liwirun stands infront of his food truck 8e8 Thai Food.

meet, we will be happy because it [is] something special, and vice versa."

The loyal following of the Stop Bye Cafe has not disappeared even in the midst of the COVID-19 pandemic. With business down about 75%, the truck decided to power through the undesirable circumstances and still give back by donating meals to health care workers combatting COVID-19. Tee, Tulus and their extended family set up shop in Whittier, Calif, in the heat of the pandemic to make 100 meals for the frontline workers at PIH Hospital. They also made 35 Indonesian-fusion-inspired meals that were meticulously crafted and delivered to Cedar Sinai Hospital in Beverly Hills, Calif. for the frontline workers.[5]

"Food trucks retain a large voice within their communities," Moe said. "When disasters hit, food trucks are there for their communities."

ACCESSIBILITY IN AN ELUSIVE INDUSTRY

Food trucks meet the audience where the audience is. Not vice versa. That is a huge advantage, given that restaurants are stationary and the consumer must go to them. The elusiveness can be a turn-off for some. But food trucks? They follow the community and adhere to their needs. However, there are potential downfalls when cooking on the

111

street. The limitations of a food truck kitchen can hold constraints on the abundance of a diverse menu.

Though food trucks are often associated with accessibility because of their ability to move, this can also lead to problems of inaccessibility as well. For instance Liwirun said the biggest challenge he faces as a food truck operator is finding parking. Some places he parks he has to move after two hours. Other times he works with a third party to find parking spots on busy streets.

This inaccessibility can extend to the customer as well. For example, visiting a food truck parked in a hard to reach location will change the audience's experience. Physical distances and barriers make trucks feel less approachable. When customers have to spend more

than ten minutes on a cold night walking around trying to understand how to access the truck they may find themselves wondering if this truck was actually open to the public and whether it was worth their time to visit. The ever changing location of food trucks can become a barrier for some customers.

Still, Liwirun says that the biggest advantage that food trucks have over brick and mortar restaurants is that they are not locked into one spot, he added, "If [one] location doesn't work, then we can move around."

However, with time and dedication, one can be forced to dive into the details of a simple dish to make it the greatest it can be, given the limitations. The uniqueness of the creations is part of what makes food truck food that much more memorable.

"For me, it doesn't matter," Tulus said. "Because I can create a restaurant menu on the food truck as well. The pros: from my cooking station, I always can see and greet my customers while I [am] cooking. The cons: since the limits of the capacity, I can only create a small menu."

FUSION IN AMERICA

How do food trucks become launch pads for such innovative fusion recipes? To appeal to the masses, many Asian-inspired restaurants and food trucks fuse together two different cultures into one menu.[6] The current menu at the Stop Bye Cafe features cultural classics Indonesian Ren-Dang Stew and Kemangi Shrimp Garlic Noodles. But the Stop Bye Cafe also has dishes for the more American palette. Fried Chicken Sandwiches with shoestring french fries are available to make sure every customer is pleased.

"Indonesian cuisine is not well known by Americans," Tee said. "By offering fusion cuisine, we slowly introduce the flavor and complexity of Indonesian foods." Tulus chimes in with his perspective on fusion cuisine in America. "[We] still use Indonesian ingredients in our foods to keep the authenticity," Tulus said. "Our food might not easily get approved by the Indonesian people, but as long as others say good, we [are] good."

Sometimes fusion means reinventing classic recipes such as the dumpling. This is the route the cofounders behind the Mad Dumplings

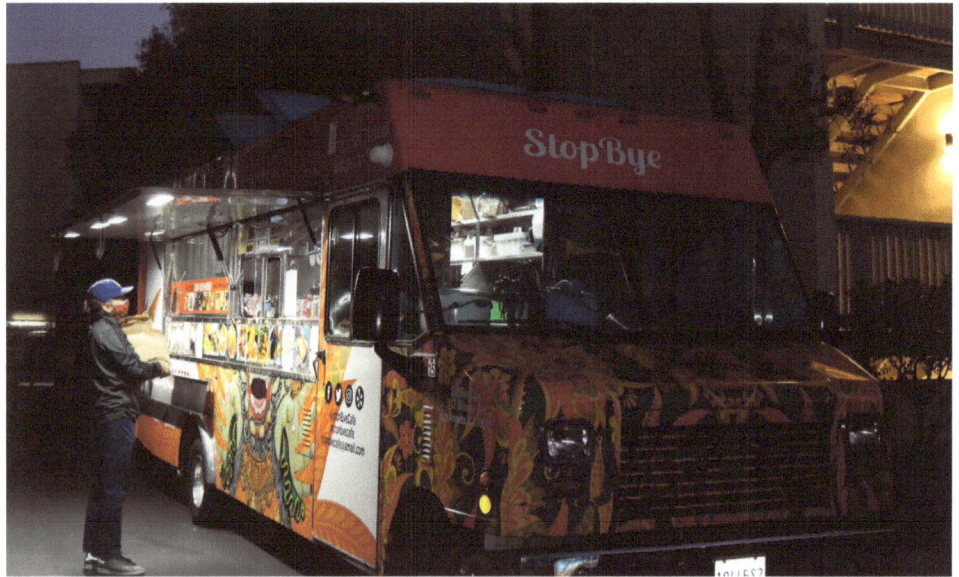

Photo by Andrea Basista

The Stop Bye Cafe parked outside an aprtment complex at Redondo Beach Cafe

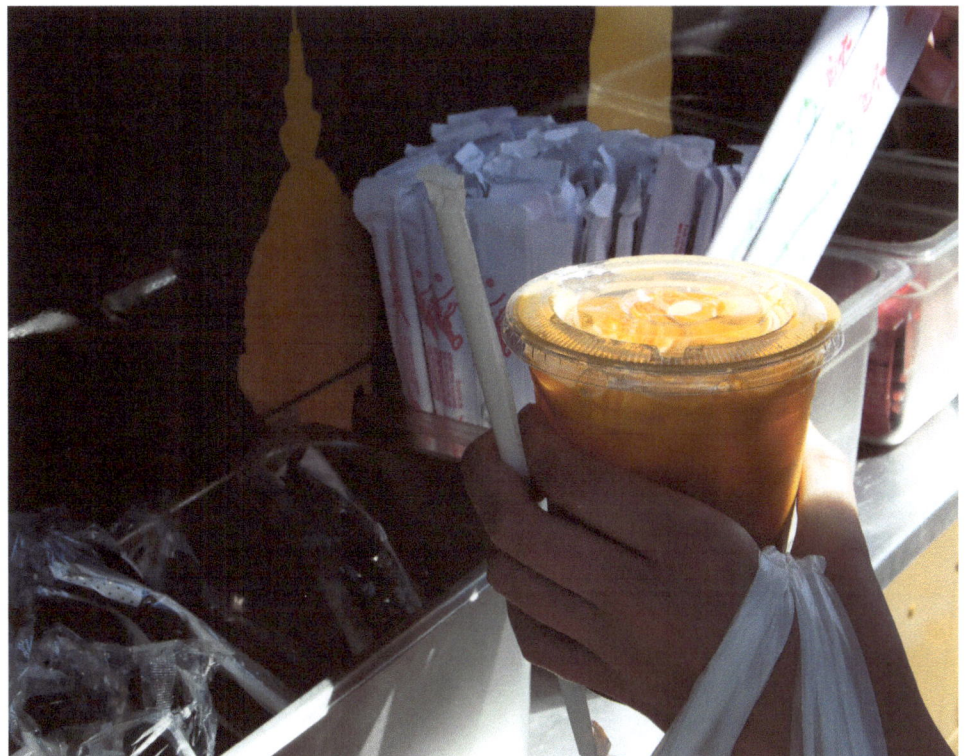

Photo by Andrea Basista

food truck decided to take. Mad Dumplings offers numerous new kinds of Dumplings such as their "Fried Chicken Dumplings" a savory dumpling stuffed with chicken and pepper jack cheese, and deep-fried in Corn Flakes, or their Mac Dumplings, another deep-fried dumpling stuffed with Mac and Cheese. These dishes are not just gourmet, they are also swiftly available.

"Fast food was never supposed to be gourmet food, until it was," Moe said. In this way food trucks are shifting rhetoric, and adding to public discourse that these two polar opposites can come together in a savory and delicious way.

STREET FOOD AND FOOD TRUCKS: SIMILAR BUT DIFFERENT

Street food in America is far less common than it is in other countries. There are many factors that contribute to why American cities have less street vendors, one major barrier is the legal status of street vendors. For street vendors on the west coast this legal process has changed drastically over the last few years. In Los Angeles, it took until 2019 to fully legalize street vending[7] though their permitting process was still far from done. L.A. Taco reports on the ten-year battle and symbolic first permit. According to L.A. Taco, a news

organization dedicated to food, art, and community news in L.A., it wasn't until February 2, 2020, that the city of Los Angeles gave out its first food truck permit.

Why is there such a glaring contrast between street vendors and food trucks? Why is one harassed by police[8] while the other is heralded as a popular new wave in gourmet cooking?

Beyond the difference in cooking styles, Nina Martin[9] explores the differences that have allowed one group to advance and the other to be left behind. Martin's writing treats the city of Chicago as a case study, where Martin says the groups are treated very differently. Martin writes, "In a society as racialized as the US we should not be surprised that the work of Latino street vendors would be criminalized." Martin continues by contrasting this to the food truck scene. "[Street vendors] embody economic and social marginality that is not 'cool', 'hip', or 'creative'." This stands in stark contrast to the relationship food trucks have with the city which is perceived as "creative".

Though both groups represent creative businesses that enrich neighborhoods, Martin says that only food trucks are seen as welcome and innovative, while street vendors are seen by cites as "a threat to public health". Street vendors and food truck services have clear differences, but they also have many similarities. Despite this their work is treated with inequity when it comes to legal and social prioritization. Nonetheless, the surge of new

113

food trucks that the cities of the United States have experienced since 2008 is likely born from similar motivations as individuals who are street vendors. Entrepreneurs looking for affordable ways to create a business.

STAND OUT PERSONALITIES

The recession of 2007[10] is a major factor in what gave rise to the gourmet food truck in America, but it wasn't what made food trucks stick. In his book, "The Food Truck Handbook", David Weber suggests the low start-up costs that made food trucks such a popular alternative for entrepreneurs is not what made food trucks stand out and stick with customers. Weber believes that it's a food truck chef's ability to zero in on one specific style of cooking or even one dish that elevates their work to an experience rather than just a meal.

Approaching the window of a food truck reveals that each food truck has its own personality. Some, like the Kogi truck, are plastered head to toe in a myriad of stickers. Other food trucks opted for a custom paint job, like Stop Bye Cafe and Mad Dumplings. Some personalities extend from their owners, like Liwirun's 8e8 food truck which is painted with the temples of Thailand and features a golden buddha sculpture on the side of the vehicle.

Appearance isn't all that stands out. Each food truck seems to find its way into a specific niche, and if you encounter multiple food trucks in one place there is rarely overlap with other truck's cuisine.

Narrowing down the menu of what a food truck serves helps create a memorable experience. Mad Dumplings has only seven things on their menu, three were specifically marked as fan favorites. On their menu itself, they presented only two types of food, dumplings and fries.

By presenting a smaller menu limited to just a few options it is easy for their customers to make a decision quickly, and easy for the staff to prepare different menu items from similar ingredients. Many of the menu items at Mad Dumplings were versions of American-Asian-fusion, such as chicken-fried dumplings or macaroni and cheese dumplings, Mad Dumplings still offered a more traditional dumpling as well. According to Maeve Webster[11], a data analyst in the food industry, in 2014 eleven percent of items on food truck menus were considered "mixed-ethnicity" dishes.

These unique menu options are definitely part of what makes an audience's experience with food trucks stand out. Add a unique setting and bold made to order flavors to the tightly curated menus and food trucks compel their audiences to hunt them down.

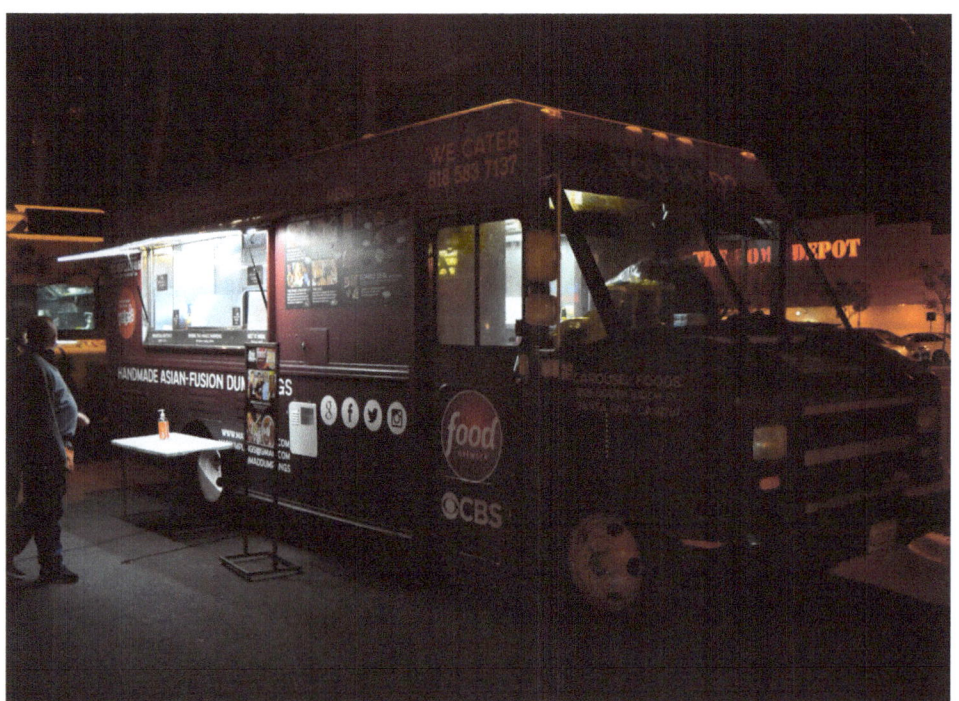

Photo by Caleb Jonker

The Mad Dumplings Truck at a food truck night hosted weekly in a Home Depot parking lot.

REFERENCES

1 https://www.thebalancesmb.com/a-history-of-food-trucks-2888314#:~:text=As%20of%20March%20of%202019,in%20some%20areas%20than%20others.

2 https://deliveryconcepts.com/taking-business-on-the-road-the-top-benefits-of-starting-a-food-truck-business/

3 Liwirun, Montre. Personal Interview, 11 March 2021.

4 Moe, Bryan. Personal Interview, 23 February, 2021

5 https://www.stopbyecafe.com/about_us

6 https://www.stopbyecafe.com/menu

7 Cabral, Javier. L.A. Issued Its First Street Vending Permit, Here's Everything You Need to Know About This Historic Moment. 6 January 2021

8 Cabral, Javier and 11. Can Street Vending Survive the Pandemic? L.A. Vendors Face Harsh New Reality and LAPD Enforcements.

9 Martin, Nina "Food fight! Immigrant Street Vendors, Gourmet Food Trucks and the Differential Valuation of Creative Producers in Chicago"

10 David Weber, "The Food Truck Handbook: Start, Grow and Succeed in the Mobile Food Business" p. 2

11 Maeve Webster, "The food truck effect: How food trucks have influenced consumers, menus" 2014

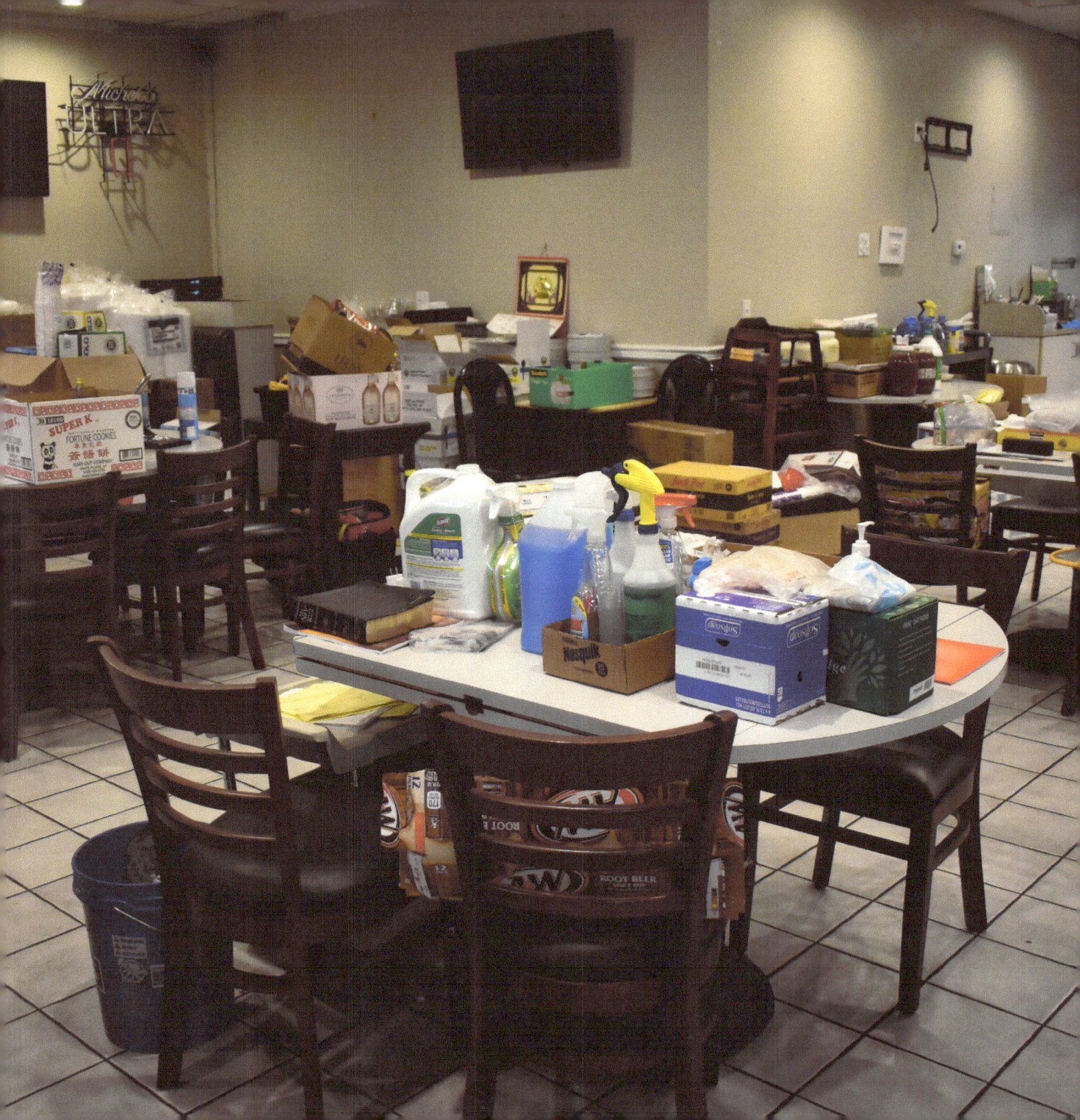

9. Enduring Empty Tables in a Pandemic

By Sarah Dougher and Angela Hom

Johnny Chen, co-founder and general manager of both locations of XLB Dumpling Bar in Walnut and Brea, California, sits on a brick wall outside his Walnut location on a breezy February evening. Wearing a blue pull-over sweatshirt, jeans and a black disposable face mask, his casual demeanor reflects his restaurant's. Inside, pop music blares over the speakers and the kitchen is bustling. The ambiance would have been seemingly conventional, except for the fact there are no tables at which to seat people. All the same, during the short time Chen sits outside his restaurant, there is a steady flow of customers entering empty-handed and exiting with plastic "thank you" bags filled with the fusion flavors XLB Dumpling Bar is recognized for. Sitting down inside of a restaurant in 2020 — a luxury that was stripped away.

> "A lot of Chinese restaurants are already dead,"
>
> — Steve Chun

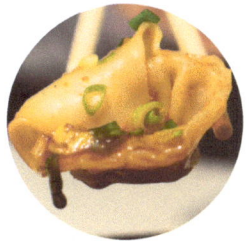

(Left) Photo by Sarah Dougher
Kung Pao Bowl's dining room was transformed into storage during the pandemic.
(Right) photo by Caitlin Gaines

Growing up in Southern California with immigrant parents, Chen and his two older brothers, who are also his business partners, were familiar with both traditional Chinese flavors and classic Californian foods such as pizza and In-N-Out Burger. Self-described as the kid sitting at a side table at a Chinese fast food restaurant doing his homework while his parents worked, Chen grew up in the restaurant business, explaining why he and his brothers gravitated toward starting their own.

"We took a lot of inspiration from the Chinese food my parents cooked for us, but [also] our experience growing up in America and eating a bunch of different things from cheeseburgers to taco trucks to al pastor and stuff like that, so our menu is a reflection of our experience," explained Chen.

Due to their ability to maintain a safe take-out method, Chen's restaurants never had to close

their doors during the pandemic. However, the National Bureau of Economic Research found that Asian American business-owner activity declined by 26% from February to April 2020.[1]

Womply, a company that helps businesses with Paycheck Protection Program loans, conducted a study in 2020 that revealed that Chinese restaurants in the United States were particularly struggling when compared to other types of restaurants.[2]

According to Womply, "By the end of March, over half of Chinese food restaurants, who might otherwise be perfectly suited to thrive in a 'takeout only' environment, stopped transacting entirely. No other type of restaurant in this group even comes close."

Due to the fact that the majority of the restaurants in the nation that fell into the

takeout grouping of eateries were operating at a manageable rate during the pandemic, the drastic slowdown of Chinese restaurant businesses was noticeable.

China Wok Express in Whittier, California, fell into the temporary closed-doors category. From March through May 2020, their doors were completely closed to business while the pandemic raged. During that time, employees at the restaurant were unable to apply for unemployment benefits for small businesses, which proved to be difficult.

On March 27, 2020, the Coronavirus Aid, Relief, and Economic Security (CARES) Act was signed into law, which extended states' ability to provide unemployment insurance for workers affected by the pandemic, according to the U.S. Department of Labor.[3] However, according to the Economic Policy Institute, for every ten people in the nation who successfully applied for unemployment, three to four more applied but did not get through, and two more neglected to apply due to the difficulty of the process.[4]

Some restaurants, such as Kung Pao Bowl in Norwalk, California, were more fortunate than restaurants such as China Wok Express because their small business received government relief funds. As a result of these funds, at the beginning of the pandemic, some restaurants were making more money than they would have with dine-in service, exemplifying the perplexing effect that the pandemic was having on the restaurant industry.

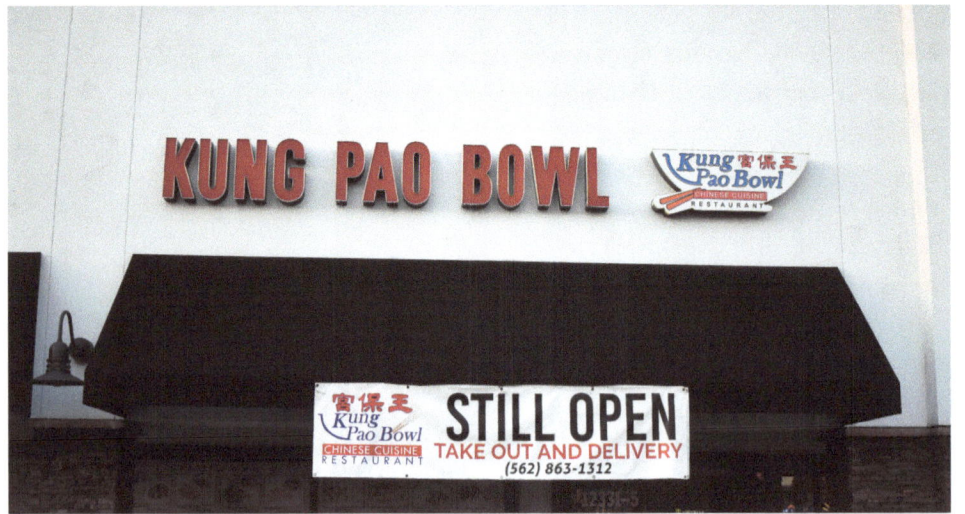

Photo by Sarah Dougher

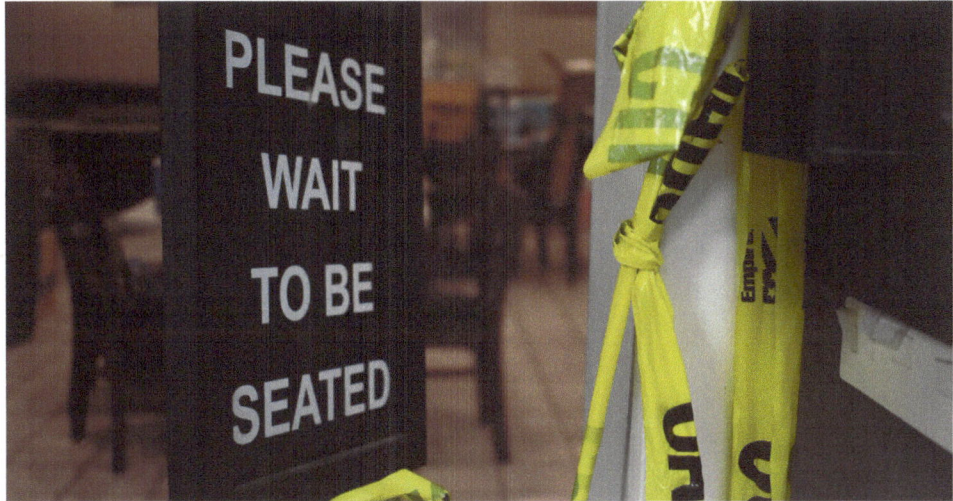

Photo by Sarah Dougher

Caution tape clung to the "please wait to be seated" sign leading into the Kung Pao Bowl dining turned storage room.

FOLLOWING RULES

On top of trying to make ends meet, there was a whole new wave of rules and regulations to which every restaurant needed to adhere. These included Center of Disease Control and Protection (CDC) guidelines such as mask wearing, social distancing and capacity limits.[5] The new rules placed restaurants in a tricky situation in trying to get customers to walk through their doors while still keeping every party safe.

"Originally we did [have indoor dining], but since the pandemic started, we decided to completely stop indoor dining, and ever since March, even when they allowed it for a little bit, like 25 % capacity, we asked how the team felt about serving people, and we understand where like people aren't comfortable with it,

so if our team wasn't comfortable with it, then we wouldn't do it," explained Chen. "We've got to protect our friends and family and the people we see when we get home from work."

Steve Chun, owner of Kung Pao Bowl since 2016, felt similarly, saying that before dine-in is allowed again, he and his workers should be vaccinated in order to feel safe.

Many restaurant owners needed to do what was best for their own establishment. For Chen, it was making his team comfortable. This is something many business owners had to tackle when the pandemic was seemingly permanent.

Chun mentioned that he remembered seeing many Chinese restaurants in his area close their doors, not because of their lack of

business, but because they wanted to avoid contracting the elusive virus.

BUMPS IN THE ROAD

Navigating regulations and rules was just one obstacle for restaurant owners. Another was having to deal with discrimation based on the type of food they served.

Because of the coronavirus's place of origin, Wuhan, China, Chinese people were abruptly thrown into the limelight. Even before California's complete shutdown, it seemed people were deliberately avoiding going to Chinese restaurants out of the fear that the virus spread simply by coming in contact with Chinese people. Chun saw this trend in his own restaurant.

Sitting outside his restaurant on a cold metal chair at a small table he cleaned with a wipe, sporting a black face mask with his restaurant's logo embroidered on the side, Chun said that March 2020 was a difficult time for a lot of restaurants, but his restaurant started seeing fewer people beginning in January simply due to the type of food it served. The weekend in March before California's first lockdown, the restaurant saw its slowest Friday, earning less than $2,000 in normal sales.

"There was no one here dining in, because, Chinese restaurant, Chinese virus," said Chun.

Once California was placed on lockdown orders on March 19, Kung Pao Bowl was open

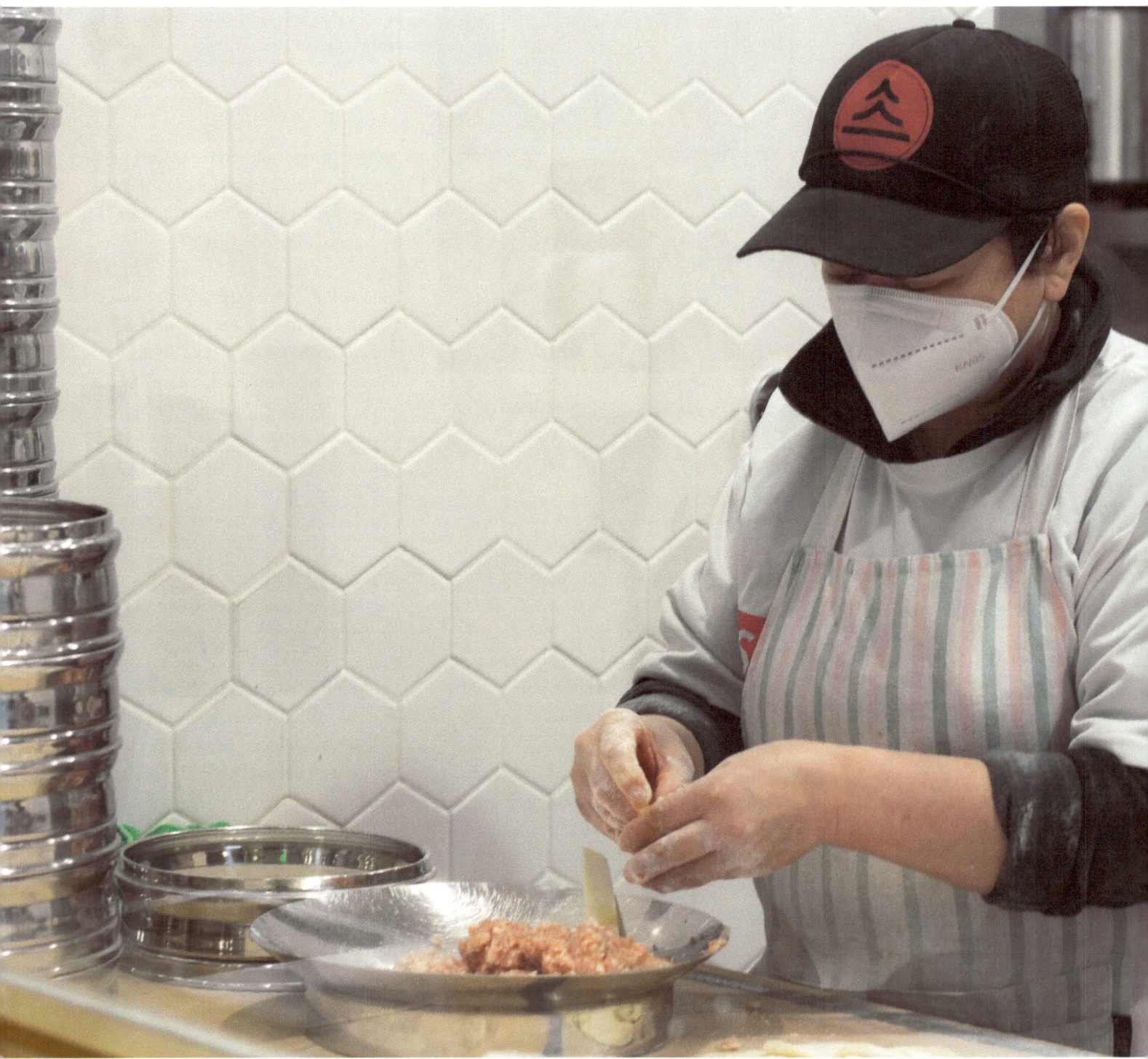

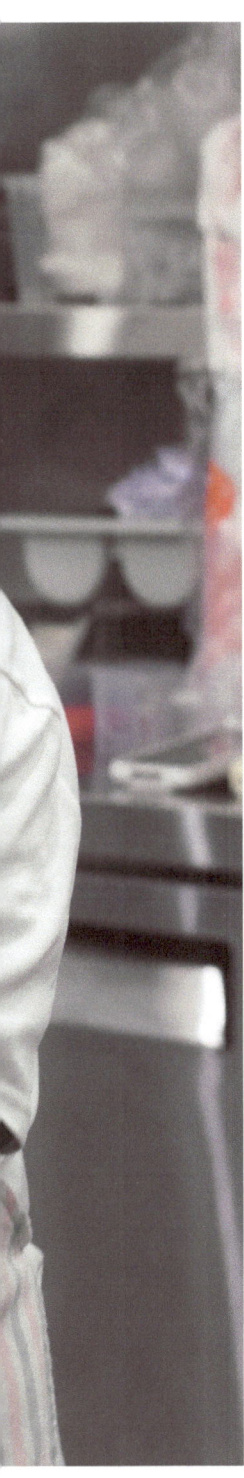

for takeout only. It only made $450 in gross sales that day, and now in April 2021, it is still only making 40% to 60% of its usual sales on a successful day.

BRINGING STEREOTYPES TO A HEAD

Some Chinese restaurants, which decided to keep their doors open, such as Kung Pao Bowl, had to handle peoples' rude comments or actions, such as deliberately coughing or uttering explicit or muttered discriminatory remarks about the restaurant solely because it was Chinese.

With the spread of the virus came the spread of new language. Politicians, the public and headlines screamed "Wuhan virus," "Kung Flu,"[6] and many more inflammatory terms directed toward those who had no control over the virus.

Chun expressed that, "China has been [made out to be] the enemy. So that doesn't help."

This was just the beginning. Following the news of the origin of the virus, many hate crimes toward Asian Americans began to spring up. According to a report from Stop AAPI Hate, they had received more than 2,500 reports of anti-Asian [hate] since March 2020 nationwide. This report was from the initial peak of COVID-19 within the States. These hate crimes and attacks not only shocked the general public, but also shook many Asian owned businesses in America.

Photo by Sarah Dougher
A woman molds dumplings behind glass at XLB Dumpling Bar.

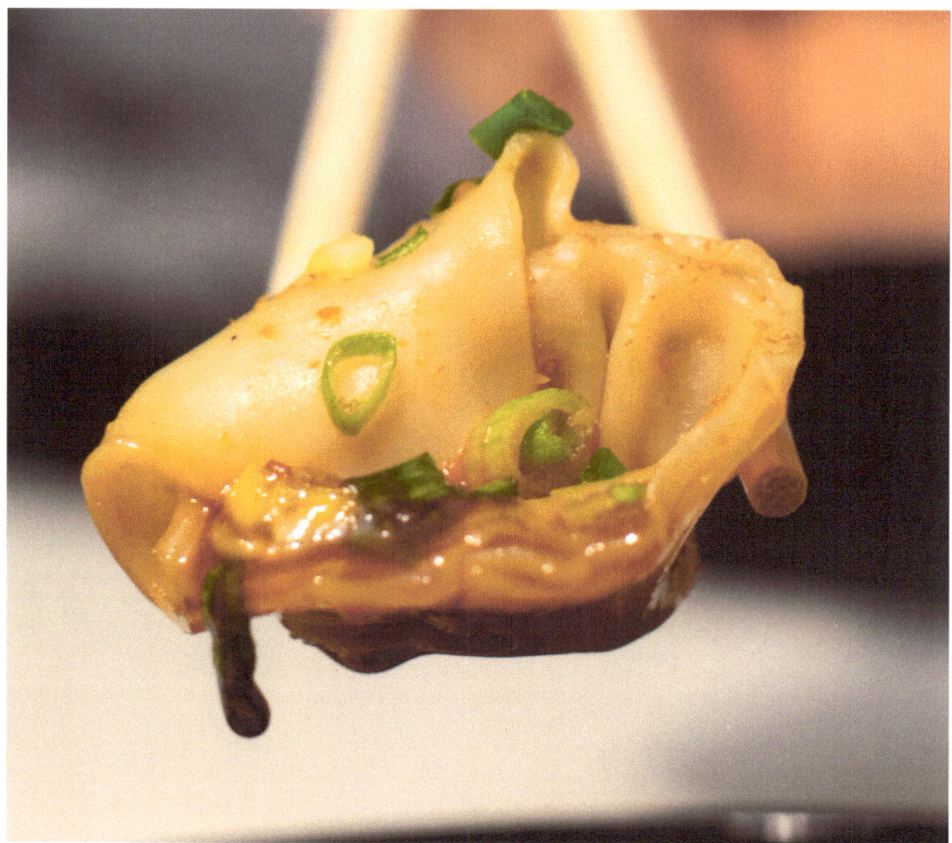

Photo by Caitlin Gaines
A dumpling from XLB Dumpling Bar.

"A lot of Chinese restaurants are already dead. Especially these mom-and-pop, dine-in types of restaurants," Chun said as he motioned toward his storefront, "There's the ones that have been here for 30 years, but this one eventually will die. It depends on your surroundings. [COVID -19 is] really affecting Chinese restaurants, and [not] Asian[s] as much, [specifically] Chinese."

COMMUNITY SUPPORT

Despite many restaurants receiving backlash, Chen has contrastingly received nothing but positive feedback from his customers and community.

"The overall community, it doesn't matter the ethnicity, they always treated us with warm welcomings and we never had to face any serious issues like that," explained Chen. "Because we're still just a take-out restaurant, and we aren't planning to change that, I think it has hurt the business, but I think everyone is going to persevere and we're going to get through this."

Whether it be in a positive or negative environment, the restaurant industry must be tenacious. When Stan Ng's family was in the Chinese restaurant business in Oxnard, California, his father would give the advice not to fear the criticism one might face while working in a restaurant. Although receiving criticism is part of the expectation in the restaurant realm, so is receiving praise. Now an instructor of Engineering at Biola

Clarence Kwan, creator of "Chinese Protest Recipes," shared with Associated Press, "In a year where Chinese and East Asian communities have essentially been blamed for the pandemic and chastised as 'dirty,' this type of narrative is completely unacceptable."

According to a study conducted in 2021 by the Center for the Study of Hate & Extremism at California State University, San Bernardino, anti-Asian hate crimes in 16 of America's largest cities increased 149% in

2020 with the first spikes occurring in March and April.[7]

According to Chun, Chinese restaurants in general have been given a bad reputation of being dirty, and the pandemic has only brought this stereotype more into the light. He also said that because of the pandemic, Chinese restaurants have started to die off both because of the pandemic and because of lack of community support.

University, Ng explained that receiving a compliment while working in a restaurant is fuel for another day.

According to Ng, kind, encouraging words such as "'Hey, we really enjoy the food and thank you for what you do,'" can make all the difference in a restaurant's morale.

PUSHING THROUGH

The year 2020 was quite unforgettable. Although vaccines are becoming more available and public places are beginning to open with limited capacity, the pandemic still exists. From finances to loss of community, COVID-19 has certainly left its impact on Chinese restaurants. Despite all of the obstacles the Chinese food scene has encountered, business owners like Chun and Chen are persevering through it all. Their food, along with many others', is still warming the hearts and stomachs of the public who are also pushing through adversity.

Although 2020 is forever in the past, 2021 brought its own troubles for the Asian American community. Stop AAPI Hate reported that in the first three months of 2021, there were 503 reported incidents of hate against Asian Americans.[8] The Asian American community is experiencing a burden not many Americans will ever understand, but is working to make the United States a place where everyone is welcome without fear of discrimination.

"The racism that Asian Americans have faced during COVID-19 has taken a tremendous toll on our community," stated Dr. Russell Jeung, professor of Asian American Studies at San Francisco State University and part of leadership of Stop AAPI Hate. "Not only are we grieving with the families of victims who've been shot, pushed and shoved, but we are also assaulted in other ways—with verbal profanities, civil rights violations, and online harassment. Ultimately, we are aiming to make the U.S. a more just and equitable nation, one where we all belong."

REFERENCES

1 Racism targets Asian food, business during COVID-29 pandemic. Retrieved February 22, 2021, from https://apnews.com/article/donald-trump-race-and-ethnicity-pandemics-wuhan-animals-4d25738ab49597d0de1517383a9108d2

2 Report: the types of restaurants most impacted by COVID-19. Retrieved February 10, 2021, from https://www.womply.com/blog/the-types-of-restaurants-most-impacted-by-covid-19/

3 Unemployment Insurance Relief During COVID-19 Outbreak. Retrieved February 22, 2021, from https://www.dol.gov/coronavirus/unemployment-insurance#CA

4 Employment filing failures. Retrieved February 22, 2021, from https://www.epi.org/blog/unemployment-filing-failures-new-survey-confirms-that-millions-of-jobless-were-unable-to-file-an-unemployment-insurance-claim/

5 Considerations for restaurants and bars. (n.d.). Retrieved February 23, 2021, from https://www.cdc.gov/coronavirus/2019-ncov/community/organizations/business-employers/bars-restaurants.html

6 Considerations for restaurants and bars. (n.d.). Retrieved February 23, 2021, from https://www.cdc.gov/coronavirus/2019-ncov/community/organizations/business-employers/bars-restaurants.html

7 FACT SHEET: Anti-Asian Prejudice March 2020 – Center for the Study of Hate & Extremism. Retrieved March 18, 2021 from https://www.csusb.edu/sites/default/files/FACT%20SHEET-%20Anti-Asian%20Hate%202020%203.2.21.pdf.

8 STOP AAPI HATE NATIONAL REPORT. Retrieved March 23, 2021 from https://secureservercdn.net/104.238.69.231/a1w.90d.myftpupload.com/wp-content/uploads/2021/03/210312-Stop-AAPI-Hate-National-Report-.pdf.

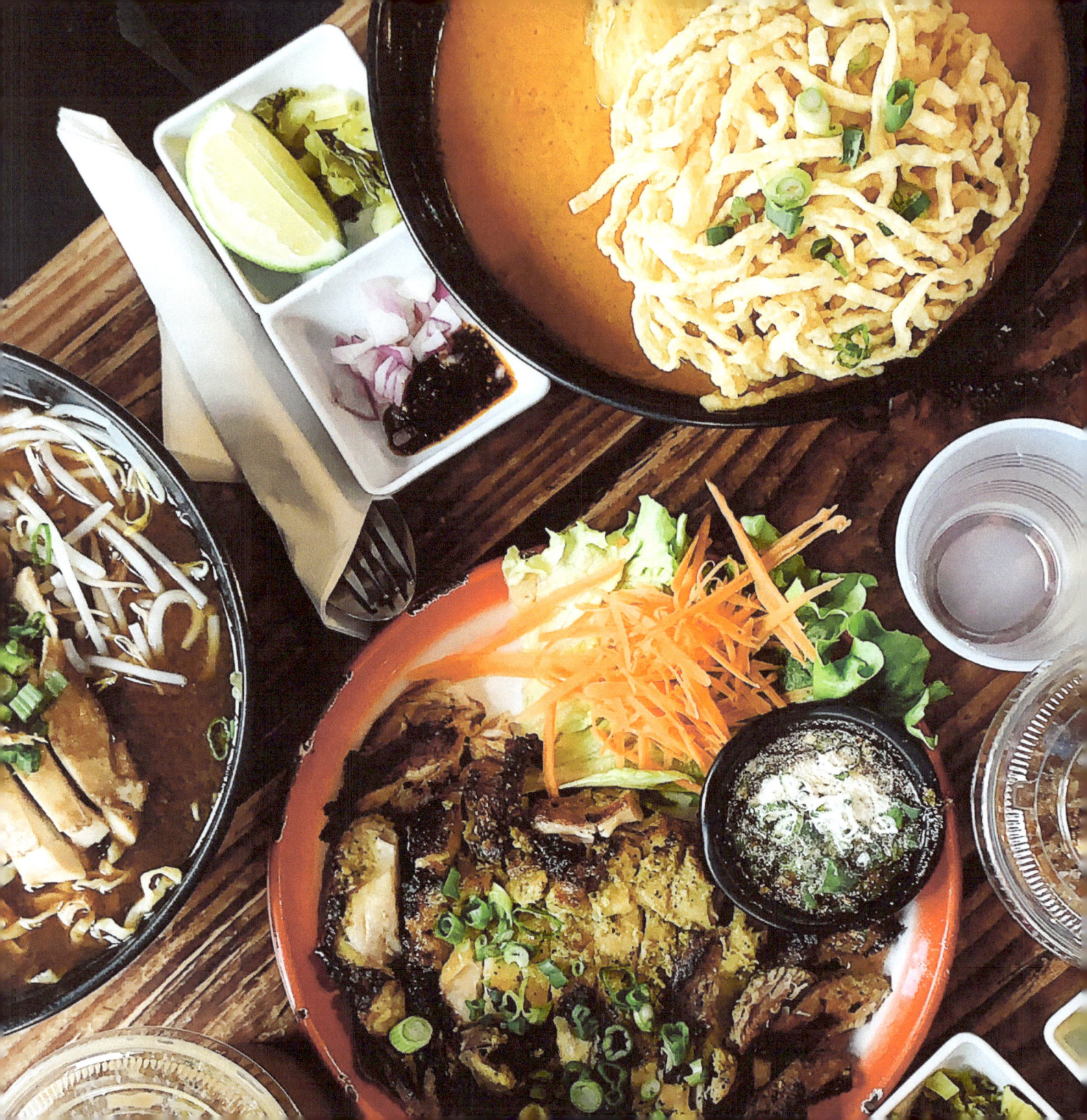

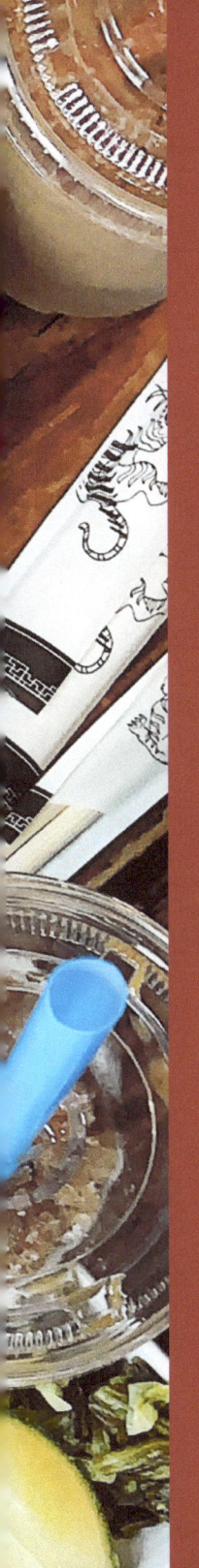

10. A Bridge Back Home: Comfort food in Thai Culture

By: Rachel Gaugler and Evana Upshaw

When Tai Nuntapramote sits down to eat the plate of fried garlic pork ribs and sticky rice, he is instantly transported back to where he grew up in Thailand, walking home from school with sticky rice in one hand and pork in the other. The "happy ribs" dish, inspired by Chef June Intrachat's desire to incorporate childhood memories and traditional Thai food, is one of many traditional plates found at Otus Thai Kitchen and Coffee on North La Brea Avenue in West Hollywood. There, a Thai-American may walk in and experience the comfort of finding their own childhood favorite
on the menu.

Comfort food is defined by its ingredients available in various regions and the values a particular group holds. The idea of food as comfort is especially true for immigrants making a life in contexts where they are the

"Food is love."

-Dr. Christina Kim

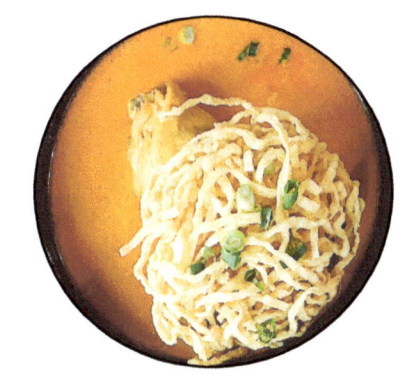

Pictured left: Khao Nom Restaurant, in Queens, New York

Photo By: Rachel Gaugler

125

minority. Immigrants from Thailand have unique experiences in regards to foods that keep them grounded in their culture and remind them of home.

COMFORT FOOD IS PSYCHOLOGICAL

Food is an integral part of the human experience, and it is often used to speak what words cannot articulate. Christina Kim, professor of psychology at Biola University, believes that eating and the act of being fed are associated with the concept of "food is love" from the very beginning of our lives—cemented through a vital act of love right after babies leave the womb.

"Even from the very earliest connections, like when a baby is born, breastfeeding is a significant source, not just of bonding or getting fed nutrition, but of comfort," Kim said. Once that initial connection is fused between food and comfort, using food as a means to self-soothe throughout our lives makes sense.

Breastfeeding is an intimate activity for both mother and baby, and the act of "comfort nursing," according to Healthline, a medical information provider, is very beneficial to babies. Comfort nursing is different from regular feeding, as its purpose is to soothe, cuddle with, bond with and relieve one's baby from pain. The bonds it cultivates also contribute to secure attachment as the child grows into adulthood. This is comfort food in its most primal form.

Additionally, our emotions are closely connected to our bodies—and especially our stomachs. Everything we put inside of us, whether good or bad, manifests in our hormones and moods. This explains the oft-referenced study of what eating chocolate does to our brains.

According to Dr. Astrid Nehlig from the French National Medical Research Institute,[1] Chocolate interacts with neurotransmitters like dopamine, serotonin and endorphins, which contribute to our mood regulation and appetite. In essence—chocolate makes us feel good, we crave it.

But when one thinks of comfort food, taking into consideration that different cultures gravitate toward different things, chocolate is not everyone's go-to. Comfort is completely relative. Although, there are some sensory concepts that are more traditionally associated with comfort.

Food and nutrition specialist Emma Laing, from the University of Georgia Online,[2] says that when it is cold outside, for example, we crave comfort foods that are usually high in fat and sugar. Similarly, when we are sick, we tend to crave foods that soothe us like soups and broths. Ken Albala[3], a food historian, has found in his research that the tradition of eating soup while sick dates back centuries, and is actually more for comfort than it is actually beneficial to our health.

There are also two broader types of comfort food: everyday food that is comfortable to eat because you are used to it, and comfort foods eaten on special occasions. The Vietnamese embrace this concept well in their comparison of rice to pho.

"Rice is the dutiful wife that you can rely on, we say. Pho is the flirty mistress that you slip away to visit." Explains Vietnamese author and consultant Andrea Nguyen.[4]

Nguyen says her mother told her that if someone ate pho every day, it would get boring, but it is widely understood by many to be comfort food. Rice, by contrast, which is eaten almost every day in many Asian countries, is associated with foods within one's comfort zone.

At its core, "comfort food is connected to nostalgia," argues Biola University professor of communication studies, Bryan Moe. "It doesn't have to do with any one particular sensory taste, it's what the person, the community, decides to replicate in a way that brings back nostalgia."

Nostalgia originally meant "homesickness," according to LeMoyne College psychology professor Krystine Batcho, Ph.D,[5] but the meaning has evolved to encapsulate "the notion of longing for or missing aspects of a person's personal lived past." The feeling of nostalgia "unites our sense of who we are, our self, our identity over time."

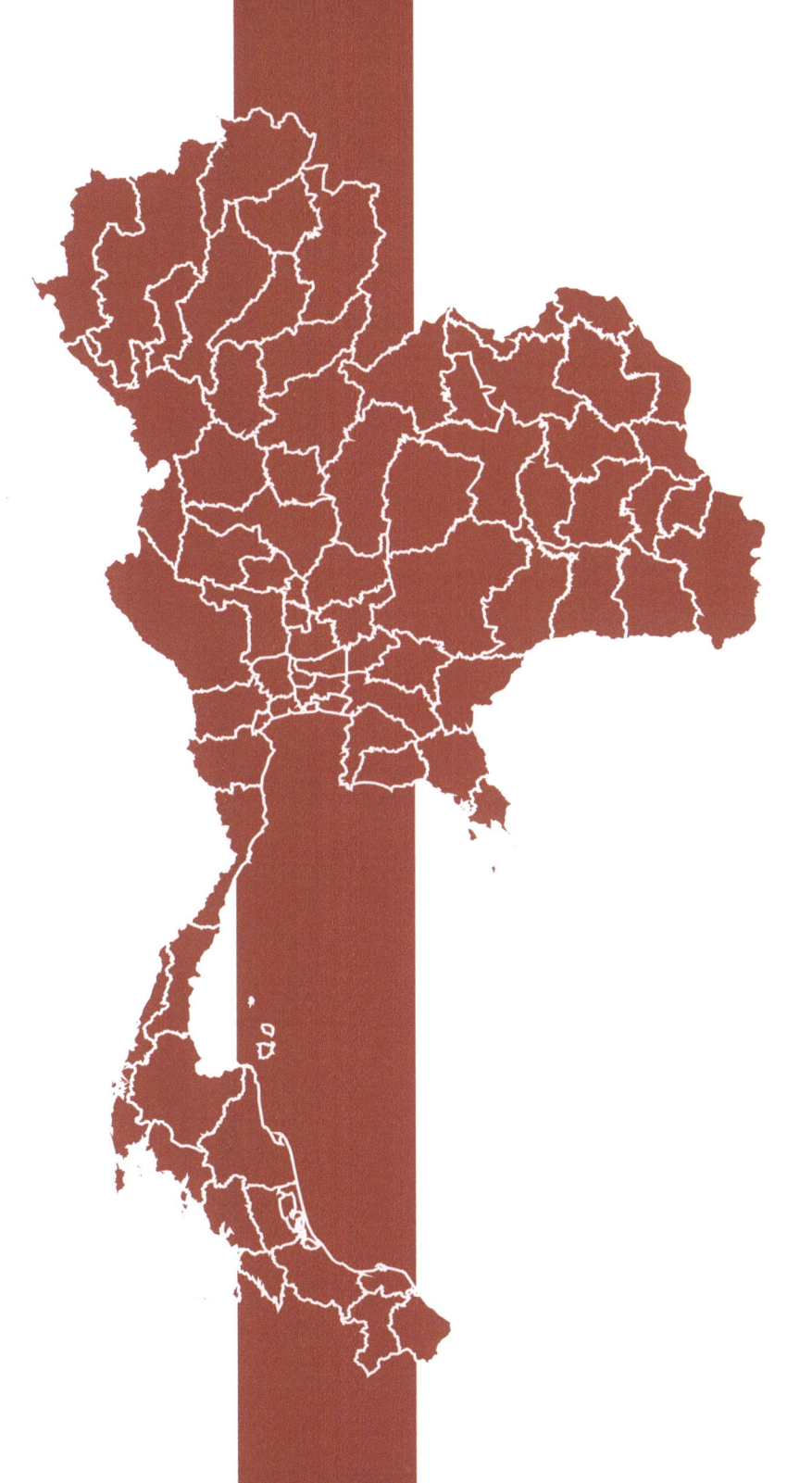

We grow, change, move and develop new relationships over time, and so it is often through food that we are called back to who we once were or where we used to be. It is a truly powerful sensation—one that feeds the soul.

FOOD THAT FEEDS THE SOUL

For many, comfort food is the avenue through which one feels most at home. For Thai-Americans, comfort food is the bridge between the collectivism of Thai food culture in the household and the authenticity of Thai food on the streets of Thailand.

According to As We Travel[6], a blog, Thai food culture is very social. Foods in Thai households are meant to be enjoyed with others and within the home. One such dish is khao tom, a rice porridge made by boiling jasmine rice with water, mixing in shallots, lemongrass, galangal or ginger and incorporating pork balls, shredded chicken, shrimps, fish or eggs.

Benya Rodthong, a first-generation Thai-American resident of Queens, New York, describes khao tom as one of the dishes her mother missed after moving to the U.S. from Thailand. In their household, khao tom is a morning food and a home remedy for sickness. She recalls countless times when her mother would carry a tray of rice porridge to her bed when she was home sick. To Rodthong, khao tom is comforting because it is associated with her mom or mae.

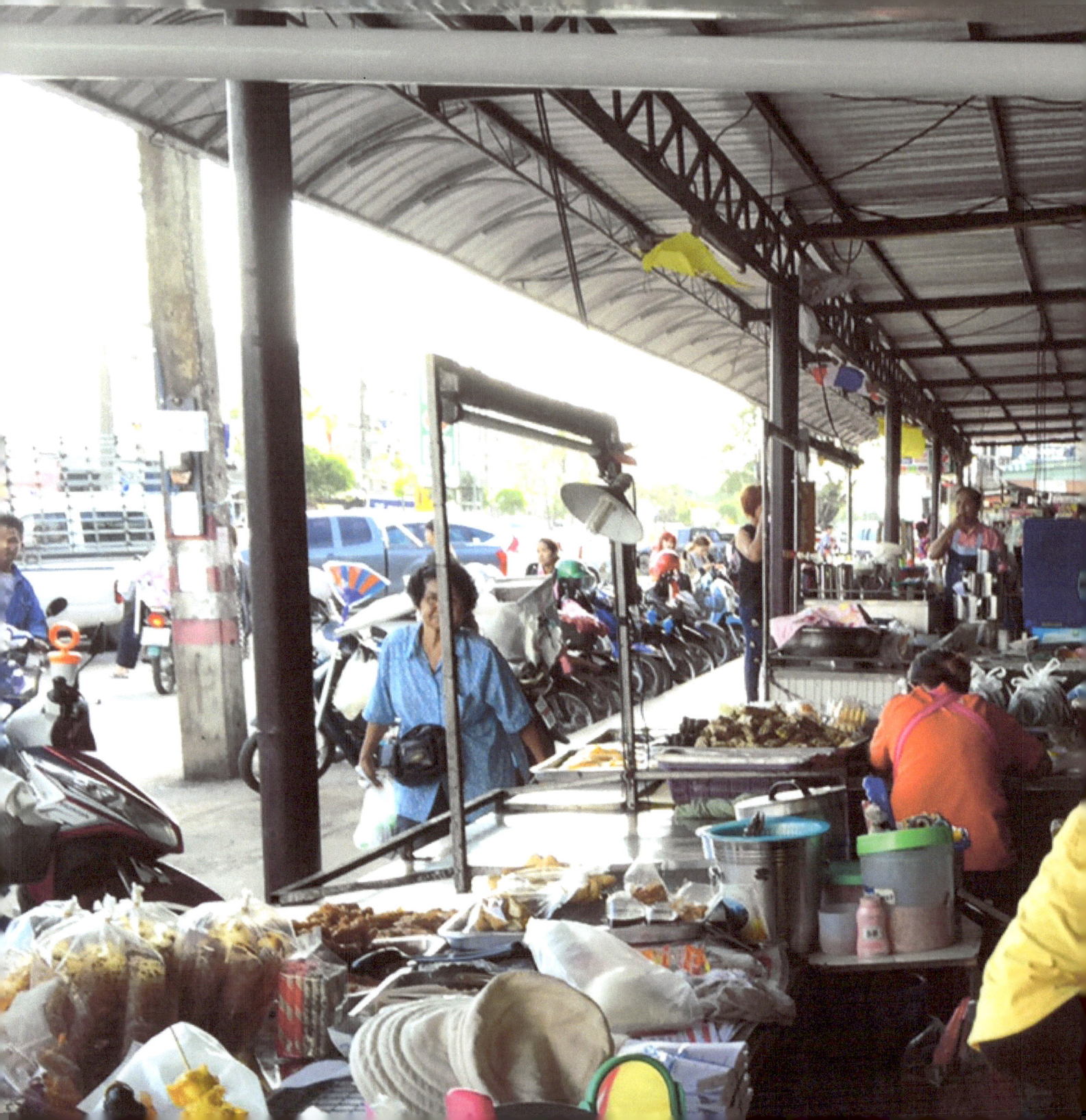

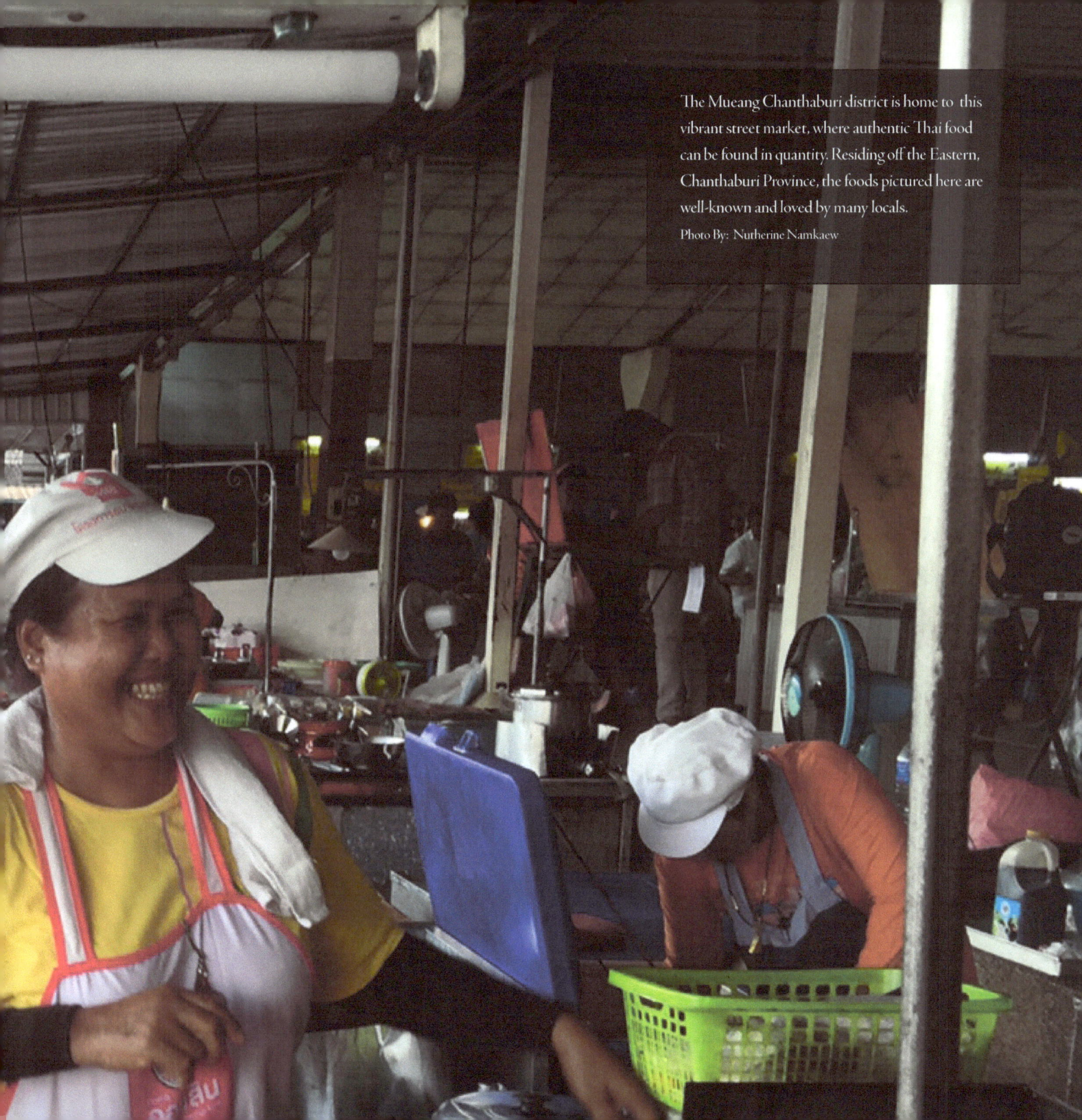

The Mueang Chanthaburi district is home to this vibrant street market, where authentic Thai food can be found in quantity. Residing off the Eastern, Chanthaburi Province, the foods pictured here are well-known and loved by many locals.

Photo By: Nutherine Namkaew

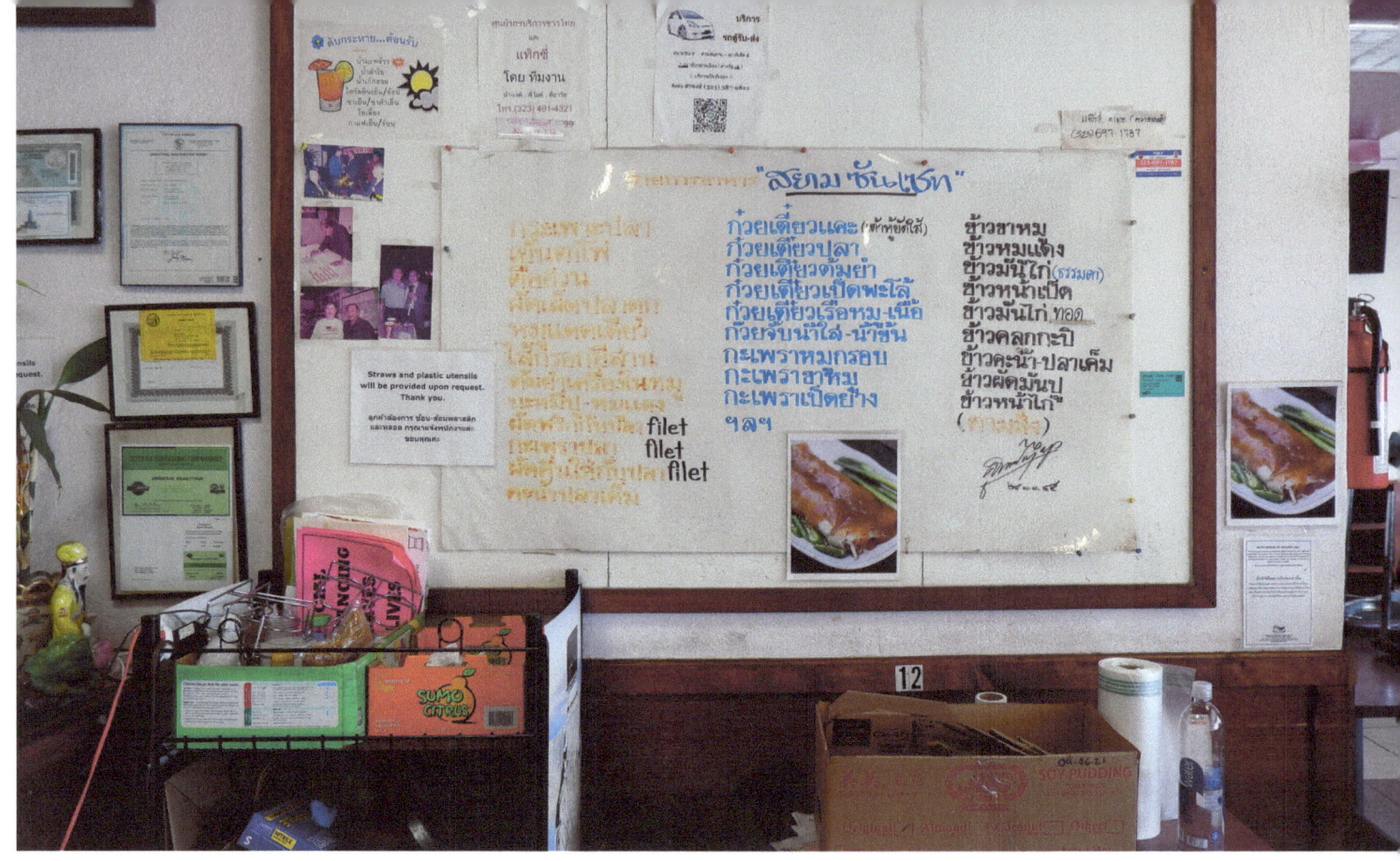

Noted for it's traditional comfort food, Siam Sunset (left) is located in Los Angeles where, Unlike many other ethnic restaurants, it is known especially for delicious Thai breakfast plates. Becuase family breakfast is cherished in Thailand, Siam Sunset's emphasis on this oft-overlooked meal is very meaningful.
Photo By: Rachel Gaugler

Although khao tom is a staple in almost every Thai household, it is made differently by each family. Her cousin, Nutherine Namkaew, for example, enjoys a different version of this traditional dish. While Rodthong would eat this morning soup with a salted egg or papaya salad on the side, Namkaew preferred the more tangy blend of mini dried shrimp tossed with chili, fish sauce, lime juice and a little bit of sugar. Though the name of the dish remains the same, the style varies according to household, adding another layer to this concept of comfort food.

Another common traditional dish is papaya salad, som tum. Like khao tom, som tum is made differently per household and acts as a staple of Thai cuisine. Rodthong describes papaya salad as an "everyday thing that every Thai household has the ingredients on deck for." One version of som tum, made with green papaya, Thai chili, green beans, dried baby shrimp, carrots and roasted peanuts, is a tasteful combination of Thailand's four harmonic elements that balance out any Thai meal: sweet, sour, spicy and salty. Namkaew describes this mixture of tastes as zabb

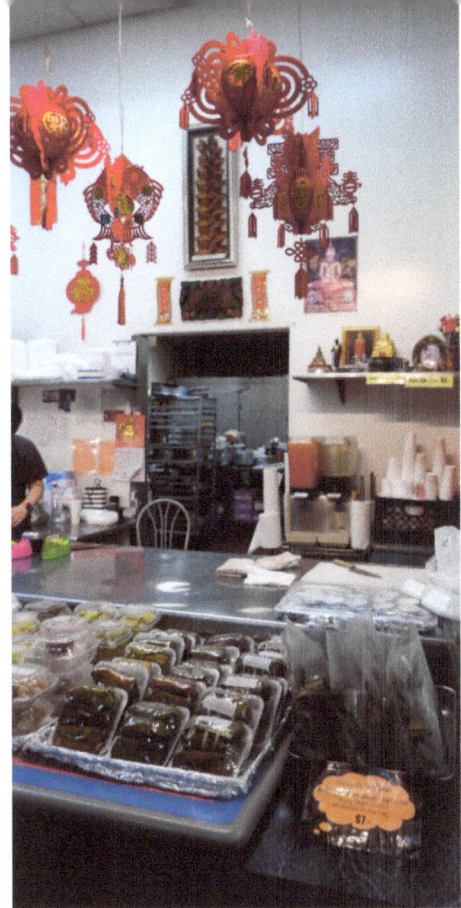

Thai Market located in Thai Town, Los Angeles (right).

Photo By: Rachel Gaugler

"There's no term for comfort food in Thai. It would just be a 'food that reminds me of home.'"

- Benya Rodthong

(แซ่บ), meaning "full of flavor." Zabb, a traditional Thai word from Northeastern Thailand, is often what separates an authentic Thai dish from a westernized version. Thai-Americans tend to stick to their homemade dishes because of the often missing flavor in American Thai restaurants. So, that raises the question—what makes certain foods taste better in Thailand and are they more satisfying to the soul because of it?

THE MISSING SPICE

According to Rodthong and Namkaew, it's the street vendors. Thai street food in the U.S. does not taste the same. Rodthong bemoaned the fact that some of her favorite Thai desserts could only be found in Thailand, like khao nom kok, which are Lao coconut cakes. The next time she returns to Thailand, she looks forward to having Pa Thong Ko, a fried doughnut usually served for breakfast with a dipping sauce of condensed milk. She missed Roti sai mai, a small and thin, pan-fried flour pancake wrapped around a bed of colorful angel hair, similar in texture to cotton candy. To Rodthong, buying one of these desserts from a street vendor in Thailand and enjoying it on a quiet morning with her family "just feels right." Namkaew shared similar sentiments as she recalled the crowded and aroma-filled corner of Mueang Chanthaburi District (เมืองจันทบุรี).

"You can find almost any type of food on each street of Thailand," said Namkaew. "Thai barbecue, papaya salad, grilled squid, Khao mun gai (Thai hainanese chicken rice). I really miss Thai iced tea and Thai iced coffee stands which we can find on every block of Thailand."

Thailand is known for its Night Market scene where tourists and locals alike can taste a wide array of foods sold by hawkers, or street vendors. The street food scene, it appears, is not something that has been replicated in the states and Thai-Americans are missing it.

That's not the only thing that hasn't been entirely replicated. According to Rodthong's mae, what's also missing is the zabb that Namkaew mentioned earlier. "The food in Thailand has more flavor and is tastier than the Thai food here," said Pengrethai Namkaew. Pad thai is an example. When visiting a Thai restaurant in the United States, the chances of finding pad thai, a stir-fry dish made with rice noodles, chicken, peanuts, a scrambled egg and bean sprouts, on the menu are high. Contrary to popular opinion, pad thai is not reflective of all of Thai cuisine. In fact, as Namkaew mentioned, pad thai in the states is rarely the authentic dish Thai people eat at home. After years of catering to the American taste, are Thai restaurants bringing back zabb?

ADD A LITTLE FLAVOR

The answer is an emphatic "yes." In 1999, when a 6-block radius in East Hollywood was officially named the first Thai Town,

131

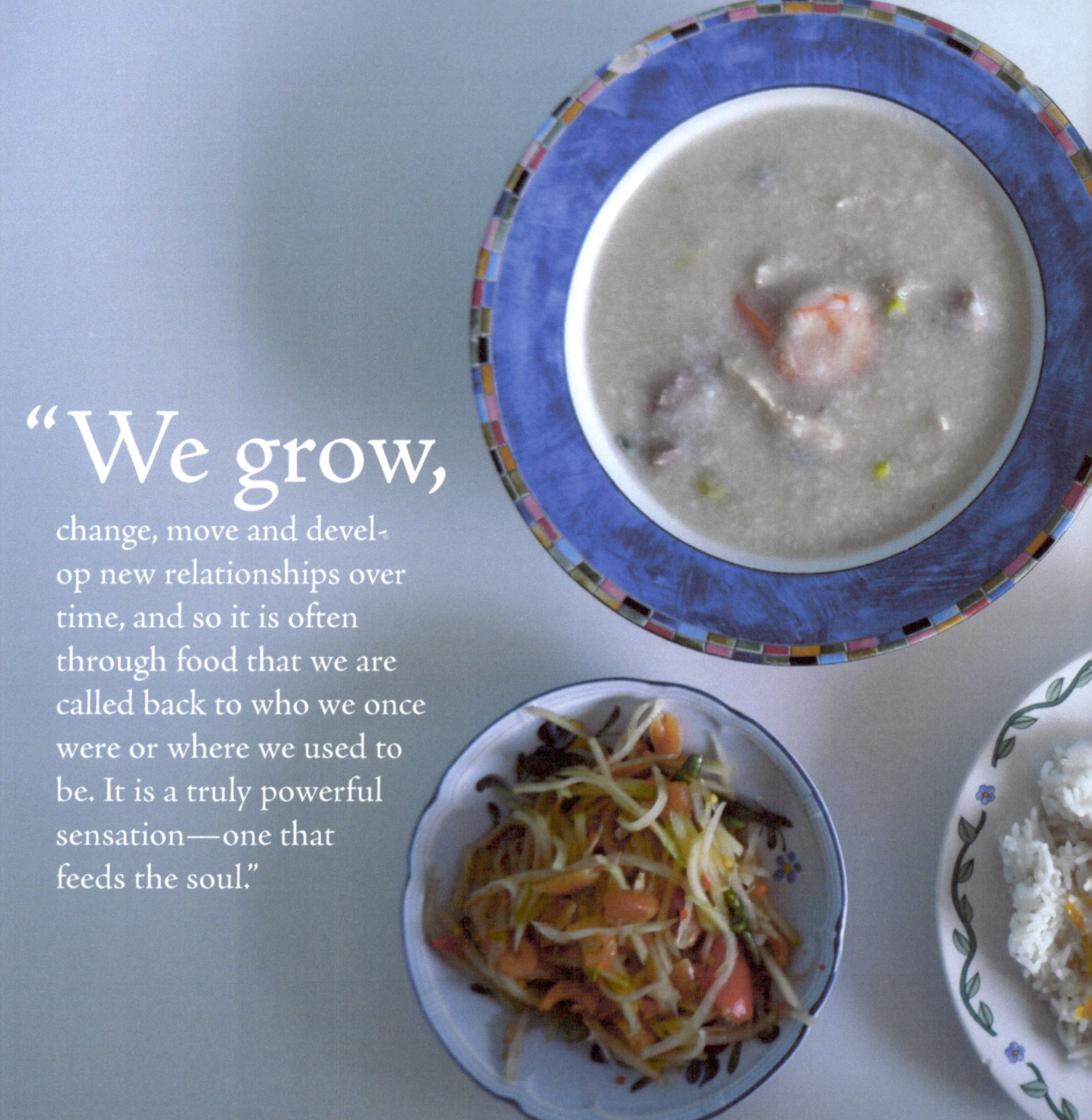

"We grow, change, move and develop new relationships over time, and so it is often through food that we are called back to who we once were or where we used to be. It is a truly powerful sensation—one that feeds the soul."

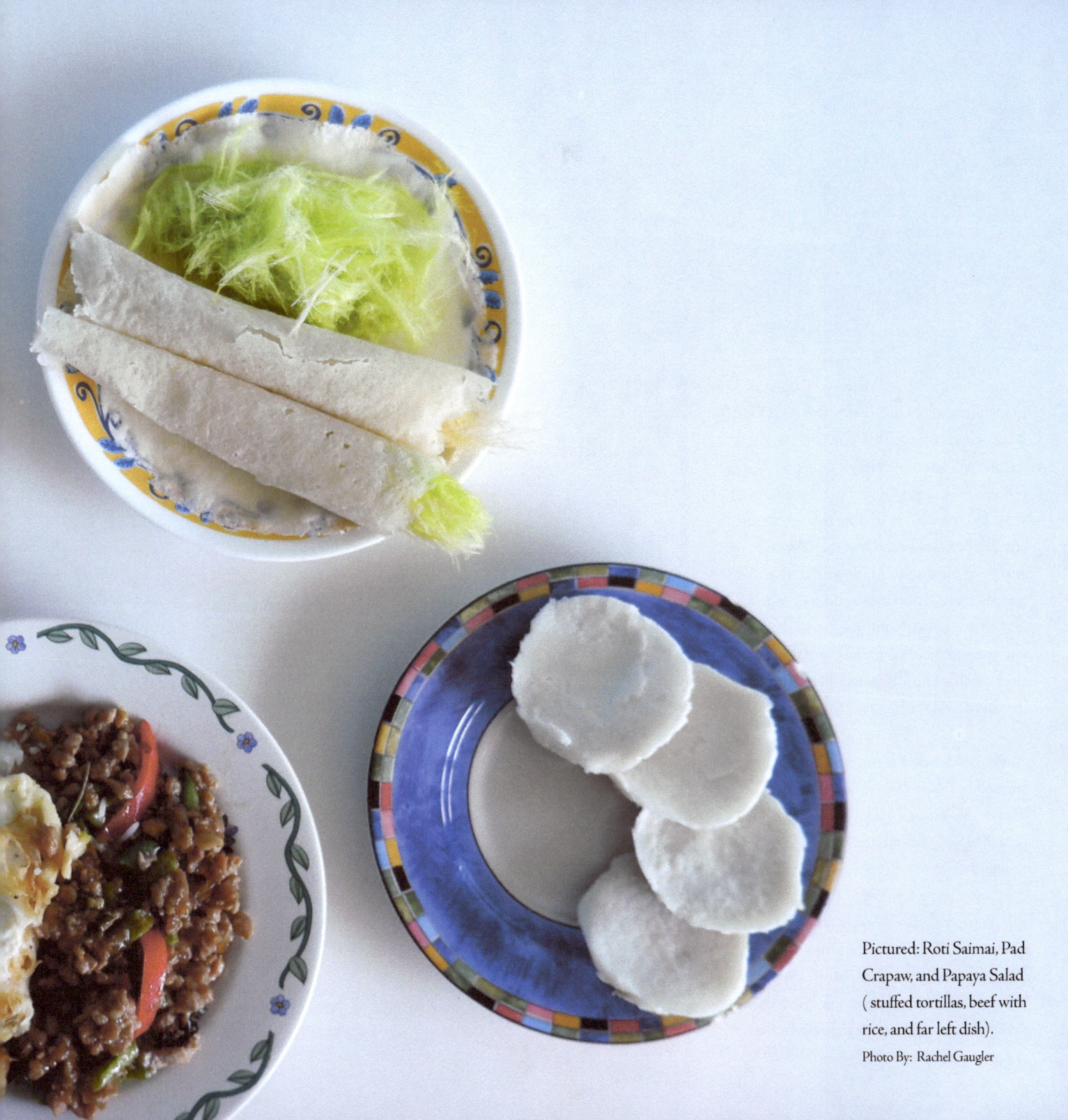

Pictured: Roti Saimai, Pad Crapaw, and Papaya Salad (stuffed tortillas, beef with rice, and far left dish).

Photo By: Rachel Gaugler

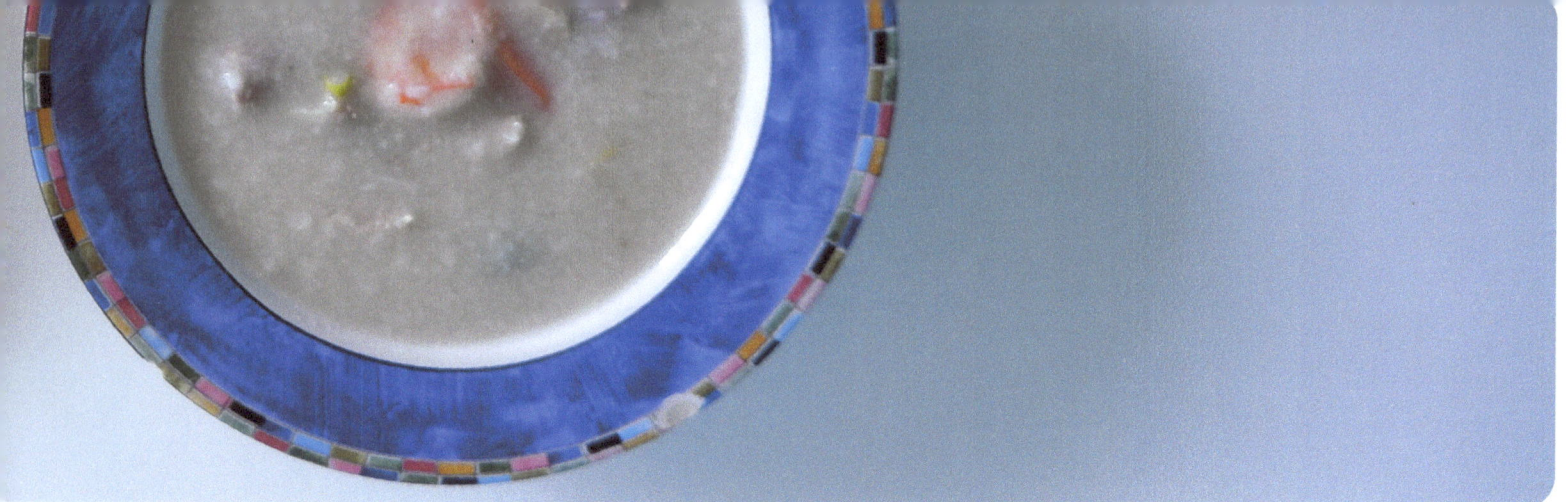

Thai-Americans began dreaming up ways to highlight their culture through their food. Now, when visiting Thai Town in Los Angeles, one will find much more than pad thai. A restaurant goer may discover Kaeng tai pla, a salty and spicy curry that hails from Southern Thailand, or find Khao soi, a coconut curry noodle dish from Northern Thailand, and a signature dish at Namkaew's relative's restaurant, Khao Nom, in Queens. Younger chefs are not holding back from zabb. Why? Because that's how they would make it in Thailand, and tradition is comforting.

As the Thai foodscape reinvents itself, young chefs are pushing the envelope in how they approach Thai cuisine, explained Jean Trinh in an article[7] published for broadcast station KCET. Gone are the timid westernized-only versions of Thai food. Now, a younger generation of Thai-American chefs are nostalgically looking back to old-school practices as they view their food through the lens of being second-generation Thai-Americans.[8] Whether first, second or even third generation, traditional food is consistently the bridge that brings one back home.

KHAO TOM MOO SAP

(A Rodthong Family Recipe of porridge with pork balls)

INGREDIENTS:

1 cup Jasmine Rice
4 cups water
1 lb ground meat (pork, turkey, chicken)
1 medium ginger
1/2 medium white onion

1/4 cup fish sauce
2 tbsp salt
1 tbsp pepper
2 eggs (optional)
Scallion to garnish

DIRECTIONS:

1. Peel the ginger and cut in half. Set half to the side. Mince the ginger and onion and place in a large bowl.

2. Add the ground meat to the bowl. Use about half of the 1/4 cup of fish sauce and combine. With your hands, combine the meat, ginger, and onions together. Add 1tbsp salt and 1/2tbsp pepper to taste.

3. Once meat is combined. Bring a pot of water to boil. Once water boils, scoop the meat mixture with a medium sized spoon and drop it into the water. Repeat until no meat is left. Let the meat cook in the water for about 5 minutes.

4. Remove the water and drain the meat. Add 1 cup of rice into the pot along with 4 cups of water. Add remaining salt and pepper. Place a lid on the pot and Let the water boil. Give the pot a good stir every 5 minutes or so.

5. While waiting for the water to boil, bring back the other half of the ginger and cut into thin strips. And chop up the scallion. Add the ginger to the pot and the remaining fish sauce. Stir the pot.

6. Continue to stir the rice until soft. Add more fish sauce and salt and pepper as needed. Porridge should be the same consistency as oatmeal or grits.

7. Let the rice cook and continue to stir for about 30 mins. Once the rice is cooked to a grits consistency, go right ahead and crack 2 eggs in and stir it until the eggs are cooked. Add the scallion at the end and enjoy! (You can add more fish sauce to your bowl if you want more flavor).

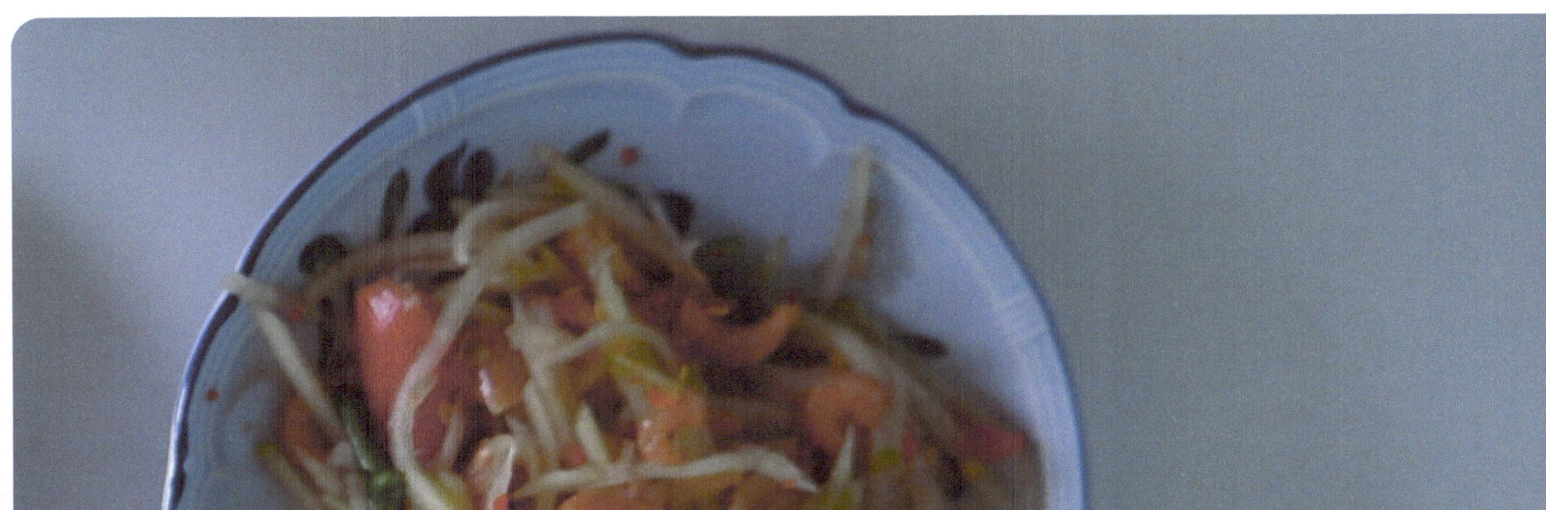

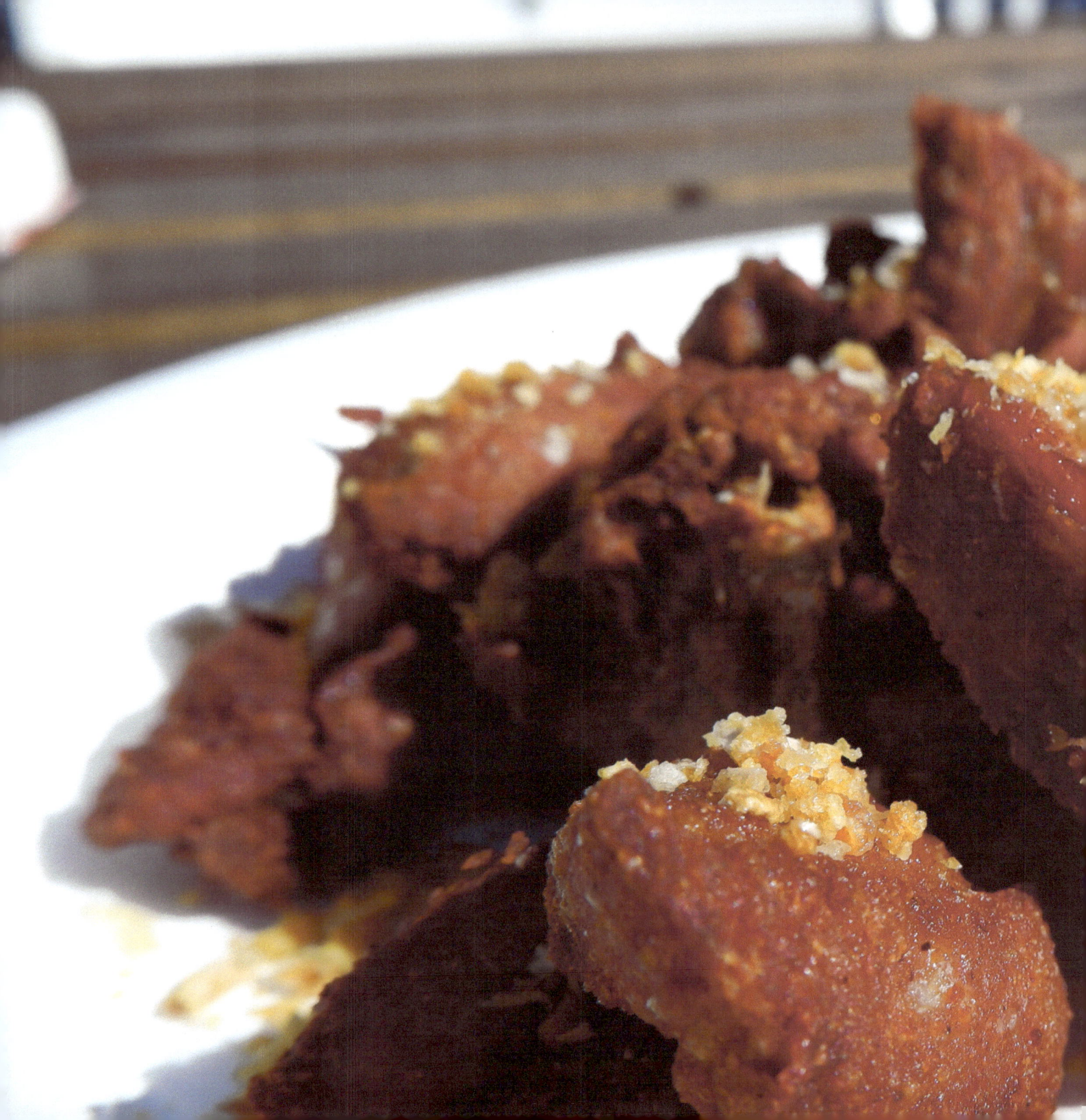

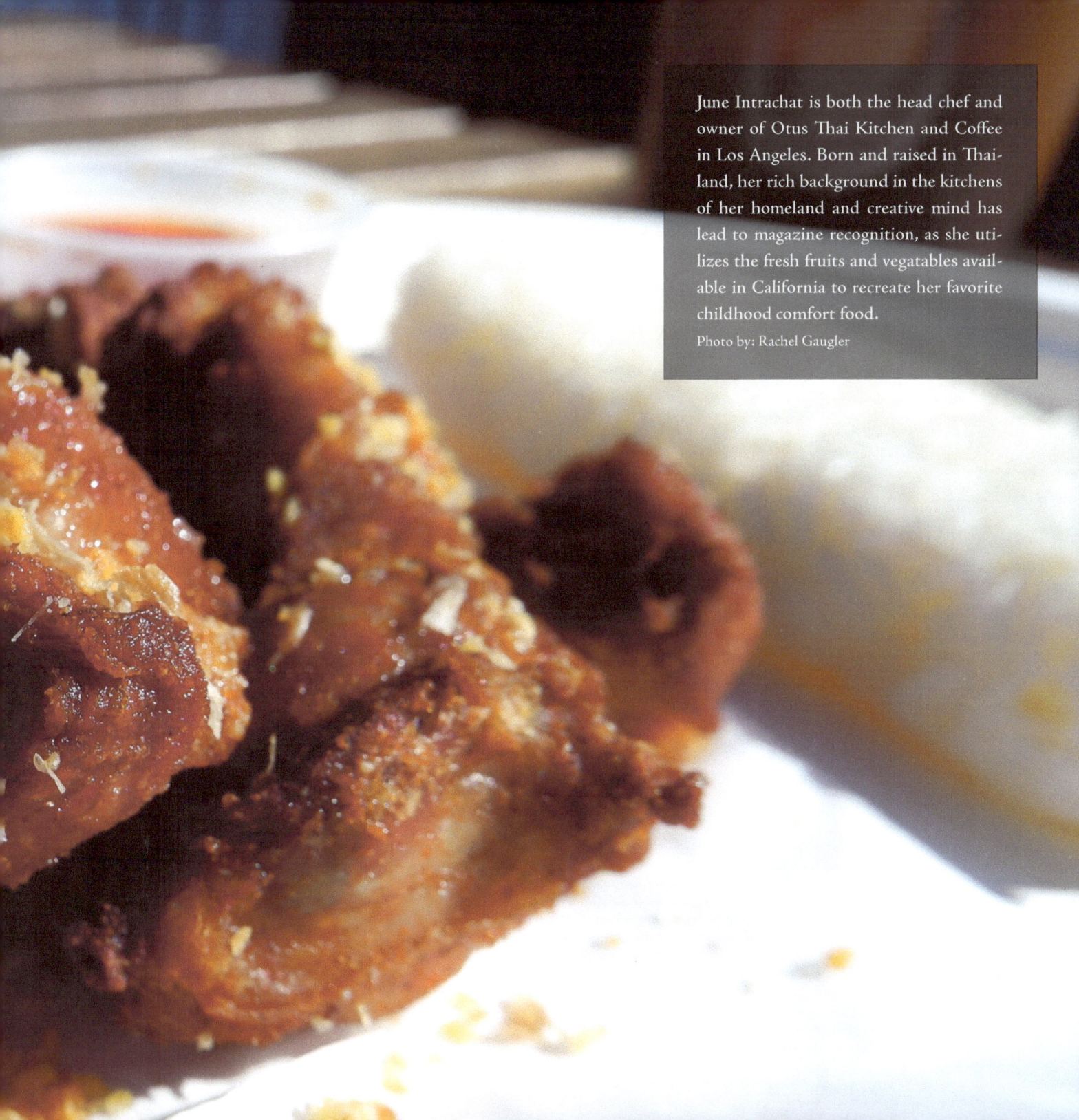

June Intrachat is both the head chef and owner of Otus Thai Kitchen and Coffee in Los Angeles. Born and raised in Thailand, her rich background in the kitchens of her homeland and creative mind has lead to magazine recognition, as she utilizes the fresh fruits and vegatables available in California to recreate her favorite childhood comfort food.

Photo by: Rachel Gaugler

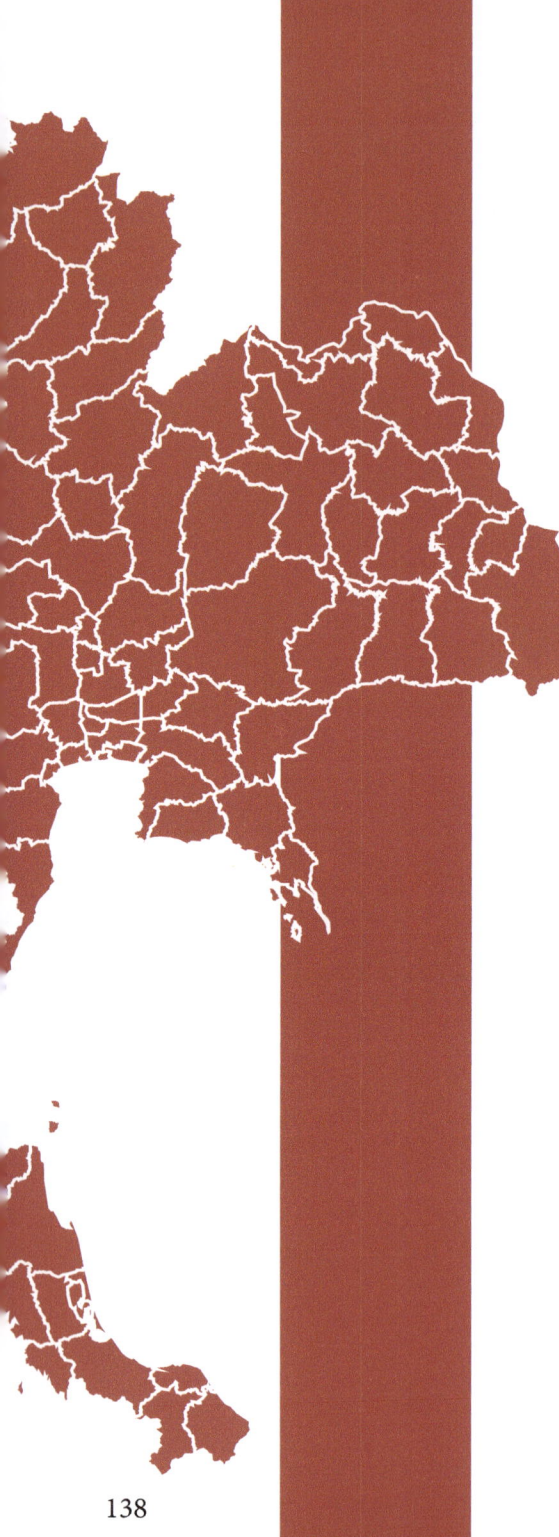

"At its core, 'comfort food is connected to nostalgia. It doesn't have to do with any one particular sensory taste, it's what the person, the community, decides to replicate in a way that brings back nostalgia.'"

Glossary

Aroi (อร่อย) - Delicious
Khao Niao (ข้าวเหนียว) - Sticky Rice, served in Northeastern Thailand, often with mangoes
Khao nom kok (ເຂົ້າຫນົມກົກ) (lao) - Lao Coconut Cakes
Khao Tom (ข้าวต้ม) - Rice Porridge
Pad Krapow Gai (ผัดกระเพราไก่) - Thai Basil Chicken
Pa Thong Ko (ปาท่องโก๋) - Fried Dough
Roti Sai Mai (โรตีสายไหม) - Angel Hair and thin rice flour pancake
Som Tum (ส้มตำไทย) - Papaya Salad
Zabb (แซ่บ) - a Thai traditional word derived from northeastern part of Thailand meaning tasty, delicious and full of flavors

REFERENCES

1. Nehlig, Astrid. The Neuroprotective Effects of Cocoa Flavanol and Its Influence on Cognitive Performance. Mar. 2013, www.ncbi.nlm.nih.gov/pmc/articles/PMC3575938/#:~:text=Chocolate%20may%20interact%20with%20some,appetite%2C%20reward%20and%20mood%20regulation.&text=Poor%20mood%20stimulates%20the%20eating%20of%20comfort%20foods%20such%2as%20chocolate.
2. "Does Cold Weather Make You Crave Comfort Food?" UGA Online, online.uga.edu/news/does-cold-weather-make-you-crave-comfort-food.
3. Taylor, Anna-Louise. "Soup: Why Do We Eat It When We're Ill?" BBC News, BBC, 8 Jan. 2012, www.bbc.com/news/magazine-16250448#:~:text=A%20healthy%20soup%20provides%20an,comes%20to%20feeding%20the%20sick.
4. guyen, Andrea, et al. "The History of Pho." Viet World Kitchen, 15 Sept. 2020, www.vietworldkitchen.com/blog/2018/03/the-history-of-pho.html.
5. "Speaking of Psychology: Does Nostalgia Have a Psychological Purpose?" American Psychological Association, American Psychological Association, www.apa.org/research/action/speaking-of-psychology/nostalgia.
6. Ettenberg, Jodi, et al. "Understanding the Culture of Thai Food." As We Travel | Travel the World, 6 Nov. 2020, www.aswetravel.com/understanding-thai-food-culture/.
7. Trinh, Jean. "The Decades-Long Evolution of Thai Cuisine in Los Angeles." KCET, 19 Jan. 2021, www.kcet.org/shows/the-migrant-kitchen/the-decades-long-evolution-of-thai-cuisine-in-los-angeles.
8. Trinh, Jean. "The Decades-Long Evolution of Thai Cuisine in Los Angeles." KCET, 19 Jan. 2021, www.

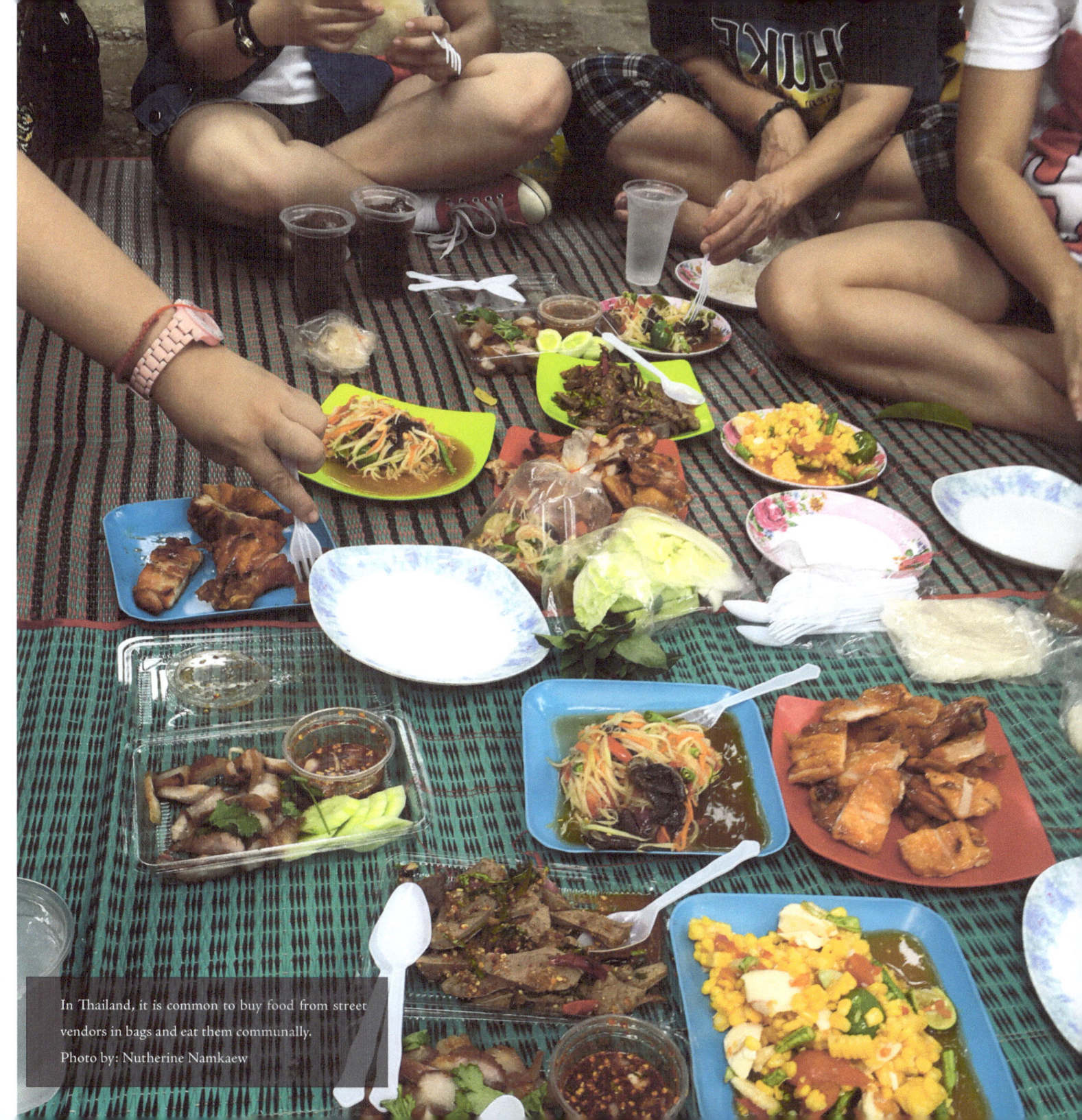

In Thailand, it is common to buy food from street vendors in bags and eat them communally.
Photo by: Nutherine Namkaew

Writers and Photographers

Vanessa Morales

Vanessa Morales grew up in a Hispanic home with beans and tortillas as staples. Diving into the Indian culture felt like an honor, one that welcomed her with open arms to experience, share and cherish. For Vanessa, food holds a special bond as it builds a community that cultivates a universal language, surpassing spoken words.

Rachel Gaugler

Rachel Gaugler grew up in the culinary passport of Queens, New York, minutes away from Indian supermarkets, Thai dessert shops and Indonesian restaurants. Recalling a childhood full of Filipino snacks and Lola's pancit, she enjoyed exploring her multiethnic heritage through the lens of Asian food and culture.

Hannah Dilanchyan

Born in Southern California to Armenian parents, Hannah Dilanchyan treasures memories of rolling up grape leaves and cooking delicious halva with her grandmother, who shared stories from her life across the globe. She is passionate about using food as a gateway for people to tell their own stories.

Bethsabe Camacho

Bethsabe Camacho grew up in a predominantly Latino community. She recalls going to Chinese restaurants during special occasions and this became her gateway into Asian culture. She hopes this chapter will help others understand the fusion between Chinese and American food a little more and what it means to the Asian community.

Grace Morales

Grace Morales grew up in a loud Hispanic household in the High Desert area of California where she learned the value of having strong bonds and great communication with those around her. While writing her chapter she appreciated the similarities between the communal values that connected Filipino culture to her own.

Corrie Myhr

Corrie Myhr spent her childhood attending an international school in East Asia. This lit a fire in her to amplify voices from all around the world. Food has always been an open invitation for her to explore new cultures and share their stories by inviting others to the table.

Briana Byus

Briana Byus grew up in the Central Valley of California where cultural diversity is lovely but limited. She wants to establish herself as a life-long learner and appreciator of God's diverse design so leaning into education on Filipino American culture blessed her tastebuds and widened her perspective of the world around her.

Angela Hom

Angela Hom is a fourth generation Chinese American from California. She is extremely passionate about her culture and sharing her story with others, and this book has been an amazing opportunity to do just that. She hopes that through this book, more people will come to understand Asian cultures and appreciate their beauty.

Sarah Dougher

Sarah Dougher grew up in Torrance, CA where many Asian cultures intersected in her schools, church and friendships. From a young age, Sarah learned about those cultures through their food, instilling in her a love of understanding other people and the lives they lived.

Zach Devane

Zach Devane is a junior journalism major from Indio, California who loves food. Having spent his whole life sharing meals with his family, he has a strong sense of the communal meaning of food and dining. His faith has inspired him to look at these things through the lens of religion.

Caleb Jonker

Caleb Jonker is from Denver, Colorado where he was born and raised. He loves sharing meals with friends and family, and how sharing food can bring us closer together. He is the oldest of four brothers and counts his brothers among his best friends.

Natalie Willis

Natalie Willis is a sophomore journalism major at Biola University. Growing up, she watched her mother prepare delicious meals that brought the family together for a moment of peace. She has learned that sharing food is sharing love.

Evana Upshaw

Evana Upshaw was born in Chicago and grew up in North Minneapolis with her mom, dad and two younger brothers. Learning about history and other cultures has always given her deep joy, especially in regards to food. Evana does not eat to live—she truly lives to eat.

Andi Basista

Andi Basista grew up in a small farm town in the Midwest. With little to no diversity, she found out the importance of cultural connections by moving to Los Angeles. The variety of cuisines discovered opened her eyes to a greater understanding of how food is a connector between different people, traditions and religions.

Maps throughout the book were adapted from map drawings available at mapsvg.com available with creative commons license.

Designers

Lailah Walker

Phoebe Vrable

Maria Wayne

Micah Kim

Dr. Tamara Welter
(Print Production Preparation)

Biola Avenue Press

Mission of Hope (2009)

Skid Row: You Don't Come Down Here Without Change! (2010)

Dominican Dream: A Passion For Baseball, A Love For Family, And a Hope for the Future (2011)

Growing Up In East L.A. (2014)

Haitian Eyes, Haitian Hands (2015)

Beyond the Wall: Migrants, Migration and the Border (2017)

Newcomers to Neighbors: Migrants and Refugees from the Middle East in Southern California (2019)

Biola Avenue Press is an imprint of the Department of Digital Journalism and Media at Biola University. The books it produces are part of two upper-level courses aimed at giving students practical experience with in-depth reporting, writing, photojournalism and graphics design aimed at guiding students in cross-cultural topics in the U.S. and in other countries.

More From Biola's Department of Digital Journalism and Media:

Newcomers to Neighbors

People from Middle Eastern cultures live within a culture of fear that has barely ebbed since the tragic events of September 11, 2001. This multimedia book project took a closer look at what it means to be a refugee or migrant from a Middle Eastern country in California. Students' in-depth, multimedia journalism in this project brought faces to our understanding of the food, the music, the schools, and the worship of people from the Middle East.

Skid Row: You Don't Come here Without Change

Biola University, under early guidance from Union Oil Company magnate Lyman Stewart, began life as a Bible Institute with a heart for the streets of Los Angeles. In this book, a group of its journalism students' reporting and writing spotlights the lonely pain of Skid Row - a portion of L.A. being helped by, among others, Union Rescue Mission.

Beyond the Wall

Separation hurts. This multimedia book project examines pain on both sides of the border wall at Tijuana. Through the eyes of families, attorneys and government officials, it unpacks complexities of immigration policy and practice in the U.S. and in Mexico. It includes the voices of women and men for whom the border has particular, and painful, meaning. Students ventured into Tijuana for their in-depth, multimedia reporting, but also into Los Angeles, Santa Ana, and the East Coachella Valley in California.

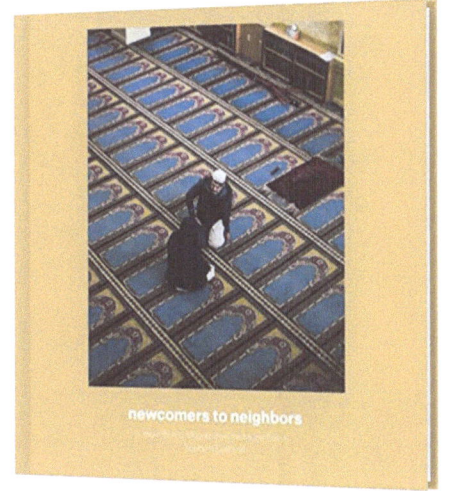

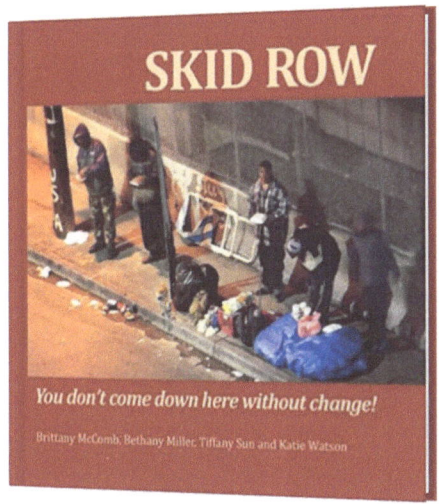

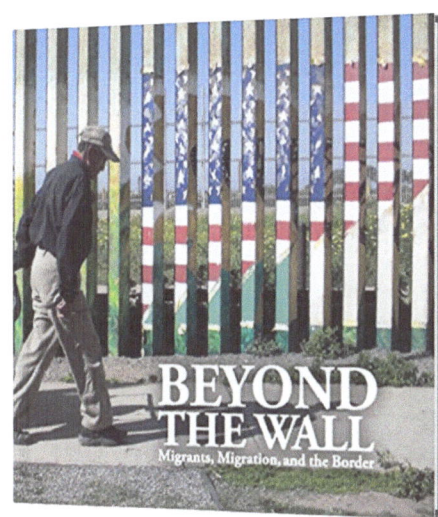

www.ingramcontent.com/pod-product-compliance
Lightning Source LLC
Chambersburg PA
CBHW050717180526
45159CB00003B/1056